Parapsychology

A CENTURY OF INQUIRY

Parapsychology
A CENTURY OF INQUIRY

D. Scott Rogo

TAPLINGER PUBLISHING COMPANY | NEW YORK

Second Printing

Published in the United States in 1975 by
TAPLINGER PUBLISHING CO., INC.
New York, New York

Published simultaneously in the Dominion of Canada by
Burns & MacEachern, Toronto

Library of Congress Catalog Card Number: 74-22890

ISBN 0-8008-6236-8

Designed by Mollie M. Torras

To Mark and Karen Wise
and Barbara Achan

Acknowledgments

Several individuals assisted in various ways in the final presentation of this book and I would like to acknowledge and thank each of them individually. First, thanks are due to Mr. J. Fraser Nicol who read over the entire book to double-check accuracy. Secondly, to Dr. Robert Morris, Eileen J. Garrett Lecturer in Parapsychology at the University of California, Santa Barbara, who read over those sections of the book dealing with experimental parapsychology. Credit is also due to Dr. J. B. Rhine, Foundation for Research on the Nature of Man, who clarified some aspects of his own work; to Mr. Charles Honorton of the Division of Parapsychology and Psychophysics, Maimonides Medical Center, and Dr. Rex Stanford, St. John's University, who also made valuable suggestions. Finally, thanks to Mrs. Winifred Rogo for general help in preparing the manuscript. Of course, responsibility for any opinions, omissions or inadequacies rests solely with the author.

Contents

FOREWORD 9

1 PARAPSYCHOLOGY AND THE ESP CONTROVERSY 11
2 THE FOUNDATIONS OF PSYCHICAL RESEARCH 28
3 ESP—THE SEARCH AND THE EVIDENCE 58
4 ESP IN THE LABORATORY—THE SEARCH CONTINUED 82
5 SPONTANEOUS ESP 117
6 ESP RESEARCH WITH GIFTED SUBJECTS 148
7 MIND, SPACE, AND MATTER—TELEKINESIS 172
8 MIND, SPACE, AND MATTER—PK IN THE LABORATORY 205
9 NEW HORIZONS IN ESP RESEARCH 226
10 PSI, DEATH, AND SURVIVAL 255
11 THE ENIGMA OF PSI 282

NOTES AND REFERENCES 295
SELECTED BIBLIOGRAPHY 305
INDEX 309

Foreword

For some time there has been a need for an introductory book on parapsychology which would present data unbiasedly and using material which most parapsychologists would consider to be the classic studies, cases, views, and theories which constitute the core of psychical research. This book has been written with this need in mind. Of course, an author will always show some bias by his choice of material, but other than this necessary evil, I have tried to keep from personal evaluations or conclusions, and present only those theories and opinions which are commonly put forward in parapsychology. Since I have selected material for this book on the basis of what I feel to be the core research and history of parapsychology and which most other parapsychologists would also consider to be essential background material, I have not tried to be particularly original in what is presented. Any attempt at novelty would detract from the goal of the book which is to arm the reader with enough hard facts and data to help him make his own appraisal of parapsychology. In doing so I have adopted a procedure commonplace in writing a basic text on any subject. I have therefore devoted the first few chapters to an outline of parapsychology's history. This material covers the earliest attempts by society to investigate psychical phenomena to the beginnings of its scientific recognition due primarily to J. B. Rhine's ESP research at

Duke University. The remainder of the book is devoted to more recent research and developments.

There are however several good general books on parapsychology written by such well-known authorities as Robert Thouless, Gardner Murphy, G. N. M. Tyrrell, René Sudre, and Raynor Johnson which will acquaint the reader with a good set of facts and figures on parapsychology. I have written this introduction to parapsychology because these books are often very personal contributions and are not totally comprehensive. Secondly, they have not been kept up to date in new editions which take into account new research. This problem is even more acute because parapsychology is such a rapidly advancing science and books soon become outdated as new developments and research confirm or invalidate previous concepts about the paranormal.

Nonetheless, it should be pointed out that parapsychologists themselves often disagree on the boundaries of psychical research and even on the validity of much of its own research, both contemporary and historic. In fact, some parapsychologists might disagree on the very existence of certain types of psychical phenomena.

Of course no book is going to be without the personal mark of its author. Many readers and colleagues may feel that my own plan of impartiality has not been successfully carried through. However, the only prejudice I have willingly brought into this volume is one shared by many in parapsychology—that parapsychology represents a vital contribution to science and psychology and that the public as well as the scientific and academic communities badly need to be educated about its findings. For this bias I see no need to apologize.

D. Scott Rogo

1

Parapsychology and
the ESP Controversy

What is parapsychology and is it a valid science? These two questions are among the first asked when the topic of ESP is brought up. Parapsychology might simply be defined as the study of psychical phenomena, or more distinctly, "behavioral or personal exchanges with the environment which are extrasensorimotor—not dependent on the senses and muscles." [1] To be a little less obscure, parapsychology deals with cognition such as telepathy or foreseeing the future that is not based on any of the five senses. It also studies those experiences where physical movements of objects are not caused by any normal power or energy source, popularly termed *mind over matter*. Any mental psychical phenomenon, such as telepathy or precognition, is grouped under the general heading *extrasensory perception* (ESP), while any physical phenomenon, such as the inexplicable movement of an object, is labeled as *psychokinesis* (PK).

It may seem that these two divisions, ESP and PK, are arbitrary and have little connection. Why then are these two divisions the basic subject matter of parapsychology? Firstly, ESP and PK seem governed by similar laws or behavior principles. Secondly, we find that most gifted individuals who have any exceptional ESP ability usually possess PK also, and those who can produce PK can usually display ESP. Thus, these two enigmatic phenomena are intrinsically related. As far back as 1914

Henry Holt, a student of psychical research, wrote of ESP and PK, "rare as are the persons manifesting either, yet generally, not always, a person manifesting one manifests the other." [2] It is generally accepted that ESP and PK will often be combined during a single experience. For example, a clock might stop running suddenly and the witness will immediately realize this to mean that a person known to him has died. Here PK, the stopping of the clock, is combined with the extrasensory knowledge that someone has died. Why ESP and PK are so linked is not known, although several theories have been advanced.

Parapsychology is very much a hybrid science, since it really is a combination of both the behavioral and the physical sciences. ESP, which deals with perception, cognition, and consciousness, is clearly a psychological problem. PK, which must use some sort of energy, is within the province of physics. Because of this paradox, parapsychology has long been thought of as an interdisciplinary study.

In the last few years there has been a marked step-up in research activities and scientific acceptance of parapsychology. Opinion polls on the scientific credibility of parapsychology taken among psychologists have never been optimistic, although one recent poll among selected members of the American Psychological Association showed that over 90 percent believed the study of ESP was scientifically valid. Nevertheless, the percentage of those accepting the evidence for the phenomenon has been gauged to be much less according to polls published in 1938 and 1952. Recent opinion polls have shown that the step-up in parapsychological research has also affected its scientific credibility. For example, in 1969 the Parapsychological Association, an organization consisting only of recognized researchers in parapsychology, was overwhelmingly elected as a component scientific organization of the American Association for the Advancement of Science. This though some years before it had been deferred. Meanwhile, a poll taken by the staid British journal, *New Scientist*, showed that 97 percent of its readers considered ESP either proved or a possibility. A poll of United States academic institutions, made in 1972, revealed that over 80 percent of their psychology departments felt that parapsychology should be covered in undergraduate psychology courses. [3]

This reaction to parapsychology has had both its benefits and evils. Unfortunately, many persons interested in parapsychology are not aware that it has close to one hundred years of organized research behind it, and just as psychiatry has its Freud and physics its Heisenberg, so parapsychology has its pioneers. The work carried out over the last one hundred years is the basis upon which this book has been built.

One problem we must face with the current vogue in "pop" parapsychology is the confusion between parapsychology and the occult. Subjects such as numerology, astrology, palmistry, and others are systems of occultism which teach certain dogmas about the world or human life. Parapsychology has little to do with these systems, since it is, above all, an experimental science. That is, its facts and theories are based on empirical studies, experiments, or observations. However, it has not been ruled out that some peripheral element of ESP might not be an occasional factor in the aforementioned pseudosciences. Also many new "sciences" and studies have developed within recent years which have been almost arbitrarily lumped together with parapsychology. Primary perception in plants, acupuncture, Kirlian photography, and even Ufology have been considered to have intricate bearings on parapsychology. This may ultimately prove to be true, but nevertheless these studies are not, nor have they ever been, parapsychological studies inasmuch as they do not fundamentally study ESP or PK.

These intrusions into the study of psi (as all psychical phenomena are abbreviated) are not rare. Years ago hypnosis and multiple personality were considered parapsychological topics. This was primarily because of their unusualness. When more light was cast upon them, it became apparent that they had little to do with ESP or PK directly. They were categorized as psychical studies because to the popular occultism of the day these things were enigmas, and parapsychology became thought of as the study of anything unusual. The problem has become so acute that J. B. Rhine, recognized as the founder of modern experimental parapsychology, recently wrote an editorial on the subject, "Is Parapsychology Losing Its Way?" in the *Journal of Parapsychology*, one of the leading journals in the field.[4] In his statement Rhine criticizes the popularization of parapsychology, arguing that this science is the study of ESP and PK exclusively and that even parapsychologists themselves have mistakenly widened its boundaries to include border areas of study such as acupuncture. While Rhine admits that these border areas might bear on the psi process, he argues that they cannot yet be considered within the proper bounds of psychical research. He blames this confusion on the mass media which link parapsychology with any controversial new study which bears any savor of occultism. However, Rhine also feels that "it must be admitted that parapsychologists themselves are not always in agreement about the boundaries of their field."

This controversy has been touched upon to point out that, like any other science, parapsychology does have a mainstream core of research and topics as its mainstay, and that this core consists of ESP and PK. Nevertheless, the terms ESP and PK are, in fact, collective nouns encompassing a great many different types of phenomena (although they probably all share a similar etiology). The very term ESP, extrasensory perception, was coined by Rhine to include phenomena which had hitherto been labeled by various other names.

ESP, the first major division of psi, entails the study of the following phenomena: (1) telepathy, the transference of thought or feelings between minds; (2) clairvoyance, extrasensory knowledge about material objects or events not obtained from another animate mind; (3) precognition, extrasensory cognition of a future event; (4) retrocognition, extrasensory cognition of a past event; (5) mediumship, the study of the ESP ability of an individual which suggests that the source of information is from a discarnate (deceased) personality.

PK is a little more complex since its various forms are not so well defined. Generally, however, the following distinctions might be made: (1) telekinesis, the spontaneous movement of objects without contact or observable force or energy; (2) psychokinesis, the direct action of mind over material objects; (3) physical mediumship, the study of those individuals around whom PK habitually manifests or who can deliberately induce it; (4) poltergeists, habitual telekinetic disturbances confined to a specific location such as a home or a person; (5) paranormal healing, PK affecting biological functions prompting recovery from disease or biological damage.

As in any taxonomy, a few constituent topics cannot be clearly labeled as purely physical or mental, but hold rather a middle ground. These phenomena are those of apparitions, hauntings, and out-of-the-body (where a person feels he has left his body) experiences.

In using these terms it must be remembered that they are merely terms of convenience. The psi process seems to be a unitary process which only manifests, although in different forms, under certain conditions. For example, clairvoyance and precognition are basically the same process but occurring under different circumstances. In this case time is the mitigating determinator. Similarly, it is often hard to differentiate between these phenomena. If one receives an impression that an accident has occurred to a relative, at which time such an incident actually did occur, this would likely be an ESP experience. But is it a clairvoyant impression of a distant event, or is it telepathy from the individual involved? Likewise, if one predicts that dice are going to be thrown to land on a double six, is this precognition or did the subject use PK to influence the fall? Thus, telepathy, precognition, and so forth are really descriptive terms for what can be called the psi process. It is well known that those individuals who can do well on one form of ESP task usually can do well on others.

If these descriptions seem to be long and labored, it is necessary that, before plunging directly into the challenging world of parapsychology, we understand exactly what parapsychology is and what it is not. Now that we have defined parapsychology, we can grapple with the next problem: Is parapsychology a science?

Although the evidence for the existence of psi is massive, problems such as fraud, self-delusion, and the elusiveness of the phenomena themselves have all contributed to what can be called "the ESP controversy." Several parapsychologists have written specifically on how parapsychology fits into our concept of what science is.

Robert Brier has convincingly argued that in order for a discipline to be scientific it need only follow certain procedures. That is, its main facts and theories can either be proved or disproved.[5] Much of the occult is not science because it is based on set principles and tenets that can neither be experimentally demonstrated nor proved to be false. Parapsychology, on the other hand, can study and demonstrate ESP and PK by using certain procedures such as determining if a subject can correctly "guess" concealed targets more often than chance will allow. With such procedures available, certain theories can be postulated about ESP and then be either confirmed or nullified by experimentation. Because of this, and more importantly, because such experimentation has led to evidence for the existence of ESP and PK, parapsychology must be considered a scientific study.

Gardner Murphy, the eminent American psychologist, has also turned his attention to the problem of parapsychology as science.[6] Murphy justly pointed out that, although unlike most sciences there is no repeatable experiment in psychical research (that is, an experiment that anyone can repeat at any time to demonstrate the existence of a reaction or phenomenon), there is evidence that certain conditions, if properly met, will help induce the appearance of psi. For example, there is now more than ample evidence that passivity in the subject will aid in the appearance of psi and, it might also be added, certain states such as hypnosis seem to help induce psi.[7] Because psi does seem to have opaque but very real laws which govern it, it cannot be doubted that parapsychology is a scientific discipline.

Murphy has added the following astute observations about the scientific validity of ESP:

> Psychical research is not, and cannot be, a systematic world philosophy. It is a field of investigation . . .
> Since psychical research aims not to become a cult, but a branch of science, many of the problems with which it deals overlap the problems of psychology, physiology, anthropology, and medicine. It is often difficult to tell whether a problem is a relevant one for the psychical researcher, or whether these other groups are adequate to the task.
> Only when we are sure that normal psychology and physiology have failed to cover the situation can the psychical researcher say that he certainly belongs in the picture, and that he has an important area of investigation which the other scholars are not fully qualified to handle within the accepted scope of their disciplines.[8]

Despite the fact that parapsychology is obviously a science and has achieved scientific credibility and recognition, there is still the problem of "the ESP controversy." It must be kept in mind that psi is a relatively elusive phenomenon which only surfaces into consciousness when many conditions, mostly unknown, are met. Contrary to the picture promulgated by mass media, ESP is a very hard-to-control phenomena. There have been relatively few great ESP subjects, and even these usually could not control their ESP or PK, often losing the ability completely in time. In order to appreciate the enormous difficulties that parapsychologists have faced while amassing the data which will be presented in the course of this book, a discussion of the criticisms against the study of ESP will help the reader grasp why, even in the face of the evidence concerning ESP, precognition, mediumship, PK, healing, hauntings, and so forth, so many scientists are wary of the study of parapsychology and why it has had such a hard struggle for recognition.

For a recent survey, Champe Ransom has listed nine major criticisms which are commonly leveled at parapsychology and parapsychologists. These arguments will be cited and discussed as they are cataloged by Ransom. The discussions, however, following each point do not stem from Ransom's own discussions of them in his paper "Recent Criticisms of Parapsychology, A Review" (*Journal:* ASPR 65: 289–307).

The foremost problem in parapsychology is nonrepeatability. That is, there is no known experiment that will always demonstrate psi. This argument speaks for itself—because not everyone can prove psi to themselves experimentally and at leisure, many scientists are reluctant to accept ESP as a scientifically valid subject for study. Arguments that are cited in rebuttal by parapsychologists are that many phenomena of nature, such as ball lightning and volcanic eruptions, are not repeatable nor can they be isolated in a laboratory. Further, certain gifted ESP subjects have been able to produce the ESP effect time and time again, and it is now known that certain types of experiments have a high likelihood of being successful when carried out by different experimenters. In surveying the evidence on the effect of hypnosis on ESP, for example, the various experiments that have been run using hypnosis do seem to indicate that it will lead to success a good number of times. In fact, Charles Honorton and Stanley Krippner of the Maimonides Medical Center, in Brooklyn, New York, in assessing all experimental studies of ESP and hypnosis, have clearly shown the staggering success of the results when analyzed all together. The importance of this point is that while parapsychology has no repeatable experiment, certain experiments have been repeated successfully by different researchers. It might also be noted that many behavioral sciences do not have a repeatable experiment. Although it is obvious that schizophrenia exists, few experimental studies of schizophrenics themselves have offered confirmatory evidence about the etiology of the disorder. The eminent American psychologist, Carl Rogers, in an address to his students, once remarked that there is more empirical evidence for ESP than for any of psychology's learning theories.

The second, and perhaps most serious, problem facing parapsychologists is that of fraud. It must be admitted that fraud has been uncovered in much parapsychological work, both in the laboratory and in the investigation of spontaneous phenomena such as poltergeists. The case of the Jones boys is one famous case in point. Glyn and Ieuan were two Welsh teen-agers who were unusually gifted with ESP. In 1955 they came to the attention of the British parapsychologist and mathematician, S. G. Soal, who set out to investigate their abilities. During these experiments one boy would try to send to the other, via ESP, the picture or symbol printed on a card. These experiments were carried out under Soal's personal supervision while the boys were in the same room, in different rooms, out of doors, separated by several feet, and so forth. When the experiments were well in progress, the boys were so successful that on one occasion they were able to succeed twenty-five times in a row on a simple type of ESP test. Yet afterward, during a less rigorously controlled test, the boys were caught by the investigators using a rather crude code. Since the boys would alternately send one of five pictures over and over again, it isn't hard to give a little shuffle or grunt to signify certain targets. If animal pictures are used, a sniff could signify a lion, shifting in the seat a zebra, and so on. This is not to say the boys had always used such a code. In fact, this is probably not the case, but it is a well-known fact that gifted psychics will often cheat to produce results as well as produce genuine psi. Nonetheless, the ESP critic does have good cause to argue that, if a subject cheats, as did the Jones boys on one occasion, it is likely that cheating had been going on all the time. This argument is hard to counter and many cases that had a high likelihood of being genuine have been marred by the disclosure of occasional fraud.

Parapsychologists themselves have from time to time been caught faking their results, and, although all sciences have these unfortunate incidents, parapsychology seems particularly prone to charges of experimenter fraud. The following exposé is representative. An Indian parapsychologist claimed to have achieved significant ESP results. The American parapsychologist, J. G. Pratt, went to India to supervise and recheck the results. During the original experiments the subjects had to guess which one of five geometric symbols was printed on a card. Pratt discovered, when analyzing the score sheets, that the experimenter had failed to fill in a certain target. It was rather damningly clear that blanks had been deliberately left on the score sheets and later filled in with the correct answers to make the results look conclusively to be ESP. Later all the evidence was published as an exposé in the *Journal of Parapsychology*.[9]

Fraud does not have to be actually discovered to be an objection to the existence of ESP. Some critics such as George Price, in an article in *Science*, August 1955, and C. E. M. Hansel, in his notorious *ESP: A Scientific Evaluation*, have used the miracle versus deceit argument. Briefly this means that it is easier to believe that deceit occurred during an experiment than to believe that a miracle (ESP) occurred. If an experiment has a loophole through which either the experimenter or the subject could have cheated, then the critic can validly assume that he did. Few experiments in any science are perfect, but this argument is valid. Parapsychologists are the first to admit that unless all normal explanations can be ruled out, we are not entitled to believe that ESP did occur during an experiment or observation. In Cumberlandism, for instance, an object is hidden. The subject comes into the room, takes the hand of the person who hid the object, and immediately uncovers it. This art is named after Stuart Cumberland, a thought reader of the Victorian era who was a practitioner of this ability. At the time this was thought to be ESP, but it is now known that the subject is being consciously or unconsciously guided to the object by his ability to read the muscle pressure of the hider's hand or by noting slight visual cues offered him by various onlookers. All such cuing must be ruled out before ESP can be accepted. Similarly, any possibility of fraud must also be dismissed before presenting a study to a skeptic as evidence of ESP.

Of course there are rebuttals to this, and it should be pointed out that when fraud is uncovered it is usually by parapsychologists themselves. Modern parapsychology uses automatic devices to shuffle cards, record responses and guesses, and even uses computer analysis of the results. All this makes simple fakery much more difficult than it was during parapsychology's infancy. The most telling argument, though, against the fraud hypothesis has been offered by R. A. McConnell in an address, "ESP and Credibility in Science," delivered at Carnegie-Mellon University and subsequently published in *The American Psychologist* (vol. XXIV: 531–38). In this address Dr. McConnell points out that so many independent scientists have confirmed the existence of ESP that the critic would have to postulate a worldwide conspiracy of an unbelievable magnitude among scientists. To add to this powerful point, it might be added that this conspiracy would have had to have been self-promulgated by parapsychologists (and other outsiders who have also confirmed the ESP effect) for a hundred years. This conspiracy would have had to include such scientists as the Nobel prizewinning physiologist Charles Richet, the physicist Lord Rayleigh (John William Strutt), and the famous psychologist William James among many others. George Price seems to have seen the unworkability of his views and has since retracted his famous *Science* article.

The third major argument against ESP is that the statistics used to evaluate tests are invalid. As is well known, many ESP tests are really games where the subject tries to guess correctly above what coincidence would dictate. If an individual attempts to guess under which of three walnut shells a pea is hidden, over a long period of time he will consistently be correct one-third of the time. There is certainly nothing unusual about that. But what if the subject consistently guesses correctly two-thirds of the time? Statistics tell us that this cannot happen by chance.

There are standard mathematical models used to judge when a series of guesses' is more than merely chance, and of course, parapsychologists use these models in their work. According to statistics 20 to 1 odds are suggestive of more than chance. In ESP and PK research, odds of 100 to 1 are usually accepted as evidence of psi. Despite the fact that all sciences use these models, one critic has written that ". . . the parapsychologists are forced to rely on the shaky evidence of statistical significances." [10] Some critics, such as G. Spencer Brown, have argued that the entire scheme of statistics is arbitrary and faulty, so that the statistics used in parapsychology are still suspect. This may be so, but if it is then parapsychology is in good company, since experimental psychology, sociology, and other behavioral sciences use the same methods. As for calling the statistical evidence shaky, some experiments with gifted psychics have achieved odds of millions to one. It should also be noted that this criticism is itself hackneyed. As far back as 1937 when the ESP controversy was first erupting due to the Rhine experiments at Duke University, the American Institute of Mathematical Statistics issued a statement to the effect that the statistics used to evaluate ESP were completely valid and that if one wished to debate the ESP issue it could not be done on mathematical grounds.

However, there are certain statistical flukes that might mistakenly appear to be ESP results. As any poker player knows, chance can produce some rather weird results. Another problem is that of statistical artifacts. Parapsychology today often uses an experiment using a one-half probability. For example, a subject might have to guess either red or green as the color of a concealed card. If twenty people run the same test, ten will probably get better than chance results. Of these ten, five may confirm the above chance scores. Of these, two will succeed on a third trial and perhaps one will succeed a fourth time. By pure chance, then, one subject will have run a test and will have confirmed it three times. If one takes *all* the results together, it would be clearly shown that only fickle chance was at work. It is sometimes argued that something of this sort, on a much more sophisticated scale, might be going on in experimental parapsychology.

At this point, it must be pointed out that this argument, like most other criticisms, applies only to one part of parapsychology—laboratory ESP. Critics often tend to think that parapsychology consists merely of a few diligent scientists running statistical tests in a laboratory. The total scope of parapsychology must also include its backbone—the spontaneous occurrences of ESP in day-to-day living: well-authenticated cases of hauntings and apparitions; spectacular cases of people who have willed objects to move in sealed containers; and other exciting areas of investigation to which statistical controversies are totally irrelevant.

These three arguments then are the main valid objections to scientific ESP and PK research. They are termed valid because, despite the fact that they have been adequately answered, the points raised are serious ones and should be taken into consideration by anyone trying to make an impartial evaluation of parapsychology.

There are, however, some invalid and demonstrably incorrect arguments that are often leveled against parapsychology and parapsychologists which Ransom cites and which will be briefly dealt with. Again, any comments on these charges are not taken from Ransom's own evaluations.

The first of these invalid criticisms is that ESP is a priori impossible. This rigid argument is similar to that of George Price to whom ESP was a miracle which would necessitate the breaking of natural law. Ergo, it just could not be. This argument goes against everything that modern science stands for, the unbiased pursuit of truth and fact, authenticated by empirical observation and experimentation. There is no room for dogma in science. Another fault inherent in this argument is that it presupposes that our knowledge of psychology, physics, and biology is total and complete. This is hardly the case, since several recognized sciences have fundamental problems which are still a mystery to them. Psychology still has not fathomed the primary cause or causes of mental illness, and astronomy has little concrete idea what those mysterious quasars are. Physicists are hard put to explain the actions of certain subatomic particles. Because of these and many others, it is rather ludicrous to say that psi is impossible because it breaks the laws that govern certain sciences of which we have incomplete or even little understanding. This reasoning is a subterfuge at best. If parapsychology is but an infant science, her sister sciences are hardly more than adolescents.

Another argument that is now invalid is that the experimental designs used by parapsychologists in running their tests are faulty, since recording errors and sensory cues could explain the results, and that when these conditions are improved, no results are forthcoming. This is erroneous for several reasons. First of all, parapsychologists are more than aware of these possible sources of error in their experiments and routinely check for them. Also, many experiments today are recorded automatically, and there are examples of "perfect" experiments where the tightening of controls has not canceled any psi effects.

There are three additional arguments which, although they might contain a ray of validity, are nonetheless irrelevant to the central issue of whether parapsychology is a science.

The first of these is that psi has not been fitted into a theoretical framework, nor has it shown any relevance to the rest of science. The latter part of this point is mere value judgment and as such is not a valid objection. Several theoretical frameworks have been offered for psi, but these are admittedly speculative. That a certain study does not offer frameworks has little to do with its scientific acumen. Frameworks gradually arise as organized facts and data are amassed. Because parapsychology is a young science, many feel that it is not yet time for such frameworks to be seriously proposed. As the parapsychologist Ian Stevenson has humorously noted, ". . . parapsychologists have no really satisfactory theory of extrasensory perception to market even to available buyers." [11] Nevertheless, this still does not invalidate the scientific credibility of psychical research. Perhaps it is to its credit that hard-core parapsychology is more concerned with fact than theory.

Other objections are that parapsychologists are not in agreement among themselves as to the quality of their own evidence (which is a problem inherent in any science), and that parapsychologists are biased in favor of the existence of psi. (To which one might respond that biologists are now biased in favor of evolution.) Several nonparapsychologists have entered into the field and have been amazed to discover not only that they could achieve psychic results, but also were quite talented at it. One need only read the barest amount of the rich history of psychical research to discover that many of the most famous parapsychologists were initially skeptics who only ventured into the study of psi after breaking through their own bias. Only after much travail did they ultimately become convinced of psi and realized that it offered a bold new world of exploration. One historical case is that of the criminologist, Cesare Lombroso. Lombroso resisted the notion of psi until he was publicly challenged to investigate the matter, and, although he consented grudgingly, he could not in all intellectual honesty refuse. Overcoming his bias he attended some experiments and seances and ended up championing the cause which he had so shunned a short time before. Lombroso's case is not unique historically. Several nonparapsychologists have similarly reported successful ESP experiments and have also reported a multitude of personal experiences.

Although these arguments were accumulated by Ransom in 1971, they showed little change from a similar survey made in 1956 which touched upon the very same objections. In a paper delivered at the Ciba Symposium on ESP, J. Fraser Nicol, a noted historian of parapsychology, pointed to four main criticisms of parapsychology: its apparent irrelevance to other sciences; nonrepeatability; disagreements by parapsychologists on the quality of the evidence; and that claims made by parapsychologists are often unsupported by the evidence.[12] This last argument was also listed by Ransom in 1971. If one is historically minded, he might wish to read an amusing book, *The Enchanted Boundary* by W. F. Prince, published in 1930, which is a survey of criticisms of psychical research. The arguments dating back to the 1890s are little different from the ones offered today.

All this material points to a seeming paradox, for although there has been little change in the charges made against parapsychology over its one hundred years, there has been a growing acceptance of it by the scientific community. Why has there been no change in the arguments against parapsychology, yet growing acceptance of it? What are the real reasons for the resistance to accepting ESP research?

As several of the critical arguments reveal, resistance to psi is often more emotional than scientific or logical. Science naturally resists innovation and abhors anomaly if these breakthroughs or events are not consistent with the current vogue of scientific thinking. In 1962 a scientific commentator and theorist, Thomas Kuhn, rocked the establishment with a little book entitled *The Structure of Scientific Revolutions.* Basing his views on the history of science, Kuhn argued that scientific progress is not a slow evolutionary process, but a much more dynamic practice. Organized science reacts against any strikingly different observation or anomaly. These new observations grow and grow and finally organize themselves into an entirely new framework which ultimately overthrows the old paradigm and replaces it with a new one. A scientific revolution has then taken place. As Max Planck once noted, young scientists grow up with this new paradigm and accept it as a matter of course. ESP was strikingly daring to the psychologists of 1934 when Rhine's *Extrasensory Perception* was published, but today's psychologists have grown up with ESP research staring them in the face. Kuhn also notes that a scientific revolution is not necessarily precipitated by bare facts, but rather occurs when the scientific community itself seems ready for a change, be it for scientific, philosophical, or cultural reasons.

Kuhn's observations, which have not gone unchallenged, do throw a clear light on parapsychology and its critics. Robert Thouless, a British psychologist and parapsychologist, has specifically commented on Kuhn's writing and its bearing on the ESP problem in the following extract from his book, *From Anecdote to Experiment in Psychical Research:*

> Kuhn's theory of scientific revolutions contains many illuminations of the problems of parapsychology; among others it suggests why we should expect to have critics . . . and why they will not be convinced merely by increased weight of experimental evidence. He points out that practitioners of normal science have always tended to resist new theories because these seem to throw doubt on what they are doing and on what they have already done. He also suggests that this resistance to change by normal science has its own value in emphasizing the fact of anomaly when a new finding does not fit normal expectations. But this resistance has always led a

number of the practitioners of normal science to refuse to recognize the necessity for conceptual change. They will not indeed abandon an old paradigm until a new paradigm is ready to take its place. We are, in parapsychology, far from the situation of being able to formulate a new paradigm. So we must expect incredulity to persist among our critics, and not expect that this incredulity will be overcome by mere increase of experimental evidence obtained under new conditions of stringency.[13]

The science of today is a remnant of what can be called Victorian materialism, when science was seen as an alternative to, or even a foe of, religion. The science of today is still enmeshed in that tradition, or at least many interpret it that way. To those of this old school of thought the idea that one mind can directly influence another mind or can influence physical objects must indeed be shocking if not actually blasphemous. Yet, our new generation of scientists is growing up in a scientific community where talk of ESP and mind over matter are commonplace. They are growing up with these new but now not so strange facts, and are not so biased against them.*

Because of the nature of scientific changes (according to Kuhn), Thouless hints that the facts of ESP and PK will gradually be consolidated into science when some bold young explorer offers a new framework for science which will incorporate the facts of psychic science, or rather offers a more acceptable framework for psi. As Thouless prophetically states of this inevitability and of the current function of the parapsychological community, ". . . we should not be tempted to see ourselves as the Einstein of parapsychology, but rather as having the task of preparing his way by increasing knowledge of the field." [14]

Although it is likely that the Kuhn–Thouless view is the main component and instigator of the ESP controversy, there still are major practical problems which have negatively colored ESP. Speaking in 1968 at the Institute for Parapsychology of the Foundation for Research on the Nature of Man (FRNM)—the old Duke Parapsychology Laboratory—J. B. Rhine, its founder, cited the fact that we can only study ESP scientifically by using

---

* These thoughts are not based on or taken from Thouless' evaluations.

methods of investigation dictated to us by other sciences. However, we are not entitled to believe that ESP will so conform. Because psi is so elusive, a basically unconscious process, and perhaps even a physical process, the psychological approach may actually be a deterrent to the study of psi.[15] This, too, must be kept in mind, though many parapsychologists would disagree with Rhine on this issue.

After diligently wading through the foregoing arguments, the reader might be tempted to throw up his hands and ask, "How can we separate fact from fiction about psychical phenomena?" The next several chapters will deal with the fundamental core of parapsychology—psychical phenomena itself. The evidence and findings are picked from a century of organized research. For despite its problems and controversies, there have been thousands upon thousands of studies offering evidence for everything from telepathy to haunted houses to alleged communications from the dead. The best evidence for these phenomena will be presented and will usually represent the major cases and studies that have been considered the core findings and thoughts about psychical research and psychical phenomena.

2

The Foundations of
Psychical Research

Although modern parapsychology, or psychical research, dates only from Victorian England, psi phenomena had been recorded and investigated for centuries before the scientific revolution. Despite the fact that the Age of Reason, Age of Enlightenment, and the Industrial Revolution all shunned what they thought to be crude superstition, no culture or era has been without tales and reports of what we today would call psychical phenomena.

No science comes into being out of the blue, as it were. An organized science only develops when enough scattered facts gradually merge into a unified body which lends itself to critical evaluation. Every science has a prehistory which, though perhaps steeped in error and even frivolity, nonetheless acts as the basis upon which a science is built. Oft cited examples of this are the well-known relation between alchemy and chemistry and astrology and astronomy.

Parapsychology had a rather wide base which over centuries gradually offered hundreds of observations and insights into psychical phenomena. These reports and observations may be found in the writings of ancient cultures, the ecclesiastical writings of the Middle Ages, the early history of hypnosis and finally in the birth of Spiritualism, a religion based on the premise that the dead might extrasensorily affect the living. In trying to understand parapsychology and why it developed the way it did, these early sources give us keen insights.

Telepathy and clairvoyance were certainly known in ancient cultures. Professor E. R. Dodds, in a scholarly discussion, "Supernormal Phenomena in Classical Antiquity" (*Proceedings:* SPR 55 [1971]: 189–237), has collected several cases from the Greek culture. He cites several cases of clairvoyance drawn from H. W. Parke's *The Oracles of Zeus* (1967), a thesis on ancient divination. One such case concerns a missing boy named Aristocritus. The lad had dived from a cliff into the sea and had disappeared. That night the boy's father dreamed that he was led to a certain spot where his son might be found. Upon waking, the father was able to recognize the location shown in the dream and recover the body of his son.

In another report a woman is said to have been searching for a lost treasure concealed by her deceased husband. During a dream a god appeared to her and revealed that the cache "will be lying within the lion at noon in the month of Thargelion." The valuables were later found by digging within the shadow of a particular statue of a lion during the month designated.

In both these accounts, which the ancients interpreted to be the divine intervention of gods communicating with the living, we need postulate little more than clairvoyance to explain these veridical dreams. Nevertheless, certain of the Greek philosophers were aware that the mind might have the ability to perceive by psychic means without the actions of godly agents. Democritus, for example, held that dreams were caused by "seepage," into the dreamer's body, of images emitted by other persons or even physical objects. By this process, Democritus believed that dreams might exhibit thoughts, emotions, and opinions of other human beings. Aristotle also disparaged belief in supernatural deities and felt that any veridical impressions could be explained by an unknown potential within the human mind. While Aristotle did not believe that one could foretell the future by means of omens, he did accept that dreams had the capacity to reveal the present and the future.

In condemning omens Aristotle was, in fact, reacting to the popular occultism of his time. Although many of the early philosophers were ardent in their appreciation of psychic events, many, like Aristotle, condemned the popularizing of these potentials which was manifested in the form of various schools of divination. These were arbitrary systems by which it was felt that one could foretell the future. There was belomancy, divination by throwing arrows about and seeing how they landed; rhabdomancy, divination by watching a falling staff; capnomancy, divination by watching rising smoke; and countless others. One could watch bird flights, look at the internal organs of slaughtered animals, and so on. The plight of Aristotle and others of his day, who abhorred this form of popular occultism, is much the same as with many parapsychologists today who often find themselves editorializing against numerology, palmistry, and other occult "sciences."

Although many schools of Greek thought argued the nature of premonitions, Professor Dodds, to cite once again his excellent thesis on the subject, points out that firsthand accounts of precognition are scarce. Much more so than telepathy or clairvoyance. Despite this rarity, a few such cases have been recorded for posterity. Quintus Cicero once dreamed that his brother almost drowned while crossing a river on horseback. The dream was ultimately confirmed.

It is rather amazing that if one were to set down a list of certain types of psi phenomena and principles about them, we would find direct parallels in the literature of the classics. Such philosophers as Aristotle and Plato were obviously aware that the state of sleep and dreaming is especially conducive to the emergence of psi. Today one of parapsychology's few solidly confirmed facts is that a percipient is more likely to be dreaming than awake in spontaneous psi experiences.

Other parallels might be pointed out. Many psychiatrists feel that the patient-therapist relationship, which is such an emotionally charged transaction, is conducive to the emergence of ESP between the patient and his therapist. Although Sigmund Freud was hostile at first to the idea of ESP, he gradually put forth these views himself scattered around in various of his writings.[1] Later, other psychiatrists and psychoanalysts, such as Jule Eisenbud, Helene Deutsch, and Jan Ehrenwald, confirmed this opinion from their personal experiences. They all point to the fact that the patient often seems uncannily aware of the thera-

pist's thoughts or his physical activities during the interims between therapeutic sessions. This pattern was confirmed and well
known to Augustine centuries ago.[2]

Augustine's observations arose from a case in which a hysteric
could only be calmed by a priest who came to talk with him
now and then. Habitually, the patient would be aware when the
priest was about to pay him a visit. His friends thought him
possessed by a supernatural being, but Augustine felt that the
hysteric's ability had nothing to do with anything but his own
uncanny mental abilities.

And so during the early history of hypnosis, clairvoyant somnambulists were also alleged to have been able to diagnose either
their own disease or the medical state of others. The fourth century thesis *On Regimen*, in a discussion of dreams, makes similar
mention of "medical clairvoyance," and how the soul, during
sleep, can survey the internal medical state of the physical body
and direct this information to the sleeping subject in a dream.
(Such incidents would not necessarily be psychic in nature,
since the dreamer might be subconsciously aware of his own
physical state.)

If the classical writers were the first to call attention to the existence of psi, certainly the writings of the early and medieval
Catholic saints and ascetics offer a rich heritage of introspective
reports about psychical phenomena. Nearly every conceivable
type of psychic experience was recorded by the saints. Saint
Angela (1540) saw an apparition of her sister who had died
without the last rites of the Church; Saint Thomas Aquinas saw
the apparition of Romanus, a teacher at the University of Paris;
and many reported more bizarre encounters. One of the most
famous of these is a case of traveling clairvoyance (where the
percipient believes that he has sent his consciousness spatially to
a distant place) reported by Cardinal Villecourt in his *La Vie de
St. Alphonse de Liguori* (1864). In 1774, Alfonso di Liguori, in
seclusion after an arduous fast, claimed that he attended the
bedside of the dying Pope Clement XIV in Rome. Rome was a
week's travel from Di Liguori's residence in Arezzo, yet his
description of the deathbed scene was later confirmed as accurate.

Some reports of miracles also seem to be more the province of mind over matter, or telekinesis, than of divine grace. Several saints reported that they had been levitated, and eyewitness reports and personal testimony have come down to us from Saint Ignatius Loyola, Saint Philip Neri, Saint James of Illyricum, Saint Dunstan, and Saint Teresa of Avila, among others.* Every culture is automatically prejudiced in believing that it, and only it, is scientific and sophisticated, and that earlier reports and studies are either invalid or suspect. Nonetheless, several miracles of the saints were well observed by independent witnesses, and so must command our attention. As for levitation phenomena, certain physical mediums have been known to be levitated during well-controlled experiments. Because of this, levitations reported by the saints probably represent a peculiar form of telekinesis.

The classic example of a well-witnessed and authenticated case of levitation is that of Saint Joseph of Copertino (b. 1603). Saint Joseph was often seen to levitate, both during religious observances and spontaneously. He lived the life of an extreme ascetic, often entering into altered states of consciousness and mystical states. There are many unsubstantiated tales of Saint Joseph's levitations, but several of these odd telekinetic displays were well witnessed. Dr. Eric J. Dingwall, who has been both a parapsychologist and a critic of parapsychology, has given a scholarly study and evaluation of Saint Joseph's life in his book, *Some Human Oddities*. Basing his account on original sources pertaining to Saint Joseph, Dingwall writes the following of one exceptionally well-documented levitation which was secretly observed:

> One of the most interesting events of this kind was that connected with Johann Friedrich, Duke of Brunswick, who died in 1679 and who was the patron and employer of the great German philosopher, G. W. Leibnitz (1646–1716). He visited Assisi in February 1651, and expressed a wish to see Joseph in the Sacro Convento. For this purpose the Duke, on his arrival and accompanied by two of his noble retinue, Jo-

---

* There have been several books written concerning Biblical narratives and how they might be explained by psi. The most important of these are G. Maurice Elliot's *The Bible as Psychic History*, and Hereward Carrington's *Loaves and Fishes*.

hann Friedrich Blume and Georg Sittig, of whom Sittig was a Catholic and the others not, was conducted to a room in the Convent which was called the Pope's Room. The next morning, which happened to be Sunday, he with his two companions were secretly taken by a private staircase to the door of the chapel situated in the Noviziato Vecchio, where Joseph was accustomed to say Mass, but on this occasion had no idea that he was being observed. There they heard him give a loud cry and saw him rise in the air in a kneeling position, passing backwards five paces and then returning in front of the altar remaining in ecstacy for some time.[3]

The duke was able to observe the phenomenon a second time. On this occasion the duke saw Saint Joseph levitated at the foot of an altar. As a result of his observances the duke became a Catholic while Blume, still a Lutheran, was deeply consternated by what he had seen.

There were also witnesses to other displays. The daughter of Charles Emmanuel I, the Great, duke of Savoy, observed levitations as did the duke of Medina de Rio-Seco. It must be remembered that these witnesses were neither credulous nor miracle-mongers, but intelligent persons of the highest education and culture, and it is difficult to believe that they all were duped by a simple man of piety. Apart from his levitations, Saint Joseph also was reported to have exhibited paranormal healing, clairvoyance, and out-of-the-body experiences.

Theology and dogma aside, Saint Joseph's abilities are understandable in the light of parapsychology. His life indicates that the saint was a man with obvious PK and ESP abilities. Catholic theologians have often had a difficult time explaining such occurrences, and one Catholic viewpoint that attempted to fit the phenomenon of levitation into the confines of academic theology was made by Oliver Leroy in his book *Levitation: An Examination of the Evidence and Explanations* (London, 1928). Leroy's hard-to-follow argument asserts that it is not the individual who is gifted or actually levitated at all, but that the Divine Will grants the onlookers the grace of witnessing a "divine hallucination." This type of hypothesis is clearly unworkable. Yet, if one surveys the evidence of telekinesis, where heavy objects have been moved and levitated, the levitations of the saints can be seen as a demonstration of a unique form of PK where some energy acts upon the body.

The Church authorities were also aware of phenomena such as hauntings and poltergeists. Although E. R. Dodds notes a specific lack of poltergeist hauntings in classical literature, there are several ancient accounts of such disturbances. In 1951 Hereward Carrington and Nandor Fodor made a historical survey of poltergeist cases, many of which persecuted the Christian clergy.[4] In 1138 it was reported that showers of stones bombarded the house of Bishop Hugh, of Maus. In 1170 Saint Godric (d. 1170) saw objects flung around his hermitage.

Modern parapsychology was born when such reports as these nudged the scientific conscience of several Victorian men who began systematically to investigate and study this type of occurrence. The same problem had been considered by the Catholic Church a hundred years before. In order to examine "miracles," the Church had to study and determine the validity of certain paranormal phenomena. By doing so the Catholic Church became the first organized body of psychical investigators.

The most important of these personalities was without doubt Prospero Lambertini (later Pope Benedict XIV), who was the Vatican's chief investigator of psychic events and miracles. It was Lambertini's duty to verify and determine the value of such reports. He ultimately wrote a thesis, *De Canonizatione*, which to all practical purposes was a highly concise and meaningful study on the nature of paranormal processes. Reading Lambertini's views today, it is obvious that he had already discovered certain principles about psi which have only quite recently been confirmed by modern parapsychology. For example, compare the following of Lambertini's views to what is now known about psi:

1. Not only saints but "fools, idiots, melancholy persons and brute beasts" could have experiences of "knowledge of things to come, things past, present events distant in space, and the secret places of the heart." (Thus, Lambertini was one of the first Churchmen to realize that precognition, retrocognition, clairvoyance, and telepathy were common experiences and not an indication of sanctity.)

2. Certain visions might include apparitions of the dead and of the living, but again these experiences had little to do with either sanctity or demonic entities.

3. That prophecy occurs more often in sleep than in waking. (Again this was also noted by the Greek philosophers and has been confirmed by modern studies of spontaneous ESP occurrences.)

4. Prophets cannot always distinguish between their own thoughts and extrasensory or divine messages. (Lambertini has here enunciated a fact that parapsychologists, working with gifted subjects today, have also uncovered—that a psychic is not always able to differentiate ESP impressions from his own thoughts and often confuses them.)

5. Predictions often come in symbolic form. (This is now a well-known feature of precognitive dreams.)

These points were all made by Lambertini in the middle of the eighteenth century, long before the advent of organized parapsychology.[5]

The ecclesiastic establishment was not the only body of elite who turned their attention to the paranormal. Several European intellectuals were also intrigued by the topic, and every so often small groups formed to discuss the subject. In 1665 one such group met regularly at the residence of Lady Conway, Ragley Hall, outside of Alcester, England. During their meetings the members reported and discussed hauntings and the like. The assemblage was distinguished by the inclusion of several notables of the day, for example, Joseph Glanvill and Henry More. The group also investigated people who claimed that they had psychic ability. It was Glanvill, however, who was the most active of the group and who wrote what might be considered the first nonecclesiastic publication on psi, although Glanvill himself was preoccupied with how the phenomena related to good, evil, and religion. His major opus was published posthumously in 1681 as *Sadducismus Triumphatus*, in which can be found one of the first analytically reported and evaluated poltergeist-haunting cases, usually referred to as "The Drummer of Tedworth."

The Drummer of Tedworth was a vagrant drummer who was arrested when his official papers were found to be counterfeit. The official who spotted the forgeries was a Mr. Mompesson who became the focus of the poltergeist. For some odd reason the drum was confiscated. During this affair Mompesson's family was terrified by odd noises plaguing their home. There were strange knockings on the door, even though no one could be found producing them. Mompesson himself witnessed these strange goings-on as they continued. Drumlike thumpings were repeated and gradually centered on the room where the confiscated drum was held. The next phase of the strange events began with the telekinetic movement of objects—often hurled around the house and sometimes at the observers. These persecutions centered mainly about the children in the house. Strange lights flashed through the residence, and phantom footsteps were heard pacing the staircase. Gradually the manifestations subsided.

This report represents a conventional poltergeist. Although it was generally believed that the Drummer was somehow to blame for the phenomena, there is little to substantiate this even though the Drummer, hearing of the events, took credit for them. However, it probably was coincidental. Glanvill investigated the matter himself, even though the odd occurrences had stopped by the time he did so. He scrutinized diary entries concerning the affair, damage allegedly done by the poltergeist, and interviewed firsthand witnesses. By modern standards Glanvill was an astute and critical investigator, and his report on the Drummer of Tedworth still remains a classic of parapsychology's prehistory.

It was inevitable, with such cases as these, that the scientific community should start looking into the matter of the paranormal. This was to be ignited by the discovery and claims of mesmerism and the subsequent rise of the Spiritualism movement.

Up until the eighteenth century the study of anything that could be classified as the occult was mainly a religious discipline. It was usually up to Church officials to determine if any paranormal (to them, supernatural) event or ability was due to demonic forces or God's grace. However, the tide turned during the middle of the eighteenth century with Anton Mesmer's discovery of hypnosis. Followers of mesmerism ultimately tried to demonstrate scientifically such phenomena as telepathy, clairvoyance, clairvoyant diagnosis, traveling ESP (clairvoyant vision over great distances), and other manifestations. No longer was psi a part of religion, and it was fast becoming a threat to the general concept of the era's scientific establishment. No longer could the responsibility of investigating these claims about the wonders of mesmerism (the term which predated hypnosis) be shrugged away, and eventually they fell into the province of scientific investigation. As with psi itself, mesmerism had to overcome a great deal of controversy, charlatanry, and resistance before it was finally accepted as a legitimate study.

Franz Anton Mesmer was born in Switzerland in 1733. He was a gifted scholar and entered a Jesuit college at the age of fifteen. Later in life, in 1773, he obtained a medical degree from the University of Vienna. Mesmer was primarily concerned with the influences of the doctor over his patients, and he discovered that passing his hands over a patient and other similar processes would induce slumber. Hypnosis had been discovered. Mesmer soon went overboard with his discovery, interpreting that vague occult forces were at work and, at times, conducting "group hypnosis" demonstrations with subjects sitting around a large tub waiting to be healed of their various complaints. Charges of charlatanry against him were soon rife, and his reputation was not helped when in 1784 a French government committee investigated mesmerism and declared the whole thing rubbish. (A later commission reversed this judgment.) Mesmer retreated from the scene but issued a pamphlet, *Memoire sur la Decouverte du Magnetisme*, in which he claimed that mesmerized subjects might perceive both the past and the future.

Proof that mesmerism was a psi-conducive state was chiefly due to the research of Mesmer's disciple, the Marquis de Puységur. De Puységur had discovered that one of his subjects, an illiterate peasant named Victor Race, could sometimes echo the thoughts darting through De Puységur's own mind. In some instances, Race would verbalize bits of information that were not in De Puységur's mind, such as events happening far away. De Puységur was also the discoverer of "clairvoyant diagnosis," in which a subject would be mesmerized and asked to give a medical evaluation of another subject or visitor. On some occasions, these diagnoses were staggeringly accurate. One case in particular might be quoted from De Puységur's own writings on medical clairvoyance, *Du Magnetisme Animal considéré dans ses rapports avec diverses Branches de la Physique générale* (Paris, 1807), and *Recherches, Experiences, et Observations Physiologiques sur l'Homme* (Paris, 1811). This extract is a patient's own testimony:

> I had certainly told no one the nature of my ailment. After giving particular attention to my head, the woman [the somnambulist] said that I often suffered pain there, and that I had constantly a buzzing in my ears—this was true. A young man who had been an incredulous spectator of my experiment then submitted himself for examination. He was told that he had obstructions in the abdomen, arising from an illness which he had had some years previously. All this, he told us, was correct. But, not content with this soothsayer, he went straight to another "doctor" twenty feet distant [another somnambulist presumably], and was told exactly the same thing. I never saw anybody so dumbfounded with astonishment as this young man. . . .

Medical diagnosis became part and parcel of the mesmeric repertoire. Medical men became interested in the possibilities of this phenomena, and in 1855, some years after De Puységur's experiments, Dr. E. Louis de Séré wrote a book, *Application du Somnambulisme Magnetique au Diagnostic*, in which he outlined clairvoyant mesmeric applications to medicine.

Until this time mesmerism had been mostly the plaything of amateurs and charlatans out to con the general public with gaudy shows and ludicrous healing claims. However, the dawn of the nineteenth century brought with it more scientific and medical interest. Notably, these more sophisticated inquirers continued to verify that this peculiar state was conducive to the emergence of psi. One of the interested medical men was Alexandre Bertrand who began teaching the art actively in 1819. In his *Traité du Somnambulisme*, he cited cases of medical clairvoyance and "community of sensations" (where the somnambulist takes on physical characteristics or reactions of the patient):

> I observed a somnambule who, I was told, possessed the faculty of discerning disease . . . So I brought her into rap-

port with a young lady whose chief malady was an attack of asthma, which afflicted her very often. When the patient came, the somnambule was already endormed, and I was sure that she could not know the person I brought her. Nevertheless, after contact for a few minutes, she seemed to respire with difficulty, and soon she experienced all the symptoms that attend a violent fit of asthma.

The somnambulist told Bertrand that the patient had imparted these symptoms to her. According to Bertrand, the subject also went on to diagnose several minor aches and pains with acute accuracy.

Such occurrences did not seem to be rare, since Bertrand, and many other fellow investigators, made prolific mention of this type of incident. Nor was psi confined to the French pioneers. Confirmation was soon to come from Great Britain as well. Dr. John Elliotson was senior physician at the University College Hospital and a professor at the University of London. His eminence in medicine also gained for him the position of president of the Royal Medical and Chirurgical Society. In 1847 Elliotson stunned his colleagues by reporting his discovery of the community of sensations. Before commissions of his colleagues and assorted witnesses, he demonstrated that hypnotized subjects could correctly distinguish tastes, smells, and other sensory experiences which Elliotson himself was experiencing, with no observable mode of normal perception or sensory cuing. Elliotson's reward for his discovery was a rude denunciation by his colleagues which forced him to give up his official positions and the medical use of hypnosis as well.

If Elliotson had somehow been mistaken or duped into believing in psi, he was in good company for another English doctor, James Esdaile in India had encountered similar incidences in his clinical experience. Esdaile was primarily interested in the use of mesmerism as a form of artificial anesthetic. His research had been showing great promise when he also discovered that telepathy might occur between himself and his patient.

It is hard to do justice to the encyclopedic literature on psi and mesmerism. In fact, claims of ESP under mesmeric influence became so widespread throughout Europe that hundreds of volumes were written on the subject and the role ESP played within it. Recently, under the sponsorship of the Parapsychology Foundation, an educational institute founded for the furtherance of parapsychological work, Eric Dingwall edited a compilation and reevaluation of all this material. The result was four volumes, *Abnormal Hypnotic Phenomena* published in 1967. Contributing to this massive work were Allan Angoff of the United States, George Zorab of the Netherlands, Ludmilla Zielinski covering Russia and Poland, Luciano Leppo on Italy, Liselotte Moser covering Germany, Erik Bjelfvenstam on Scandinavia, and Dingwall himself on Great Britain, France, and South America.

All these cases and reports give rise to two different approaches to the study of altered states of the mind. James Braid, an English doctor working during the middle of the nineteenth century, discovered that all the mesmeric practices of "magnetic healing" and "life fluids" which supposedly induced the state were actually not pertinent to inducing hypnosis. He discovered that *suggestion* alone caused the peculiar sleep. The discovery that suggestion was the true root of the state spurred medical and scientific recognition of hypnosis. On the other hand, enamored by the theories of Mesmer, complicated schools of occult thought sprung up searching for "psychic fluids" which they felt were the cause of the mesmeric state and accompanying psychical displays. Several scholars such as Baron von Reichenbach spent years in diligent quasi-scientific work searching for evidence which would prove that these forces, and the principles upon which they worked, existed.

It is extremely hard to make a critical evaluation of these cases, for even though it is clear that they had an appreciable role in alerting science to the subject of thought transference (since the term telepathy had not yet been coined), we have little to go on in trying to judge the validity of this claim. Surely there must have been some paranormal fire hidden beneath the proverbial smoke of claims and demonstrations. But how much? The major problem is that, with rare exception, the psychic wonders recorded by the early investigations have not been so commonly witnessed by clinical hypnotists today. While the experimental literature of parapsychology suggests that hypnosis can raise the success level of subjects during statistical ESP

tests, this is a far cry from the "community of sensations," clairvoyance (medical, traveling, and otherwise), and other marvels
so fully recorded by the early researchers.

Charles Honorton, who has been successful with a number of
hypnotic ESP tests, in commentating on the Dingwall survey,
noted that we really cannot judge the role hypnosis played.
Those patients and somnambulists who did exhibit ESP might
just as well have had ESP ability while awake. In fact, it was
not for years that researchers even began to think in terms of
ESP occuring during waking states. When J. B. Rhine started
his famous Duke University experiments, he began by employing hypnosis and only later discovered that the normal waking
state was also conducive to psi. Honorton also suggests a cultural effect which was originally pointed out by Dingwall who
noted that psychic individuals may have naturally gravitated to
the mesmeric movement. With the rise of Spiritualism—a religion whose basic tenet is that the dead may still influence and
communicate with the living via some sort of ESP—shortly after
the heyday of mesmerism, and as an outgrowth of it, psychics
may have simply been drawn to the new movement just as naturally.[6] This left the mesmerists without many gifted subjects.

While the Dingwall-Honorton view may be cogent, some men
of science during the mesmeric renaissance were realizing that
they could no longer achieve the results that they had attained in
their earlier years. In 1865 an aged John Elliotson wrote that, although he was positive of his earlier results, he could no longer
achieve the types of mesmeric results he had been able to obtain
years before and could not account for it.

Some further scholarly remarks on this issue have been made
by A. R. G. Owen in his book *Hysteria, Hypnosis and Healing: the
Work of J. M. Charcot*. Owen suggests that the growing scientific
acceptance of hypnotism coerced the scientific establishment to
guard rigidly against the shady reputation of its beginnings. The
upshot of this is obvious—researchers did not witness psi because they were either not looking for it, or were hostile to it.
This could very well account for the lack of mesmeric feats of
clairvoyance today. The subjects had no motivation, as did the
early ones, to display psi. Few clinical hypnotists have actually
looked for evidence of ESP.

These thoughts are merely speculations about why claims of ESP gradually faded away from the mainstream development of clinical hypnosis. There is, of course, another reason. In light of the difficulties of strict parapsychological research outlined in the previous chapter, it is not hard to understand that the early mesmerists and scientists did not have the expertise to check for such phenomena as subliminal perception, sensory cuing, and hypersensitivity which might often be mistaken or pass for psi. Few of these cases were reported in such a way that one can be completely assured that the conditions were foolproof. Even in 1891, Dr. Julien Ochorowicz, in his treatise on thought transference and related phenomena, *Mental Suggestion*, was offering normal explanations for much of what had been reported during hypnosis' adolescence.

Despite all these formidable objections, two things might be said of the import of mesmerism on the ultimate development of parapsychology: (1) It is clear that ESP was to some degree repeatedly and scientifically observed during these years. (2) The mesmeric movement transfered the research of ESP and the rest of the paranormal from the dominion of religion into the clear light of scientific evaluation.

The major precipitating factor in the development of psychical research was the Spiritualist movement which began in the United States in the middle of the nineteenth century. American popular culture was enmeshed in an occult revolution. Mesmerism had migrated to the United States and with it came healers, trance speakers (who spoke "wisdom" while in mesmeric trance), and exhibits of psychic wonders. One such speaker was A. J. Davis who heralded the Spiritualist movement. In his trance state he would lecture on subjects of which he claimed no previous knowledge. He also alleged possession of psychic and healing abilities, and contact with the dead. The time was right to bring forth this new addition to the mesmeric repertory—extrasensory contact with the dead. As far back as the 1780s European mesmerists were studying not only hypnosis, but also the problem of communications with the dead, but it had never been in vogue.

This claim, which had its beginnings in popular occultism (although the belief has been widely held for centuries that the living and the dead could commune by extrasensory processes and via gifted psychics), was primarily due to Emanuel Swedenborg. Swedenborg was an eighteenth-century Swedish savant and scientist who turned his back on technology (of which he was a genius) to study religion. He apparently was a gifted psychic as well and wrote several books on his communications with the dead. Some of his displays of clairvoyance had been well witnessed which added to his credibility. Swedenborg's philosophy and writings had a great influence on the occultism of his day and when A. J. Davis first began his preachings, he claimed Swedenborg as one of his contacts.

The situation in American society in the 1840s was this—a highly emotional period where religion was just beginning to be challenged by science, and would be actively when Charles Darwin's *On the Origin of Species by Means of Natural Selection* ultimately appeared in 1859. Industrialization was on the rise, and in addition to all this there was an upsurge in popular occultism, a potpourri of mesmerism, Swedenborgianism, faith healing, phrenology, and so forth. Something was bound to give. And it did in 1848.

On December 11, 1847, John D. Fox, his wife and daughters, Margaret (aged fourteen) and Catharine (Kate, age twelve), moved into a small wooden home in Hydesville, New York. The Foxes had another daughter, Leah, who had married and was living in a neighboring town. The cottage had a reputation of being haunted. However, the events that gave Spiritualism, and for that matter parapsychology, its impetus began in March of the next year when percussive sounds were heard on the walls of the cottage. The height of these disturbances came on the eleventh of April, 1848. Mrs. Fox's own deposition on the noises reported that, having just gone to bed, the family once again heard the raps. The children tried imitating the sounds and the raps answered back. Experimenting further, the girls found that if they commanded the raps to thump out certain numbers, they were immediately answered.* With the working out of a code, the raps could answer simple questions.[7]

* This phenomenon is not a rare one in poltergeist cases. Sir William Barrett, a physicist who later turned his full attention to psychical research, investigated a poltergeist where he asked the raps to show the number of fingers he held outward in his pocket. This experiment,

These events were so startling that neighbors were called in to witness the proceedings. Two of them, William Duesler and Mr. Redfield, questioned and witnessed the rappings. Again, the intelligence behind the rappings answered private questions, the correct answers of which only the inquisitors knew. Another witness, Chauncey P. Losey, remarked in his testimony, "I think that no human being could have answered all the questions that were answered by this rapping." [8]

So upset was the Fox family by these manifestations that they all, with the exception of Mr. Fox, spent the night with neighbors. Fox and Redfield stayed behind, and on questioning the raps came to believe, at the raps' claim, that the intelligence communicating was a Charles Rosma, an itinerant salesman, who had been murdered in the cottage and robbed by a former occupant, John Bell. A former maid of the Bells, Lucretia Pulver, came forth and verified that a salesman had arrived at the Bell residence and that some suspicious goings-on had followed. Moreover, she claimed to have heard typical haunting-type sounds herself, such as footsteps and knockings. Bell denied the whole thing and the story was never verified. Years later a newspaper carried an article claiming that a disjointed skeleton had been found in the cellar of the house when an old wall collapsed. This story though, like so many that come out of the Spiritualist movement, had little clear corroboration (*Rochester Democrat and Chronicle*, November 23, 1904).

The sounds centered on the two Fox girls, Kate and Maggie. There was, and would be for several years to come, controversy as to whether the girls were faking the phenomena. According to one contemporary authority, E. W. Capron in his *Modern Spiritualism*, the raps were heard while the girls were away from the house as well as when they were in it. Soon the two girls were joined by the older sister, Leah, and the three began to preach a new gospel—that the dead could communicate with the living. Spiritualism as an organized religion was under way.

The Fox sisters traveled about the country, giving demonstrations of their ability to bring forth raps. Usually a hall was

---

which shows some sort of extrasensory awareness on the part of the intelligence behind the raps, was successful in several instances.

rented and a lecture given on Spiritualism. Afterward the sisters would give a demonstration of the raps. This all reeked of commercialism, yet several commissions were set up to investigate them privately, and although these probes were often severe, no trace of fraud could be found. The newspapers had a field day. The *New York Excelsior*, for February 2, 1850, ran the following story about its reporter's meeting with the Foxes. "The morning . . . of the following day, we called upon them again . . . in a very light room, many questions were asked concerning ourselves and were answered correctly [by the raps] without a moment's hesitation. It is impossible that the correct answers to these questions could have been known to any person present, by ordinary methods of obtaining the information." Several examples were given. And further, "A table standing in the room was moved without any visible agency—not withstanding all our efforts to keep it stationary."

The whole story of the Fox sisters is complex and many modern writers have seriously distorted it or have left it incomplete. These demonstrations were given for years, but unfortunately two of the girls succumbed to alcoholism. Years before, a medical team had claimed that the raps could be produced by the snapping of toe joints. This explanation was given in pseudomedical phraseology which, when analyzed, really said nothing. Both Kate and Maggie fell back upon this explanation when they offered confessions of their fraud. The reason for the confessions was not only to reap a rich bounty for selling them when the girls were destitute, but also in order to discredit their older sister, Leah, who was still going on with the demonstrations after a serious family argument had alienated her from them. (One of the few sources to go into this affair in depth is Alan Gauld's *The Founders of Psychical Research*.) These confessions were later retracted, although Kate and Maggie had already discredited themselves by publicly demonstrating toesnapping. Witnesses soon discovered that these demonstrations had little relation to the raps heard during the sisters' heyday.

Despite this affair, careful investigations of the Fox sisters individually were made by various commissions. Often skeptical, the commissions were left to walk away puzzled. The most notorious of these inquiries was the infamous Seybert Commission, set up by Henry Seybert, and upon his death to be carried on by representatives from the University of Pennsylvania. Their superficial report appeared in 1887 as the "Preliminary Report on the commission appointed by the University of Pennsylvania to investigate Modern Spiritualism in accordance with the request of the late Henry Seybert."

The Seybert Commission was openly antagonistic to Spiritualism, and its main technique was merely to expose several of the top mediums of the day. It was partially successful and did find clear evidence of fraud with one famous medium, Henry Slade.* This commission also investigated the raps of Kate Fox, now Kate Fox Kane, a mature woman and no longer the girl who had, while merely a child, started the Spiritualist movement. The Seybert Commission, although critical of Kate Fox, could find no explanation for the raps they heard in her presence. Fully cognizant of the toe-snapping explanation, the Seybert Commission required that Kate Fox stand on glass tumblers so that she could be completely controlled. On another occasion further raps were heard at some distance from the medium:

"Raps were produced as members of the Committee stood with the Medium around the desk in the library, and close to a book-case. Raps were produced according to the Medium on the glass door of a book-case, upon which Mr. Sellers placed his hand. Mr. Sellers felt no vibration on the glass, but raps were heard somewhere in the vicinity."

The commission left puzzled, claiming that it would continue the investigation of Miss Fox. However, the chairman of the committee, H. H. Furness, reported that, on discussing the matter with Miss Fox, both had mutually agreed not to go on with the investigation at that time due to Miss Fox's health. She did invite them to contact her later, but the invitation was never acted upon.

* Slade had previously impressed the German scientist, Professor Johann Zoellner, who set up a theory of the fourth dimension after his experiments with Slade, and wrote a book, *Transcendental Physics*, about the experiments. Although Zoellner could easily have been duped, the Seybert Commission, in order to discredit Slade, charged Zoellner with senility and insanity, both provably false charges. A complete rebuttal to the Seybert Commission was later published by A. B. Richmond as *A Reply to the Seybert Commissioners' Report* (1888).

Meanwhile, Spiritualism had traveled to Great Britain in 1852 with a visit by Mrs. Hayden, another spirit-rapper. Margaret Fox also went to England, and her raps were tested by Professor William Crookes, a famous chemist of the day who was later knighted for his scientific work. Crookes witnessed not only raps but telekinesis as well. In his report he says of the raps:

> . . . in the case of Miss Fox it seems only necessary for her to place her hand on any substance for loud thuds to be heard in it like a triple pulsation. In this manner I have heard them in a living tree—on a sheet of glass—a tambourine—on the roof of a cab—and on the floor of a theatre; I have had these sounds proceeding from the floor, wall and when the medium's hands and feet were held—when she was standing on a chair—when she was suspended in a swing from the ceiling—when she was enclosed in a wire cage—and when she had fallen fainting on a sofa. I have heard them on a sheet of paper, held between the fingers by a piece of thread passed through a corner. With full knowledge of the numerous theories which have been stated, chiefly in America, to explain these sounds, I have tested them in every way that I could devise until there has been no escape from the conviction that they were true objective occurrences not produced by trickery or mechanical means.[9]

Unfortunately Crookes was not careful in his recording of the exact conditions of many of his experiments with Miss Fox which he wrote up for the *Quarterly Journal of Science* in 1874. But, it must be remembered that Crookes was a noted scientist of his day and he had entered into the investigation of Spiritualism as a rigid skeptic expecting to expose the entire movement. His scientific colleagues applauded his entry into the controversy; however, when Crookes began publishing his successful experiments and his own beliefs in telekinesis and other phenomena, they turned on him and tried to discredit his work. Crookes felt the source of the phenomena to be a new force unknown to science, not the spirits of the dead—an issue that he was never able to resolve clearly in his own mind.

While this type of critical investigation was going on among scientists delving into the question of Spiritualism, American and English society were undergoing a tender romance with Spiritualism which had become somewhat the rage. A typical list of the types of phenomena recorded by the Spiritualists was printed in *The Spiritual Magazine* in 1860. Note that even though these phenomena are often exaggerated, they do contain the roots of ESP and PK. Although the form of these paranormal manifestations was gilded in fraud and delusion, it is more than suggestive that a real element of psi pervaded them: rappings; spirit writing (appearance of writing independent of any human being such as on sealed slates); trance speaking (this would later turn into trance mediumship, a state wherein the psychic often demonstrates extreme psi abilities); clairvoyance; luminous phenomena (lights and so forth which later would be well observed as a peculiar form of physical phenomena); spiritual impersonation (where the medium takes on the characteristics of a dead individual); spirit music (usually plucking strings on instruments often levitated, a form of telekinesis); visible and tactile manifestations; spirit intercourse via mirrors, crystals, and so forth. (This is merely using such devices as objects upon which to focus attention. Often ESP impressions could be elicited by creating a psi-conducive state of consciousness.)

Other phenomena included were apparitions; visions and previsions; dreams (psychic ones, it is presumed); presentiments (precognitive experiences); spirit influence; involuntary utterances while the psychic was still partially conscious (a form of trance mediumship); and possession (also a type of mediumship).

Unfortunately, to most people involved in the Spiritualist controversy, these phenomena were either caused by the dead or by demons, or were fraud. Only a few scientists of the day, such as William Crookes, were aware that many of these displays could be due to a PK force inherent in living organisms or ESP from living persons—not necessarily from the dead.

Usually these phenomena occurred during darkened seances. The medium would sit at a table with a circle of observers about her, the lights were turned off, and telekinetic effects would allegedly be produced. Tables would levitate, objects would be hauled about, and phantoms would sometimes appear. If the question came down to whether the phenomena witnessed were due to spirits or fraud, each side had an armed battery with which to enter the fray. On one hand, there were many eminent scientists such as Professor R. M. D. Hare of the University of

Pennsylvania (who pioneered the use of mechanical apparatuses to test the force issuing during telekinesis), and Professor James Mapes, an eminent professor of chemistry, who along with William Crookes avowed that the facts and phenomena of Spiritualism were genuine although not necessarily the Spiritualist interpretation of them. On the other hand, it did not help the Spiritualists at all when their favorite mediums were caught time and time again faking their manifestations, nor when some of them, hardly more than con men, started writing their confessions for publication and handbooks on how to fake psychic phenomena began to appear. In 1891 an anonymous medium wrote *Revelations of a Spirit Medium*, a book so damaging that the Spiritualists themselves tried to suppress every available copy.

Yet, beyond this morass of delusion and deceit, it was obvious that at the heart of the matter was PK and ESP again molded by its practitioners to fit into the current mode of expression—from mesmerism to Spiritualism. If all of this sounds overly naïve and the reader finds it hard to believe that Spiritualism was taken so seriously, remember that the generation of the 1850s–1880s had little idea about the bounds of meaning of ESP and PK. These were new and astounding phenomena and the public had no means of evaluating them. Secondly, the large number of the cultured who openly sponsored the phenomena, as well as the hearty newspaper coverage, only encouraged the movement and belief in the often exaggerated claims.

There also were sociological causes for the rise and rapid spread of Spiritualism. American society was in turmoil, especially the East Coast region which has been called the "burned-over district" because it gave birth to several offbeat religious movements during this era, including Mormonism and Adventism. According to the sociologist G. K. Nelson, in his *Spiritualism and Society* (1969), the rise of Spiritualism was abetted by a mixture of psychological and sociological conditions. Nelson argues that the East Coast area was a great mixture of immigrant cultures, so no cohesive cultural pattern had yet been formulated. Initially, Spiritualism was an answer to this chaos, since it was a religion which offered its investigators demonstrations of its chief tenet—that man could consort with the dead. This chaos was also brought about by the Darwinian revolution which burst upon the scene while Spiritualism was still spreading at a quick pace. Evolution was a serious challenge to the religious establishment. To those already in social upheaval, Darwin's writings were but a further spur to find new idols to worship. To them Spiritualism, which was termed the "scientific religion," was a logical movement to join.

However, with the onset of the Civil War, exposures of many prominent mediums, lack of organization, coupled with fanaticism and crackpotism, the movement in the United States faltered. Yet, in Great Britain Spiritualism flourished and was a constant challenge to the scientific community. Eminent scientists such as Alfred Russel Wallace had endorsed the movement and had embraced its creed. As with the ill-fated Seybert Commission (which never published anything beyond its preliminary report), a similar committee was set up in England in 1869 by the London Dialectical Society, which gathered testimony and investigated claims. The committee had several subsections, forming into two large groups that tried experiments for self-psychic development to determine if they could develop telekinetic effects without the use of a professional psychic. Both groups were successful. Their report, including several first-hand testimonies of psychical phenomena, was published in 1871 and was favorable to the genuineness of the phenomena.

The scientific establishment was still wary of lay committee work or claims, and conversions to Spiritualism of some of their own workers did little to help. What was clearly needed to jolt the scientific establishment of Victorian England was a great psychic, and an eminent scientist to investigate him. It was William Crookes, the famous chemist, who unwittingly paved the way for scientific psychical research by his ingenious experiments with the medium, D. D. Home.

D. D. Home was the most famous medium of his day. Unlike his confreres, he was never detected in fraud and displayed both ESP and PK (or more properly, telekinesis). Home's phenomena were often well observed in daylight. Even in 1972, ninety years after the founding of organized parapsychology (usually dated at 1882, the year of the founding of the Society for Psychical Research in England), the 1972 Convention of the Parapsychological Association, meeting in Edinburgh, Scotland, listened to a paper delivered by the Dutch parapsychologist, George Zorab, reevaluating Home's psi abilities.

Home was born in 1833 in Scotland but was raised in Connecticut by an aunt. By the time he reached adolescence, raps and other spontaneous displays of telekinesis often occurred in his presence in a manner similar to the Fox sisters. These manifestations were first investigated by a theologian and Orientalist, George Bush. Bush was very impressed by what he saw, and his validation was soon endorsed by Professor David A. Wells of Harvard and Professors Hare and Mapes. Home, sitting in order to induce phenomena deliberately, soon developed not only raps but stronger telekinesis, including levitation of objects and his own body. His fame quickly spread, and for the rest of his life he traveled over Europe, a welcomed guest in royal houses and among the elite.

The first attempts at scientific examination of Home's abilities came in 1867–1869 during his association with Lord Adare. Adare and Home traveled together and shared residence for long periods of time during which careful notes were made of all the psychical manifestations witnessed, both experimentally and spontaneously. These included telekinesis, fire immunity, levitation, ESP, and visual phenomena—ghostlike phantoms which would suddenly appear in Home's presence. Adare's *Experiences in Spiritualism with D. D. Home* was privately circulated in 1869 and published later in an edited version which was rereleased by the Society for Psychical Research in 1924. Here are two brief extracts from Adare's account. The first is from his notes on a sitting held while the percipients were sitting around a large wooden table. This was in 1868. The second is a spontaneous telekinetic display which Adare witnessed:

> . . . We felt strong vibrations on the table which was moved about, Augusta's couch was moved, (no one touching it) as was the screen at the head of her couch (no one touching it). The spirits also answered, and gave messages by rapping on the couch, altogether it wasn't a bad seance for convincing sceptics.

During the sitting, all the participants were seated around a circular table. The movement of objects and the raps occurred on the other side of the room which was not being used by any of those present. Home was, of course, visible and remained seated throughout the display.

The second extract reads as follows:

> . . . Last night I slept in Home's room at Ashley House. I did not go to bed till past three. Soon after I was in bed, there were evidences of a very strong influence in the room; and we saw lights and heard sounds, as if some one was endeavoring to make their voice audible to us; and we heard a sound like footsteps . . . There is a plaster of Paris crucifix, about one foot in length, hanging on the wall over Home's bed. We heard something being moved on the wall, and presently saw this crucifix waving in the air between us and the window. I could see nothing holding it; it appears to move by itself . . .

Reports such as these were typical and unlike most of the other mediums of the era, Home was completely open to any request for a scientific inquiry into his abilities.

When William Crookes entered the picture, he was already one of the most famous chemists of his day. He had invented several scientific gadgets such as the radiometer and had discovered the element, thallium. Before actively beginning his research, Crookes had announced his intention in the *Quarterly Journal of Science* (July 1870). Harshly criticizing the claims of the believers, Crookes stated that, in the face of all the tales of movement of objects, he would wish to see only a balance of his own moved with no contact. He also hinted that had mediums been willing to subject themselves to the confines of the scientific laboratory and the scrutiny of mechanical tests and experiments, the issue of the reality or sham of telekinesis could easily have been determined long before.

The scientific community applauded Crookes. They felt sure that if a man of such keen intellect and integrity were to explore the matter he would make short shift of the issue and expose for good the claims of Spiritualism which had become a scientific headache. These same colleagues bitterly turned on him when a year later, in 1871, again in the *Quarterly Journal of Science*, Crookes prefaced his report by saying:

> Opportunities having since offered for pursuing the investigation, I have gladly availed myself of them for applying to

these phenomena careful scientific testing experiments, and I have thus arrived at certain definite results which I think it right should be published. These experiments appear conclusively to establish the existence of a new force, in some unknown manner connected with the human organization which for convenience may be called the Psychic Force.[10]

Crookes's conversion was due primarily to D. D. Home who eagerly participated in well-controlled experiments—some of which were similar to the type of PK experiments on static objects carried out today in parapsychology. Other manifestations that Crookes witnessed with Home were more sensational. When research in parapsychology turned to the experimental study of ESP, the types of phenomena exhibited with such mediums as D. D. Home seemed to disappear. Several other physical mediums arrived on the scene during the next several decades, but none of these incredible displays have been witnessed by parapsychologists since the 1930s.*

Crookes witnessed exactly what he hoped to verify with Home. He was able to keep Home under good control while a table levitated. He was also able to measure the PK force by having Home exert his PK on a balance and on a table hooked to a balance. Several startling displays of telekinesis occurred in the laboratory, including not only the movement and floating of untouched objects, sometimes in enclosed cages, but the spontaneous appearance in the room of phantom forms. In one experiment a cage was constructed with an accordion inside. The cage was placed partially under a table so that there would only be room for one hand to hold one end of the accordion. Crookes devised this test to see if under these conditions Home could affect the object:

> Mr. Home took the accordian between the thumb and middle finger of one hand at the opposite end to the keys. . . . Having previously opened the bar key myself, and the cage being drawn from under the table so as just to allow the accordian to be passed in with its keys downward, it was

* Nonetheless, the European parapsychologists, notably in France, Germany, and Poland, continued with the study of gifted physical mediums up until the 1940s and witnessed similar phenomena as were recorded with D. D. Home with such subjects as Franek Kluski, Rudi Schneider, and others, as chronicled in chapter 7.

pushed back as close as Mr. Home's arm would permit, but without hiding his hand from those next to him. Very soon the accordian was seen by those on each side to be waving about in a somewhat curious manner; then sounds came from it, and finally several notes were played in succession. Whilst this was going on, my assistant went under the table and reported that the accordian was expanding and contracting; at the same time, it was seen that the hand of Mr. Home by which it was held was quite still, his other hand resting on the table.

   . . . the sequel was still more striking, for Mr. Home then removed his hand altogether from the accordian, taking it [his hand] quite out of the cage, and placed it on the hand of the person next to him. The instrument then continued to play, no person touching it and no hand being near it.

Toward the end of this experiment Crookes sent a battery current around the cage and the telekinetic motions ceased. Several of Crookes's colleagues criticized these experiments harshly, but he answered all of them in detail in the *Quarterly Journal of Science*. Although Crookes was to be the center of controversy because of his support of another medium, Florence Cook, his experiments with whom were poorly reported, he eventually retired from psychical research and would have little to do with it even though he was elected president of the SPR in 1896. In 1898 when he was elected president of the British Association (a highly regarded scientific body), he again confirmed his support of psychical research and his past observations. He made a similar statement in 1917, two years before his death.

So far it would appear that most scientific research was devoted to telekinesis and not ESP which is the focus of contemporary parapsychological interest. The reasons for this are many: they were the crux of Spiritualism at the time; they were more easily observed and tested; and they were well within the province and interests of the physical sciences, which were more developed than the barely developing study of psychology which eventually undertook the study of ESP. In spite of the major interest focused on telekinesis, ESP also was being investigated by a few pioneer scientists during the emotionally heated days of the Spiritualist controversy.

The pioneer of ESP research at this time was Sir William Barrett who was interested in the reports of ESP occurring during hypnosis. After a critical evaluation of the problem he offered a paper on the subject to the British Association in 1876. The very topic of thought transference raised heated objections. Finally, by a close vote the paper was read before the subsection on anthropology, but not published. Barrett's presentation created a stir, and the physicist soon found himself in correspondence with several witnesses to ESP-type experiences and performances. What was novel to Barrett was that many of the phenomena stemmed not from subjects in the hypnotic state, but in the waking state. After 1876 Barrett started an exploration of waking thought transference.

By the 1880s it was clear that the scientific establishment and the intellectual elite could no longer ignore the problem of psychical phenomena. In 1882, as noted earlier, several scholars joined forces to form the Society for Psychical Research. The Society included some of the best minds of its day. William Barrett had suggested the idea of such a society in conjunction with some Spiritualist leaders who were interested in the scientific orientation of research. However, the society soon developed into something more than just another amateur organization. It became a disciplined and scientifically oriented body whose leading lights included its first president, Professor Henry Sidgwick of Cambridge, F. W. H. Myers, also of Cambridge, the physicist Lord Rayleigh, and the scholar Edmund Gurney, among others.

The purpose of the SPR was outlined by its various committees, each set up with the task of investigating a certain aspect of psychical research. These committees were to study the following: (1) thought-transference; (2) hypnosis and claims of clairvoyance and other phenomena alleged to occur during the mesmeric state; (3) the study of Reichenbach's theories (see page 40) and the gifted psychic; (4) apparitions and haunted houses; (5) physical phenomena reported by the Spiritualists; and (6) the study of literature and history bearing on psychical phenomena.

Psychical research was now born as a topic for scientific discovery. The early SPR set out to determine certain criteria of evidence, methods of research, experimental programs, and to collect spontaneous cases of everything from telepathy to apparitions. From the date 1882 when we speak of psychical research we are speaking about the research undertaken by this body which became the nucleus for all parapsychological work until the universities began taking an interest in the subject. The SPR was very much preoccupied with studying whether psi indicated survival of death. This was natural, since the best psychics available usually claimed that their ESP impressions stemmed from the dead. Nonetheless, the early SPR members were also interested in telepathy (a term coined by Myers in 1882), and allied phenomena which did not bear on the survival question. Because of this, early psychical research soon began to move away from the study of telekinesis and oriented itself more to ESP-type phenomena displayed by gifted psychics. From this, parapsychology in the United States and England became primarily the study of mental phenomena, and over the next few decades the study of PK became the province of continental parapsychologists. The fact that parapsychology in the United States and England is ESP-oriented stems from this historical development.

From 1882 onward psychical research was no longer to be a seance-room, cops-and-robbers affair, not a pseudoscientific occultist study, but a rigorous and disciplined experimental and descriptive science organized by some of the best minds of the era. Many of the Spiritualist elements who helped form the SPR soon fell away as they realized that the new society, while sympathetic to the survival question, was more eager to approach any topic with incredulity and armed with vigorous plans and designs for experiments. If one were to study spontaneous cases of apparitions, precognitions, or telepathic experiences, there were rigorous criteria of evidence (similar to legal evidence) by which such cases could be evaluated. The Spiritualists, more interested in the direct and simplistic religious aspects of the subject, ultimately abandoned the SPR completely. For years a feud existed between the Spiritualists who saw the SPR as unnecessarily skeptical and the SPR which saw Spiritualists as credulous or simplistic.

In 1885 a similar body was organized in the United States, but due to financial difficulties, merged with the British society in 1890. In 1887 Richard Hodgson, a skeptical and dedicated researcher, took charge of the American branch until his death in 1905. Then Professor James H. Hyslop, formerly of Columbia University, took over the reins of the branch and reinstituted it as a reconstituted, separate entity as it so remains today.

Throughout these years investigators accumulated the first large body of scientifically acceptable evidence for ESP and PK and developed the techniques for research and evaluation which are the mainstay of modern parapsychology. The research carried out by the SPR and the ASPR became the major force of world parapsychology until the 1930s when J. B. Rhine began his ESP program at Duke University and a new era in psychical research dawned. It was at this time that Rhine coined the term estrasensory perception and adopted the old but unused term "parapsychology" to replace the term "psychical research."

From a scientific standpoint, the founding of the SPR in 1882 began a century of inquiry into psychical phenomena.

3

ESP — the Search and the Evidence

When psychical research was born in 1882, the evidence which compelled its scientific recognition stemmed from two different approaches to the study of the subject. Firstly, there was the evidence that scientists such as William Barrett collected from experiments in thought transference. Secondly, there was the background which led to experimental displays of ESP, spontaneous cases of psi, such as telepathic dreams reported by credible witnesses. From the beginnings of organized research, psychical research was both an experimental science and a descriptive science. Even today there are some parapsychologists who argue as to which approach is the more fruitful or important. In 1962 the *International Journal of Parapsychology* invited some of the foremost authorities on parapsychology to answer a series of questions on the future of parapsychology.[1] Among the participants were Professor C. J. Ducasse of Brown University; the psychoanalyst Jule Eisenbud; Professor Hornell Hart, formerly of Duke University; the pioneer of psychoanalysis, C. G. Jung; Henry Margenau, the well-known physicist; Dr. Gardner Murphy; J. Fraser Nicol; J. B. Rhine; Gertrude Schmeidler of the City College of the City University of New York; Ian Stevenson; the pioneer French parapsychologist René Warcollier, and others who have identified their professional careers with parapsychology.

One of the questions asked during this survey was whether or not the future of parapsychology should be slanted toward quantitative (experimental) or qualitative (case study) approaches. A few of the participants, notably Henry Margenau, felt that parapsychology is above all an experimental science. He wrote that ". . . qualitative work is merely incompletely analyzed work, all good work is quantitative." This posture was challenged by another physicist, Joseph Rush, who wrote that ". . . we are now in a position to relax our anxiety to prove the existence of psi phenomena by quantitative exploration. . . . The processes of subjective experience cannot yet be tagged and numbered, but they have to be dealt with. Certainly I would not depreciate the role of measurement and mathematical analysis in scientific investigations. But insight is essential also."

However, the majority of those responding felt that parapsychology is at heart an integral combination of both natural observation and experimental confirmation. J. B. Rhine adroitly answered that, while quantitative work is of extreme importance in judging the evidence of a certain phenomenon, quantitative methods (such as statistical measurements) are not the only criterion of evidence and that the evaluation of spontaneous cases need not be mathematically calculated to be valid. These views point out that parapsychology is a combination of a natural and an experimental science, neither approach of which negates the other. Although in the following chapters the specific contributions that both quantitative and qualitative approaches have made to parapsychology are outlined, in this chapter a consideration will be given to how psychical phenomena have been studied in each of the two methods and what type of evidence has been achieved.

While some experimental work was being done during parapsychology's early years, the emphasis was on the collection of spontaneous cases. The chief result of this research was the SPR's *Phantasms of the Living*[2] written chiefly by Edmund Gurney and coauthored by F. W. H. Myers and Frank Podmore who joined at this same time. Edmund Gurney was born in 1847, attended Trinity College and studied music, but later switched to medicine at University College, London. Finding that medicine did not suit him, he turned to law with an interest in philosophy. It was this last discipline that brought him into contact with Henry Sidgwick and F. W. H. Myers and their preoccupation with Spiritualism. When the SPR was founded, Gurney became its second honorary secretary and soon began work on *Phantasms of the Living.*

The idea for *Phantasms of the Living* came from the cases collected by the Literary Committee which was amassing spontaneous cases. The most common experiences that had been assembled were "crisis cases." In these incidents an individual would either see an apparition or have an ESP-type experience at the same time a close friend or relative had an accident or died. There was an enormous bulk of such incidents which Gurney and others set out to evaluate. Gurney and Myers did the actual writing while Podmore was a chief investigator. Of the types of cases collected for *Phantasms of the Living,* several forms of spontaneous psi experiences were at hand: crisis apparitions; experimental telepathy (thought transference engendered by conscious will of one of the parties involved); spontaneous telepathy; and telepathic experiences in which either a voice or even a physical sensation was telepathically hallucinated, concordant with a crisis the agent was undergoing. The authors of *Phantasms of the Living* believed that all such experiences were a product of telepathy. Even apparitions were interpreted to be not physical, but merely a hallucination of sight catalyzed by thought-transference. Several early psychical researchers debated this point, but Gurney felt that, since only rarely did apparitions leave any proof of their objective existence (such as moving objects, opening doors, and so forth), they were probably not hallucinations but very real visions conjured forth by the mind as a reaction to a telepathic message. If more than one person saw an apparition, Gurney argued that the initial percipient "infected" the others. It was the difficulty in stretching the pure telepathic theory that eventually led Myers and others to revise or reject the telepathic apparitional theory. Nonetheless, all these forms of crisis cases were interpreted as having a common base in telepathy.

However, more important than what the evidence pointed to was the problem of just how one can critically evaluate these types of personal experiences. For instance the following crisis telepathy case is from *Phantasms of the Living.* It was the duty of

Gurney and Podmore to figure out criteria of evidence by which to evaluate such cases.

> My father and brother were on a journey during the winter. I was expecting them home, without knowing the exact day of their return. The date, to the best of my recollection, was the winter of 1871–2. I had gone to bed at my usual time, about 11 P.M. Some time in the night I had a vivid dream, which made a great impression on me. I dreamt I was looking out of a window, when I saw father driving in a Spids sledge, followed in another by my brother. They had to pass a cross-road, on which another traveller was driving very fast, also in a sledge with one horse. Father seemed to drive on without observing the other fellow, who would without fault have driven over father if he had not made his horse rear, so that I saw my father drive under the hoofs of the horse. Every moment I expected the horse would fall down and crush him. I called out "Father! Father!" and awoke in a great fright. The next morning my father and brother returned. I said to him, "I am so glad to see you arrive quite safely, as I had such a dreadful dream about you last night." My brother said, "You could not have been in greater fright about him than I was," and then he related to me what had happened which tallied exactly with my dream. My brother in his fright, when he saw the feet of the horse over father's head, called out, "Oh! Father, father!"   —Hilda West

Since Gurney and his colleagues were searching for not only bulk, but also strong evidence for psi, it is easy to see why his legally trained mind should be impressed by this type of case. In *Phantasms of the Living* not only is Mrs. West's own statement printed, but also a statement verifying the incident, and the recounting of Mrs. West's experience by her brother who had been involved in the incident. A Mrs. Bidder who had heard the story shortly after it occurred also signed a statement to that effect. Mr. Crowe, the brother, stated that Mrs. West recounted parts of her dream before he had told of their experience. To the legal mind, the evidence was satisfactory. This was the type of evidence that became a prerequisite before the SPR would seriously consider a report.

Gurney himself was especially interested in the evidential

aspects of his cases and in *Phantasms of the Living* wrote quite a bit on this matter. He argued that he did not think that faulty memory could account for distortions in the testimony which would make the cases any more evidential. Thus, he pointed out, these experiences were often accompanied by bizarre actions on the part of the percipients, such as waking up a relative from sleep to relate a dream, which would certainly etch itself in the witness's mind. The pure bulk of such cases and the fact that so many were similar ruled out the theory that all of them were a product of falsification. Further, Gurney also asserted, though this was not a major point of his argument, that he had been very impressed by the sincere emotional responses he had seen during his own interviews with the various witnesses.

Gurney's first point, that faulty memory could not account for the cases, is one of the most controversial issues in psychical research. The problem of malobservation was of special interest to Richard Hodgson, who in conjunction with a conjurer, A. J. Davey, published a paper, "The Possibilities of Malobservation and Lapse of Memory from a Practical Point of View" (*Proceedings:* SPR IV [1887]: 381–495), a year after *Phantasms of the Living* was published. Hodgson was working on another problem which had an ultimate bearing on the evaluation that can be made of such cases. He wanted to see if an individual, given the task of watching a medium carry out a demonstration of alleged psi, would in his report correctly report the transactions. In his experiment the conjurer, Davey, gave a demonstration of spirit slate writing, where written messages would appear on sealed slates. This was a popular phenomenon of the day which was enmeshed in very complicated methods of fraud. When the testimonies of the witnesses were scrutinized, they often bore little resemblance to what had actually taken place. This led many of the early psychical researchers to consider human testimony as worthless in its relation to psi.

Hodgson had required his witnesses to observe complex transactions, but spontaneous psi impressions are usually rather simple and uncomplicated. One only had to observe himself and his experience, not another person reporting. The large amount of corroborative evidence for the validity of the cases also offsets the malobservation/memory lapse argument. Chronic memory faults would necessitate our believing that many independent individuals made the same errors in their memory of the same incident. Gurney did find some discrepancies in the testimonies, but these were usually trivial. Another criticism of *Phantasms of the Living* was the age of the cases. Many of the reports had not been written down at the time of the incident but had been reported after several years. Critics argued that after long periods of time a person might unconsciously elaborate on the evidential aspects of a case and gloss over discrepancies to make the case look more impressive.

Gurney had used a great deal of corroborative evidence to check for this effect. However, a revealing rebuttal to this argument came years later. It is generally believed that if there is a long period between a psychic occurrence and the written records of it, memory lapses might easily lessen its value. In 1931, W. F. Prince, an American psychical researcher, collected a series of spontaneous cases, *Human Experiences,* published by his own Boston Society for Psychic Research. In writing up these cases for his monograph, Prince discovered that some of the correspondents who had sent him cases had also contributed to *Phantasms of the Living* back in the 1880s. Prince compared the common cases and came up with definite conclusions about them: (1) that the cases sent to him were not copied by the percipients from their earlier contributions to *Phantasms of the Living;* (2) that the discrepancies that did occur were trivial and did not usually affect that portion of the report dealing directly with the psychic experience being narrated; and (3) that these few discrepancies actually weakened the case, not strengthened it by elaboration as the critics had claimed.

However, when *Phantasms of the Living* appeared in 1886 the popular press went in for the attack. The criticisms broke down into two major groups: that there was no contemporary evidence such as written letters describing the experiences as occurring on the date claimed by the witnesses and that there was not enough consideration offered the reader on the psychological and medical competency of the witnesses.

The evidential aspects of these cases has been emphasized, since this factor was the crucial one that Gurney and his collaborators faced in trying to prove psi to the scientific world. Nonetheless, certain patterns and principles about psi and how it appears in daily life began to emerge from *Phantasms of the Living*. For one thing, the SPR authors had made an important shift in the study of psi from the professional psychic or gifted subject to the common man. The fact that everyone might have a potential for psychic experiences was well illustrated and emphasized by this early case collection. *Phantasms of the Living* also revealed that if a large body of cases were collected, they tended to fall within certain categories of experiences, for example, crisis apparitions, telepathic impressions, and other forms that were previously mentioned. A third point that Gurney uncovered was that such occurrences were well beyond mere coincidence. Many people dream of death, and it is not unlikely that once in a great while an actual death corresponds with such a dream. In analyzing the number of cases of crisis apparitions and by comparing them to the death rate in Great Britain, Gurney calculated that the SPR cases represented a close correspondence between the psi event and death at the ratio of trillions to one. This is well beyond coincidence.

Of course, *Phantasms of the Living* also offered interpretations on the nature of psi as evidenced by the reports which filled the huge two-volume book. This led to the debate on whether apparitions were merely telepathic or something more.

In order to answer several criticisms leveled at *Phantasms of the Living* and make the evidential case for psi even stronger, a committee was formed under the direction of Professor Henry Sidgwick with instructions to amass another collection of spontaneous cases. Work was begun in 1889, a year after Gurney's tragic death by chloroform either by accident or suicide.

The Census of Hallucinations, as it was called when published by the SPR in 1894,[3] was a survey of cases reported in response to the following question put to large groups of the English public: "Have you ever, when believing yourself to be completely awake, had a vivid impression of seeing or being touched by a living being or inanimate object, or of hearing a voice, which impression, so far as you could discover, was not due to any external cause?"

Four hundred volunteers served as case collectors while the actual report was the combined effort of Professor Sidgwick, Alice Johnson, Frank Podmore, and A. T. Myers (F. W. H.

Myers' brother). The *Census of Hallucinations*' questionnaire was given to large groups of people so that the collectors would not seek out only those whom they knew to have reported psi experiences. Also this was done in order to get some idea of the percentage of a normal population which had had ostensible psi experiences. Seventeen thousand replies were received, of which 2272 reported such experiences. However, when various normal explanations could be suggested to account for the experiences, only 1684 respondents remained who reported a total of 1942 occurrences. This gave a percentage of 9.9 percent of the general population which had what they felt to be psi experiences. Notably, women answered more affirmatively than men, which suggested not that women are any more prone to having ESP encounters, but that they more readily report them. Of these experiences, eighty were crisis apparitions coinciding within twelve hours of death of the individual represented by the form. From these eighty cases, the authors of the *Census of Hallucinations* selected for in-depth analysis thirty-two cases which were more evidential than the rest. A broader range of cases can be found in the *Census of Hallucinations* than in *Phantasms of the Living*. These include death coincidence, unrecognized apparitions, experimentally induced hallucinations (via ESP), apparitions coinciding with illness, collective cases (seen or heard by more than just one witness), apparitions of the dead, and so on.

The emotional level and descriptions of these cases are similar to those in *Phantasms of the Living*. The following is a typical case where the experience had both a visual and an auditory effect:

> It occurred at Bury (Lancashire), about fourteen years ago; I was awakened by a rattling noise at the window, and wakened my step-brother, with whom I was sleeping, and asked him if he could hear it. He told me to go to sleep, there was nothing. The rattle came again in a few minutes, and I sat up in bed, and distinctly saw the image of one of my step-brothers (who at the time was in Blackpool) pass from the window towards the door. Time, 2:30 A.M.
>
> I was in good health and spirits. Age eighteen.
>
> I had not seen him for some time. He had not been home for two or three months. We heard next morning that he had been taken ill and died about 2:30 A.M.
>
> Three step-brothers and myself slept in the same room. I

awakened them, but they could not see anything. My father, hearing the talking, got out of bed, and came into the room. I told him what I had seen, and he got his watch and said, "We will see if we hear anything of him."

Since corroboratory material was required by the SPR to substantiate such anecdotes, the percipient's brother sent in a statement verifying the report.

Other cases from the *Census of Hallucinations* included solely auditory experiences, such as hearing one's name called by a recognizable voice coincidental with either death or accident. In these cases, as with some apparitional cases, the "hallucination" was collectively perceived.

When a statistical breakdown was made of the *Census of Hallucinations* cases, it was clear that more visual than auditory experiences were recorded. The vast majority of them reportedly emanated from living persons, followed by experiences relating to deceased persons. These took precedence over cases reported of religious figures, unrecognized phantoms, animal forms, and so forth. The great majority of individuals responding reported that they had had only one such experience; several others reported having had two alleged encounters with psi; and a very few had between three to six. This pointed to a similar principle uncovered by *Phantasms of the Living*—that persons having spontaneous psi perceptions are not necessarily gifted with ESP.

In judging the conditions under which psi seems to operate, the main finding was that apparitions were most often seen either when the percipient was up and about but indoors, or lying awake in bed. The *Census of Hallucinations*' main single contribution was that apparitions were most often seen, or reported, within one year of the agent's death and then trailed off as the years went by. Postmortem apparitions seen ten years after death were relatively rare. These general findings were basically confirmed in the analysis of auditory and tactile cases.

The preeminent achievement of the *Census of Hallucinations* was that its undertaking was armed with the experience of *Phantasms of the Living*. The SPR could proceed with the investigation of spontaneous cases bearing in mind the criticisms they were bound to receive. In this light, the *Census of Hallucinations* achieved an evidential standard far exceeding any prior collection or similar census taken during the same period in France, Germany, Russia, and Brazil. (The idea of the *Census of Hallucinations* had grown out of the 1889 International Congress of Psychology held in Paris in which many SPR officials took an active part. Further conferences were held in London and Munich. It was hoped that eventually psi research could become international; little was it realized that psychology, faced with its own struggle for scientific recognition, would turn its back on psychical research for decades.)

The implications and force that the *Census of Hallucinations* had on its day and to parapsychology have been ably summarized by Dr. Alan Gauld, an authority on the early history of psychical research. In his critical and authoritative evaluation of early SPR research, *The Founders of Psychical Research*, Gauld writes:

> The methods by which the Census was conducted were of course antiquated and would certainly not be regarded as satisfactory today. None-the-less it was a work on a considerable scale, and one cannot easily point to any conclusions drawn by the Census Committee which the data do not justify. *The Report on the Census of Hallucinations* without doubt threw the onus on the critic. It was no longer up to psychical researchers to give reasons for supposing that there is a correlation between deaths and crisis apparitions. It was up to whoever disputed this to find stratagems ingenious enough to explain away the evidence.

Phantasms of the Living and the *Census of Hallucinations* represented the two major attempts at the qualitative case collection approach to parapsychology. There were others. Myers, for instance, made a special collection of apparitions of the dead. Case collections have been made throughout parapsychology's history. In France the celebrated astronomer Camille Flammarion published a huge collection of such cases, *L'Inconnue et les problèmes psychiques* in 1900 which later appeared in English as *The Unknown*. This was followed by a three-volume set, *Death and Its Mystery* (consisting of *Before Death*, *At the Moment of Death*, and *After Death*). Several contemporary parapsychologists have seen the need for continued case material. Thus in the 1960s, Rhea White, and others, published a collection of modern cases closely paralleling those of *Phantasms of the Living*.[4] Meanwhile, when the ESP controversy exploded at Duke University in Durham, North Carolina, many hundreds of anecdotal cases were submitted to the Duke Parapsychology Laboratory (now off campus as the Institute for Parapsychology of the Foundation for Research on the Nature of Man). These cases were collected and filed, as they are today, by Dr. Louisa Rhine who has often used them in her writings and in her book, *ESP in Life and Lab*.

For the claims of a science to be taken seriously, it must be able to control its phenomena to some extent. Even psychology, which deals with something as delicate as human and animal behavior, has repeatable experiments. Learning paradigms is one. If an animal is constantly rewarded if it behaves in a certain manner, it will eventually be able to carry out complex tasks. During World War II, B. F. Skinner proposed teaching pigeons to fly bombers by pecking controls for food. Although his plan was met with humor, there is little doubt that the plan was feasible. Unfortunately for parapsychology there have been few subjects who can control ESP or PK very well during experiments, and this is one reason that so much of psychical research in its early years was devoted to case studies and the problems of evidence. However, even from the first, pioneering parapsychologists realized that it was possible to at least demonstrate psi in the laboratory by using games of chance, so to speak. It was J. B. Rhine, of course, who shifted parapsychology's entire emphasis to this type of procedure when he demonstrated its efficacy during the 1930s. However, Rhine's work had considerable precedent.

One of the first to attempt experimentation was a well-known physicist of his day, Professor Oliver Lodge (later Sir Oliver Lodge). Although Lodge is usually remembered for his research into the study of life after death, his first inquiries were into thought transference. He was also one of the first scientists to report his results not only to other psychical investigators, but also to the scientific community at large through the voice box of the scientific establishment, *Nature* (vol. XXX).

In his *Nature* communication Lodge reported how he was invited to join Malcolm Guthrie in a demonstration of telepathy with a group of inquirers to which Guthrie belonged. In those experiments one subject would be blindfolded while two agents would try to "send" the subject a picture, a drawing, or whatever was used as the target. In his experiment, Lodge used a large sheet of paper with a square on one side and a Saint Andrew's cross on the other, each agent concentrating on only one target. He set the target between the two agents used in the experiment. The use of two targets was unusual, but finally the percipient drew a square with a cross in it. The percipient had correctly received both impressions. In the experiments several other targets were used. Unfortunately, Lodge did not devise any method of statistically evaluating his experiments; instead while his procedure was experimental, his evaluations were not. If the reproduced drawings resembled the target, it was judged a hit, if not, a miss. Some of the reproductions were astoundingly similar to the targets.

Lodge later adopted a mathematical technique of evaluation in his experiments with two girls in Carinthia which he summarized in his book, *The Survival of Man* (1909). Control of the experiments was unfortunately poor, and the two girls were permitted to hold hands even though a wooden panel separated them. This did not rule out the possibility of some sort of code between them. Lodge had highly significant results with playing cards as the targets for one to send to the other. Out of sixteen initial trials, ten were correct, six incorrect. Lodge calculated this as odds of ten million to one. When the girls were not in contact, their scores fall nearly to chance, so the critic would be correct in judging the experiment as worthless as scientific evidence for ESP.

The use of cards became quite common in early telepathy tests, and such experiments were carried out in Germany, France, and England with varying degrees of success. Usually the experimenters were working with gifted subjects, often under hypnosis. For example, experiments of this type were carried out by Mrs. Sidgwick, Miss Johnson, Professor Sidgwick, and A. T. Myers in which two-digit numbers were used as targets. The hypnotist was G. A. Smith and supervision of the tests usually fell to Mrs. Sidgwick. The prize subject was a Miss B. Mrs. Sidgwick reported in another paper that in the first experiment 131 numbers out of 644 were correctly guessed. This is far above chance. The subject could not have second-guessed the numbers (a critical problem in such experiments), since they were drawn randomly from a bag.[5]

While trying to "send" cards and pictures was very popular in early thought-transference experiments, the first scientist to show that telepathy tests could be mathematically analyzed was the French physiologist, Charles Richet in an article he presented in the *Revue Philosophique* in December 1884. In this experiment the subjects had to guess the suits of playing cards, a one in four probability. Out of 2927 trials, 789 correct hits were made. This is 57 more than what guesswork would allow.

While telepathy experiments were going on all over the world (Ochorowicz on the Continent, Gurney in Great Britain, Blair Thaw in New York, and Max Dessoir in Berlin*), the main objection to so much of the work was that rarely were the experiments reported in such a way that the reader, especially the suspicious scientist, could be sure that fraud could not have taken place. Although it is doubtful if many of these early experiments were due to fraud, there always was that possibility. The early SPR leaders had been favorably impressed by the alleged thought transference of the Creery sisters and had written of them in their publications only to learn later that a code had been used during at least some of the experiments. What science really needed was a fraud-proof experiment.

This very type of controlled experimentation was carried out in 1920 at Groningen University, Holland. The experiments were so ingeniously done and the results so striking that they have become famous. The tests were conducted by two professors of the university, G. Heymans and H. J. F. W. Brugmans, and a psychiatrist, A. A. Weinberg. None of the three was primarily a parapsychologist and after these experiments made no other notable contributions to the subject. The impetus for the research came when Heymans discovered a student, A. Van Dam, who was a gifted telepath. In the experiment two rooms of the university's psychology laboratory, one atop the other, were used. The experimenters ran the test from the upper floor and Van Dam was on the lower floor. In order to observe Van Dam, a window was cut in the floor and was acoustically sealed.

* It was Dessoir who coined the term parapsychology.

Van Dam was blindfolded and seated in front of a screen that was closed over by a curtain. Only his hand could extend through the curtain to a specially prepared board placed in front of him which was also visually blocked off by the curtain. The board was a checkerboard with 48 lettered and numbered squares. Van Dam was to move his hand over the board and then stop to designate a square which was being concentrated upon by the experimenters. The target squares were picked by a random selection of letters and numbers from a shuffled pack. Van Dam was also often hooked to a primitive physiological apparatus by which the experimenters could determine when he was in a very passive state of awareness which they felt to be conducive to psi.*

The results were amazing. In just the first series, Van Dam achieved thirty-two out of eighty correct responses. Since the odds for each success were 1:48, the resulting data were analyzed as giving odds of one in seventy-nine quintrillion! More successes followed.[6] The success rate of the Groningen experiments were highly correlated with Van Dam's "feeling of passivity."

The Groningen experiments have become a classic of ESP research due to the care with which they were carried out. Thus the quantitative approach did demonstrate that, like the qualitative approach, it could also uncover both evidence for psi and data concerning the principles by which it is governed. When J. B. Rhine wrote *Extrasensory Perception* in 1934 he stated that the

> . . . study of Brugmans' at Groningen (with Professor Heymans) is a double-step forward, for it aimed to go beyond the first problem of proof and to try to find facts of natural relationships in the direction mainly of physiological measurements correlated with success in "telepathy." And the results of Brugmans are striking also in proof-value, as well as contributing something to our knowledge of conditions. The 187 trials yielded 60 successes as against 4 for chance expectation. The conditions for exclusion of sensory perception were elaborate and appear highly satisfactory.

* This apparatus was similar to a galvanometer. It is unique that these Dutch experimenters foreshadowed the use of psychophysiological devices to find psi-conducive states.

The Groningen experiments illustrated another step forward in ESP research, that is the gradual shift of research from organized psychical research societies to the university campus. The reason for this is twofold. Firstly, the ASPR and the SPR were not carrying out ESP research, but were instead still engaged in other areas of parapsychology. Secondly, psychology had begun to develop as a science and had established itself as a standard university study. Even though parapsychology was still *persona non grata* to the academic and psychological establishment, studying ESP could be done using standard research techniques developed by the infant science of experimental psychology. Usually these investigations, abortive as they were, stemmed from endowments.

In 1912, Stanford University offered such an inducement for the study of psychical research and Dr. John Coover undertook the project. This was a rather unfortunate choice, since Coover was extremely biased against belief in ESP and could not have been considered even an honest skeptic. He began his research with the criterion that, for any experiment to be considered evidence of ESP, the odds against chance had to be 50,000 to 1. This was a preposterous standard, since odds of 100 to 1 are clearly considered to be statistically significant in any scientific experiment. Coover used playing cards minus the face cards. One hundred subjects made one hundred guesses each. It is here that Coover made his most humorous *faux pas*. Coover designed his experiments to prove the existence of telepathy only, not clairvoyance, precognition, or other psi effects. In order to test only for telepathy, he had his subjects guess at the cards while they were being concentrated upon by an agent, and fifty trials where the card was laid flat down without "telepathy" being attempted. He then compared the two sets of data and found no difference. Because of this, he wrote, "various statistical treatments of the data fail to reveal any cause beyond chance." The modern reader can see that Coover had been unaware of the possibility of clairvoyance ("clear-seeing"), a type of psi effect from a physical object that would not necessitate anyone's being aware of the target number in order for the subject to discern it. As stated, Coover stopped only at comparing the telepathy scores (when the agent tried to send the target) to the control series (in which the agent left the card face down). Since he found no statistical difference in the success rate between these different conditions, he concluded that no evidence for telepathy existed. Coover, of course, worked from the stance that there was no such thing as clairvoyance. Coover did not, however, check to see if the level of successful guessing was above chance during the total experiment. He did not analyze the *entire* set of calls which would include telepathy *and* clairvoyance. It was only later that experimental parapsychologists discovered that a subject could use ESP to ascertain target numbers or symbols on cards without anyone trying to "send" the target. Had Coover combined his two sets of data and counted the excess of correct guesses and then compared them to what chance would allow, he would have found that his own results showed an excess of success at 200 to 1 odds against chance. This is far below his criteria that evidence for telepathy would have to show odds of 50,000 to 1, but is above what chance would allow.

Coover also compared the results of psychics to a normal population in a similar test and found no difference. Again, he worked from the faulty premise that only certain gifted subjects could exhibit psi. This was a commonly held notion in the 1910s, but it has since been shown that a large group of subjects could often show a mass ESP effect. That is, while no one member of a group scores above chance significantly, the total group score *is* significantly above chance. Coover engaged in a few more investigations of ESP and other psychical phenomena and issued a huge and padded monograph, *Experiments in Psychical Research* (1917). The rest of the endowment was shifted to other less-than-psychic projects.

A second major intrusion of psychical research on the college campuses was made by L. T. Troland at Harvard. Several years earlier, William James had set up an endowment for the study of psychical phenomena there and Troland took advantage of this. Aided by an enthusiastic donor, he carried out his experimental work during 1916–1917.

Troland used a novel apparatus for his tests. The subject peered into a specially built box and had to guess which side of the box was to be lit up. An electric switch randomly illuminated either side of the box and the subject made his choice by

hitting a second switch which automatically recorded his call.*
Unfortunately, Troland, like Coover, was extremely superficial
in his research. He carried out only 605 trials which showed no
clear evidence of anything.[7]

A happier story came from Harvard in 1925–1926 and was
due to the experiments of George Estabrooks who used standard
playing cards for his tests. In his first set of experiments the subjects and experimenters were separated in a double room by a
door. When the subjects were to make their guesses, a red light
flashed on in their partitioned area. Eighty-three sets of twenty
guesses were made, a total of 1660 guesses. The results showed
over one hundred correct guesses above the chance level at odds
of 10 million to 1.

For a second set of experiments the subjects were in an entirely different room, sixty feet away. However, instead of
achieving scores above chance, the subjects scored below
chance. This is now called the "psi-miss" effect. It later became
well known that if subjects were not comfortable in the test situation, their scores would drop to chance. If conditions were
worse, their scores would dip below chance as a sort of psychic
sabotage of the experiment. Estabrooks could not appreciate this
in 1925–1926, although he did make an observation that has
since become very important in parapsychology: that over time
ESP scores gradually decline. (This was not a novel claim, since
Ina Jephson of the SPR found a similar feature in her tests and
as far back as the Guthrie experiments declines were commented
upon. However, Estabrooks was the first to observe it in the
truly experimental milieu.) The psi-miss in Estabrooks' experiments were only at odds of 100 to 1. This is significant but not
beyond being an artifact or fluke. Unfortunately, neither Estabrooks nor anybody else will ever know, since he discontinued
his experiments at that point.[8]

Both the qualitative and the quantitative approaches have contributed immensely to our knowledge of psi. However, this is

* In order to appreciate the novelty of Troland's experiments, similar
completely randomized and automatic recording devices did not become commonplace in parapsychology until the 1960s. The pioneering
experiments were initiated in France, and then American researchers,
mostly at the Foundation for Research on the Nature of Man (FRNM)
adopted the technique as a standard research procedure.

not to say that all research into ESP can be so easily labeled as belonging to one or the other. Some very important work has been a combination of both methods.

A typical example is that of Gilbert Murray, a professor of Greek at Oxford University. Murray discovered that he had ESP ability during informal guessing games with his family. Drawing upon the technique of the guessing game, he devised a system of ESP tests with himself as subject. The agents were usually his daughters. Murray would leave the room and one of his daughters (either Agnes Murray or Mrs. Arnold Toynbee) would choose a target, speak it aloud, and write it down. Murray would reenter the room and describe his impressions out loud. The following are some of their successes:

(1)

Mrs. Toynbee: Mr. Fisher and Mr. B. drinking beer in a café in Berlin.

Professor Murray: It's got something to do with a public house—no, it's beer. It's Fisher and somebody else drinking beer—somebody who has nothing to do with Fisher. I can't be at all sure—I should think little B.

(2)

Mrs. Toynbee: I think of a scene in a Strindberg play—two people sitting in a round tower and a man has a fainting fit and the wife hopes he is dead.

Professor Murray: This is a book and a book I haven't read. No—not Russian—not Italian. It's somebody lying in a faint. It's very horrible. I think somebody is fainting and his wife or some woman is hoping he is dead. It can't be Maeterlinck—I think I have read them all—Oh! it's Strindberg.

Mrs. Toynbee: Can you get the place?

Professor Murray: I thought of them in a great round tower. That was why I thought of Maeterlinck.

(3)

Mrs. Toynbee: The little crocodile in the captain's trunk, and him showing it to Isabel and me.

Professor Murray: Where's Denis' lizard gone? Because I thought it was Denis' lizard pursuing you and Isabel—the lizard on a bed in a cabin and you and Isabel looking at it.

These experiments were carried out from 1910 through the 1930s. Later experiments have been uncovered dated 1946.[9]

Although the Murray experiments are important, they are considered to be overrated. Their importance lies in the fact that Murray was a very prominent man of letters and his report of such repeated ESP successes had to be seriously considered by his academic colleagues as at least a prima-facie case for paranormal cognition. Mrs. Sidgwick once called them the most important evidence for ESP presented to the SPR.[10] History is, however, most cruel, and evaluating Murray's experiments today would lead the critic to be less impressed with them. The conditions were informal and lax. Other than one series witnessed by two officials of the SPR, Mr. and Mrs. W. H. Salter, the experiments were not supervised. A last criticism is the most difficult to overcome: Murray's success was a little too significantly successful. ESP has not been found to be concise over long periods of time, yet Murray's phenomenally accurate successes went on and on at a staggering rate. It was unfortunate that the targets were usually spoken aloud. Could it be that he was able to hear the targets being discussed? Murray said he was out of earshot; however, it is argued that he could have been responding to subliminally perceived voices. (That is, he unconsciously heard them at a level below the conscious threshold of direct perception, but not to his unconscious perception which then impressed this data onto his conscious mind. Such a phenomenon could easily have struck Murray as ESP.)

Although there is no direct evidence for this, there is some inferential support for the theory. Firstly, the actual floor plans and exact dimensions of the rooms used were not given in the reports. Secondly, when the targets were not verbalized, Murray did poorly. Thirdly, some of the "misses" seem to be misinterpretations of barely perceived audile cues which would be consistent with the subliminal-perception/hyperesthesia theory. When Murray's last experiments were finally published in 1973, Eric J. Dingwall made a critical review of this problem in his discussion, "Gilbert Murray's Experiments: Telepathy or Hyperaesthesia?" (*Proceedings:* SPR [1972], pt. 55). For example, the following seems to be a perfectly natural misperception:

Mr. Mellor (agent): I'm thinking of the operating room in the nursing home in which I was operated.

Professor Murray: I got an impression of a theatre. No. I can't get it. I'm now guessing—Covent Garden and Oedipus.

To Dingwall it was obvious that Murray heard the word "opera" in "operating" and "operated" and this subliminally brought to mind Covent Garden, London's prime opera house. Of course this does not prove the subliminal perception theory, but it is consistent. However, Dingwall does admit that some of Murray's successes are suggestive of ESP, but he adds that because no exact data is given on what was said by other members of the experimental group during casual conversation before the actual experiment, Murray's results just cannot be held up to be clear evidence of ESP. Themes could have arisen during these conversations which were later used as targets and guessed by Murray.

A more rigorous attempt at combining both quantitative and qualitative methods was made by Whately Carington, an English psychical investigator, using drawings. Carington based his work on earlier telepathy experimentation such as that done by Oliver Lodge. Striking successes were reported by amateur investigators years before. In one series two men, F. L. Usher and F. P. Burt, would try to send simple diagrams to each other. Some of their ESP tests using playing cards were carried out between the cities of Bristol and London. (See vol. 8 [1909] of the *Annals of Psychical Science* for full illustrations.)

In 1905 a similar project was undertaken by Miss C. Miles and Miss H. Ramsden in their search for long-distance telepathy. While on her travels, Miss Miles tried to send Miss Ramsden either written ideas or visualized pictures. These were often successful. Miss Miles wrote in her notebook from London: "October 27, Spectacles." Miss Ramsden in Buckinghamshire recorded "Oct. 27, 7 P.M. Spectacles. This was the only idea that came to me after waiting a long time." [11]

Carington utilized several nonpsychic participants for his research. He would draw a picture and hang it in his house for one night. He did this successively for ten nights. So his subjects would not second-guess his drawings, he opened a dictionary at random and sketched the first drawable object to which he came. After the experiment was over, he compared the target drawings to the results of his subjects. To score the pictures, Carington used an impartial method to avoid value judgments as to what was a hit or a miss. He thus had judges compare the unmarked guesses to all his targets without knowing from which night the various guesses were made until after each drawing had been assigned for a night. If a majority of guesses were assigned to the correct target, this would be evidence of ESP. Carington made a surprising discovery. Some of the participants' drawings were very accurate, but they were for the wrong night. Sometimes an obvious success for Tuesday's picture was a residue from Monday—latent ESP? Sometimes Tuesday's drawing was uncannily similar to Wednesday's target—precognition? The pictures were too obvious to be just flukes, but Carington carried out some further tests to verify the displacement effect. In this case outside judges were again used and the effect confirmed.[12]

Although Carington's picture-drawing tests did not show a phenomenally high rate of ESP, a paranormal factor was obviously present. And he made one of the most important discoveries in experimental ESP research, that is that telepathy, clairvoyance, precognition, and retrocognition were all constituents of a unified process and not truly independent phenomena.

It would be hard to describe Carington's ingenious experiments without at least mention of the picture-drawing experiments carried out by the writer Upton Sinclair and his wife as reported in his book, *Mental Radio* (1930). Mrs. Sinclair was a gifted subject, and during the experiments the agent (usually Sinclair) would go into another room and try to send her a simple drawing. Sometimes other agents were used and tests were carried out over substantial distances. Mrs. Sinclair would then try to visualize the drawing, reproduce it, and describe it. Two hundred and ninety experiments were carried out with 23 percent successes, 53 percent partial successes, and 24 percent failures. Often the partial successes revealed more about the psi process than the clear-cut ones. If complex geometric figures were used, certain elements that combined to form the figure would be separated and drawn independently. For example, Sinclair's secretary drew an oblong diamond. Mrs. Sinclair drew two bottomless triangles, one inverted, under and to the side of the other. If joined together the lines would have produced an oblong diamond. In other experiments Mrs. Sinclair would be able to receive only part of the diagram. For one experiment Sinclair used a rough sketch of a vase and flowers. The stems were drawn simply as lines coming from the top of the vase with black dots for the flowers. Mrs. Sinclair could only draw a similar bunch of random dots. Finally, she would often be able to draw a correct representation of the drawing but her interpretations would be curiously mistaken. Sinclair once drew a volcano consisting of an inverted cone with billowing blackish smoke. Mrs. Sinclair drew a fine representation of the figure but could not discern what it was and described the smoke as a "black beetle." Her ESP impression was obviously correct if we judge from her drawing. But had the experimenters merely judged by her verbal or written description, it probably would be considered a miss.

The most extensive series of drawing experiments were those carried out by René Warcollier. These experiments, in which Warcollier served sometimes as agent and sometimes as percipient, were carried out between different parts of France and with Gardner Murphy between France and the United States when Murphy was a professor at Columbia University. The major records of the first work appeared in Warcollier's 1921 publication, *La Télépathie*. He instituted several novel procedures, one of which was collective telepathy in which a group of agents tried to send a target picture to a group of percipients. René Sudre, in his *Treatise on Parapsychology*, gives an excellent summary of these attempts:

In 1920 Warcollier founded a society for telepathic studies the principal object of which was to set up posts for collective percipients, about ten persons to a group, placed in two rooms separated by a third, in which was the controller. External percipients, often abroad, concentrated at the same times. The attempt was made to transmit attitudes and visual images (playing cards, the time on a clock-face, printed words, drawings, etc.). Sometimes these last were projected on a luminous screen. Many coincidences were obtained, but usually with the same people. It did not appear certain that the effect of a group of agents is cumulative. Sensations were most successfully transmitted. A sympathetic relationship between agent and percipient did not seem to be necessary.

There were good and bad sittings. The long-distance trials (France-America) were more successful than the short-distance ones. A kind of mental contagion between the percipients was observed . . . The best agents proved to be also good percipients.

Mental contagion is one of the most intriguing of the characteristics that Warcollier found. During group sessions several percipients of a group often would have markedly similar drawings as though they were picking up the image not from the agent but from one another.*

During long-distance experiments between France and the United States, Warcollier noted that the best results occurred with participants of the United States who had visited France and mingled with the French group. He also noted that in all his tests the telepathic impressions often might not be received verbatim, but in a disguised or associated form. When Warcollier used the name "Socrates" as a target, a percipient received only associated themes, a figure of a head and a Greek temple. In 1948 the English edition of his work *Mind to Mind* appeared in which Warcollier went on to offer several observations about the psi process.:

1. Parallelism—if geometric figures are transmitted, the components of the figure may be disjointed and apparently received independently. In one experiment a rectangle enclosing five egg-shaped circles was received as several circles and a few drawings of angles ($\sqcup$, $<$, $\wedge$, and so forth).

2. Latency—the figure transmitted may not be perceived instantaneously but only later, from a few minutes to a few days. The figure laying in the subconscious may be distorted or reassembled during this time.

3. Dissociation—reception of the telepathic impression is often dissociated so that the figure or theme may be received symbolically or imperfectly.

* Sir Alister Hardy, a British zoologist, carried out a group ESP test and observed that people near each other shared impressions even if the group extrasensory effects had little to do with the actual target. This study has recently been published in Alister Hardy's coauthored book, with Robert Harvie and Arthur Koestler, *The Challenge of Chance* (New York: Random House, 1973).

4. Analysis—the image may be completely broken down into component parts. In one of Warcollier's illustrations a butterfly with circles in its wings was broken down into four components: the gross figure of the insect, four lines representing antennae, circles for the wing design, and a fourth form representing the contour of the sides of the wings.

5. Synthesis—in which separate components of the target image might be amalgamated.

6. Syncretism—where the components of the image are not received independently, but as a vague, "global" representation of the whole, received with no detail.

7. Movement—a drawn image is perceived by the percipient not as static, but with an element of motion to it. A group of overlapping arrow targets with a figure of a plane superimposed was reassembled as a circular wheel with flags (vaguely resembling the planes) attached to each side like some sort of spinning wheel apparatus.

8. Prägnanz—a target and its background will be assembled together into a "gestalt," as though the background were just as important as the actual target.

With the exception of Murray's last experiments, all of this work covers the period from the beginnings of organized parapsychology up to the 1930s. The reason for this is obvious. Parapsychology's face was drastically changed during the 1930s when all previous work was synthesized, elaborated upon, and a new rigorously controlled program of ESP research was undertaken at Duke University, spearheaded by J. B. Rhine and his wife, Louisa Rhine, under the sponsorship of William Mc-Dougall. While there had been well-controlled experiments prior to Duke, such as the Groningen studies and Estabrooks' Harvard experiments, these romances with ESP were brief and the impetus came from a sole experimenter or small groups. It was Rhine's idea to start a large-scale ESP research project, carry it out at length so enough data could be amassed for an impressive analysis to be made, and repeat the experiments under the most stringent controls. This research and its findings, to which we shall now turn, begins the birth of what is usually called modern parapsychology.

4

ESP in the Laboratory
— the Search Continued

When J. B. Rhine and his wife, Louisa Rhine, came to Duke University in Durham, North Carolina, it was not with the intent of shifting parapsychology into a new era of experimentalism. The Rhines originally earned their doctorates in the biological and botanical sciences due to their interest in plant physiology. But by 1925 they both were becoming preoccupied with the study of the paranormal and how it could be scientifically approached. During the 1920s, Spiritualism and spirit mediums were still the rage. In fact, the great tragedy of World War I had spurred a mild renaissance for the movement. As with several other psychical researchers, it was the claim that the dead could influence the living that began the Rhines' careers.

In 1926 the Rhines met William McDougall who had long been a champion of daring thinking in psychology, including psychical research. Although McDougall had done little research in the field, he had written several articles propagandizing for its scientific recognition. When he left Harvard University to take over a position at Duke, the Rhines followed, and began identifying their professional careers with parapsychology, as the new science of ESP research became known, replacing the term psychical research.

At first their studies were oriented toward mediumship and the question: When a medium is receiving veridical information about a deceased personality, is the medium getting this information from the deceased agent or through ESP (a word Rhine coined and popularized) from the living? After analyzing records and conducting experiments with the famous medium, Eileen Garrett, the Rhines realized that the issue was a stalemate. There was no way one could resolve the problem. If a medium were to give an accurate description of a postmortem personality and even, as a "test," give a nickname by which he was called in life and which the medium had no normal way of knowing, this information could be a combination of telepathy and clairvoyance and have nothing to do with a surviving entity wishing to communicate to the living. Because of this realization the Rhines shifted their research to the experimental study of ESP. By doing so, they left survival research and took most of parapsychology in the United States with them as they explored what they felt to be the more fruitful study of ESP between the living.

ESP research began at Duke University, spearheaded by J. B. Rhine in conjunction with McDougall, Dr. Helge Lundholm, and Dr. Karl Zener. Lundholm's main concern was the use of hypnosis to elicit ESP, but his work was not very successful and he ultimately withdrew from the program. Zener, an expert in perception, was consulted by Rhine on what type of target material was most neutral and could be used for ESP testing. The upshot of this testing was the development of Zener cards or ESP cards which have been commonly used for ESP research ever since. The Zener cards consisted of a pack of twenty-five cards, five cards each of five simple geometric figures—star, circle, cross, wavy lines, and rectangle (later changed to a square). Zener, too, withdrew from the program to devote attention to more main-line psychological research. Ultimately, J. B. Rhine carried the main burden of research alone. The basic testing technique was for the agent to try to send one percipient the symbol on the card. Each card would be concentrated upon and the subject would make a call. During a run of twenty-five calls, on the average five would be guessed by chance. However, if a subject could consistently guess more than five per run, then something more than chance was operating.* Later packs were used with an irregular or randomly selected number of the five symbols which were called open decks.

J. B. Rhine's preliminary tests were promising, but it was the discovery of his first gifted ESP subject that got things rolling at Duke. In May 1931 A. J. Linzmayer dropped into Rhine's laboratory. He had participated in some of Zener's tests and had done well. Rhine haphazardly asked him to guess the card he was holding. Linzmayer was reclining on a laboratory couch and Rhine was standing at a window out of his line of vision. Linzmayer guessed correctly. Rhine tried the experiment again, and again; Linzmayer was able to call nine correct responses in a row. The performance was repeated again the next day. Linzmayer liked to be tested best when slightly distracted, so Rhine took him on a country drive. Stopping the car and improvising a test, Linzmayer achieved fifteen correct calls in a row. He also scored well on other better controlled experiments. However, after several initial successes his scores began a downward slope and eventually he lost his ESP completely. In these experiments Rhine used two types of tests. In the first procedure Rhine looked at the cards directly (telepathy or GESP—

---

* It is not the intent of this book to explain the mathematics of probability. However, simple probability is analyzed by the following method: During random guesses there will be a certain standard deviation from exact probability. For example, if one did five ESP runs he will achieve approximately twenty-five hits, perhaps twenty-two or twenty-seven. After a test is done, one counts the actual observed deviation. This is divided by the standard deviation. This gives a critical ratio (CR) which gives a probability rating. The standard deviation in ESP tests is calculated by doubling the square root of the number of runs. If one did sixteen ESP runs the standard deviation would be 8 ($2\sqrt{16} = 8$). If the subject guesses sixteen extra hits, this would give a CR of 2.0 ($\frac{16}{8} = 2$). A CR of 2.0 is equal to odds of 20 to 1 or (p. = 0.05). Odds of 20 to 1 have been calculated to be significantly above chance. In ESP research odds of 100 to 1 or (p. = 0.01) are considered to be evidence of ESP. This is only the most elementary calculation used in ESP research. Other measurements will be explained, but the actual mathematics can be looked up in any standard statistics book. See also the J. B. Rhine and J. G. Pratt text, *Parapsychology—Frontier Science of the Mind*, for further details.

general extrasensory perception, since clairvoyance could account for the results). The second procedure consisted of clairvoyant tests in which no one looked at the cards. Linzmayer did well on both types.

Rhine soon discovered other gifted subjects, but the most prominent of them was Hubert Pearce. Unlike Linzmayer, Pearce usually did not achieve long runs of successes, but consistently scored above chance to a mild but avalanching degree as success after success kept stacking up. However, there were exceptions. Once when Rhine jokingly bet Pearce one hundred dollars that he couldn't call the correct response, Pearce proceeded to give a perfect 25/25—one of the few perfect scores ever recorded in parapsychology. By this time Rhine had been joined by three assistants—C. E. Stuart (who was originally a high-scoring subject himself), Sara Ownbey, and J. G. Pratt (who eventually made parapsychology his lifework). Pratt tested Pearce during one series of experiments in what was to become a classic in parapsychology, popularly called the "Pearce–Pratt Experiments."

As can be seen, much of the early ESP research was too informal and the methods were faulty. When all of this work was published by Rhine in his monograph *Extrasensory Perception* (1934), one of the main criticisms of the book was that the exact conditions under which many of the experiments were run had not been given. It was therefore difficult to evaluate the results critically, since the experimental conditions were not fully outlined, and the skeptic could easily believe that some fault in the conditions led to the success: fraud, sensory cues, and so forth. For example, in ESP testing the following experimental precautions must be rigorously adhered to:

1. The target card should not be written down until after the call is made. This is so that the subject cannot discern the correct card by sensory cuing such as hearing, even subconsciously, pencil strokes by which the symbol used to record the target might be identified. ($0 = 0$, $\sqsubset = \square$, $== = \approx$, $\wedge = \star$, $+ = +$). Or the subject should be isolated from the recorder. Prearranged random decks can also be used.

2. The subject, if a closed deck (five each of the five symbols) is being used, should not be told if he is right or wrong, since

the subject could then increase his chances of getting correct responses by pure inference of what the next card might be.

3. The cards should not be hand-shuffled, since imperfect shuffling might lead the target sequence to be similar to the preceding run. If the subject has a certain guessing habit in his call sequence, high scores might result due to an accidental concordance between bad shuffling and the subject's guessing pattern.

4. Onlookers should be discouraged, since they might be in collusion with the subject or cue him unconsciously in some way.

5. Different ESP packs should be used. If the subject sees a pack over and over again, he might be able to identify a card, even unconsciously, because of a mark or scratch on the back of the card.

6. The recording of the targets and responses should be carried out by another party, or independent parties, to check against unconscious or conscious recording error.

These precautions have been outlined by Robert Thouless in his *From Anecdote to Experiment in Psychical Research* but have been modified, abbreviated, or emphasized for the purposes of this book. Because of these procedural problems in ESP testing, the exact conditions under which experiments are conducted must be explained in full detail. When critics examined the Duke experiments, certain faults were discovered. For one thing it was not ruled out that the subject could not possibly see through the backs of the first roughly designed Zener cards. Such criticisms as this, and the above, can be offset by removing the percipient physically from the experimental area as was done in the Groningen experiments. This is what the Pearce-Pratt series attempted to do.

This series of experiments was run in 1933 from what was then the Physics Building at Duke University. Pratt was seated in one of the rooms there while Pearce walked over to another building, 100 yards away, and in another experiment, 250 yards away. At a set time Pratt began the clairvoyant-condition experiment by placing one target card aside from the pack and isolating it for one minute. Then the next card was similarly placed until all twenty-five cards had been used as targets. In order to offset any criticism of fraud, both Pratt and Pearce kept duplicate sets of their cards and call guesses. One copy of each was given to Rhine for an independent check. Using this technique, four experiments were run. A total of 1850 guesses were recorded of which 558 correct responses were made when chance could only account for 370. If one remembers the argument that critics of parapsychology employ of "shaky evidence of statistical significance," the shaky statistics of the Pearce–Pratt experiments were calculated as 22 thousand million to 1 odds against chance.

In spite of all precautions there have still been some criticisms of the Pearce–Pratt series, notably by C. E. M. Hansel, in his book *ESP—A Scientific Evaluation.* Hansel claims that Pearce, being uncontrolled, could leave his building, sneak back to Pratt's building, peek through a window transom, and copy or memorize the card sequences as Pratt turned them over to be recorded. Or that an accomplice could have done this for him. Hansel's criticisms are valid in the respect that Pearce should have been controlled; however, his interpretations are not workable when applied practically. In the *Journal* of the ASPR for July 1967 (vol. 61, pp. 254–67), Ian Stevenson has reviewed Hansel's charges by comparing this argument to the actual layout of the experimental rooms. Stevenson argues that the position and angles of the transoms are such that a spying procedure could not have been used as the desk top could not be seen from the transom.

Rhine's work with Pearce also incorporated attempts to determine what conditions favored ESP success. He found that if an observer was introduced into the experiment the delicate conditions favoring ESP would be disrupted and Pearce's scoring would diminish, gradually rising once more when the new situation became comfortable. Different drugs were tried on Pearce, notably caffeine which increased his scoring, while sodium amytal destroyed it.

Most work with Pearce was done under clairvoyant conditions, but Rhine did incorporate telepathy tests as well. When these were first introduced, Pearce's scores dropped considerably, and at that point it could not be determined if he was a poor telepath or if the change of experimental conditions brought about the abrupt scoring change. Rhine initially changed from clairvoyant testing (no one looking at the cards) to GESP tests (as already described), and he wrote of this change in procedure:

> . . . While at first Pearce dropped off considerably if I looked at the card, he came eventually to do even better than when I did not look at it. Omitting, then, the first 175 transition trials which gave an average per 25 of only 6 . . . we have 350 trials of the combined conditions (allowing both telepathy and clairvoyance), giving an average of 14 hits per 25. This is an extraordinary high average for Pearce or anyone else, and is significantly elevated above Pearce's usual level of about 10 in 25. It may well be the effect of the combined extrasensory activity from the two sources (the card and the agent), or, of course, may result from the possibly greater attention stimulated in the percipient by the combined possibilities. Or, again, it might have been the effect of suggestion arising out of the expectation that such results would occur. At any rate, a refinement of test procedures was necessary.[1]

These new procedures consisted of placing a screen between the experimenter and the subject which prevented Pearce from knowing (that is, normally and unaided by ESP) if Rhine was using clairvoyant or GESP tests. When the results were tallied, Pearce still achieved better scores on the GESP runs. But when pure telepathy tests were recorded, his scores were highly above chance.

Pearce was Rhine's all-time star subject, but as chance would have it, one day he went to Rhine obviously disturbed. He had had a letter with distressing news and Pearce's ESP disappeared after the shock.

Several other high-scoring subjects appeared during this period, among them Sara Ownbey and George Zirkle whose results were also written up by Rhine in his *Extrasensory Perception*. When Zirkle and Ownbey worked together, some surprising results were obtained. They initiated a lengthy study on the effect of various drugs on Zirkle's ESP, pure telepathy being his best manifestation of psi. In pure telepathy tests no cards are used, the image of the Zener cards are visualized by the agent and then set on the score sheet after the guess is made. Zirkle could achieve an average of 14.8 hits per run against 5.0 expected by chance while using telepathic testing techniques. If caffeine was given to him, his score was approximately the same. Rhine and Ownbey wanted to determine what the results would be if Zirkle were first given sodium amytal and then caffeine to offset the sluggish state the first drug would produce. Neither Ownbey nor Zirkle knew which drug would be given at what time during the test, nor did they know what to expect the ESP scores to show. For the formal experiment Zirkle was first given sodium amytal. He was in one room, Ownbey in another, and he was able to signal the agent by striking a telegraph key to begin the experiment. As the drug took affect, his scores systematically dropped from 13.6 hits per run to 7.8 hits—still above chance but significantly lower than his earlier scoring pattern. When the drug took its full effect, a very sluggish Zirkle could only score at a 6.2 level. When caffeine was given, his scores began to soar once again, and ended with a 9.5 average.

In another pure telepathy experiment, Zirkle, two rooms away from Ownbey, not only achieved a run of 23 out of 25, but a total score of 85 out of 100. After Miss Ownbey and George Zirkle married, the ESP abilities of both sagged.

One of the most important discoveries made during this early Duke work was that the best subjects also became the best agents. Of the five top ESP subjects (after Pearce and Linzmayer), Miss Ownbey, Mr. T. C. Cooper, May Turner, and June Bailey also seemed able to elicit higher results than their confreres when working as the agents. C. E. Stuart also gave up his role as percipient to become a highly successful agent. This led Rhine to believe that ESP might be able to help the agent "send," just as ESP seems to be the ability that "receives"—in other words, ESP might work in either direction.

The upshot of the early Duke successes was to spur on not only other experimenters in their attempt to confirm the ESP effect, but also more daring tests from the Duke Parapsychology Laboratory itself. One such Duke experiment was conducted between Miss Ownbey and Miss Turner over long distance. In this pure telepathy test Miss Ownbey stayed at the Duke laboratory while Miss Turner was 250 miles away. They arranged a test for a daily run of twenty-five calls, one each at five-minute intervals. They both sent their calls and target sequences to

Rhine for a third-party check, and Ownbey brought the first three-day experimental reports directly to Rhine from the post office. Rhine himself opened the communication and compared it to Ownbey's records. The success rate was staggering—19, 16, and 17 hits per 25. Unfortunately, the next several days showed much lower scores, and Turner once more verified a typical pattern in ESP testing—a gradual decline effect from success to only chance scoring. Many other researchers and subjects had found the same pattern.

When Rhine wrote of the early Duke experiments in his *New Frontiers of the Mind*, he said of the Ownbey–Turner experiments:

> To many people there must appear something fantastic in such results. They will think of the hills, woods, towns, fields, roads, rivers, even of the very curve of the earth itself separating the two women who conducted this experiment. And yet two times out of three one of them knew what was the shape of an image held in the thought of the other. Whatever power it was that they possessed, it plainly was totally unaffected by distance, for these three scores were among the highest ever attained in our work on telepathy. Space as ordinarily conceived in our everyday thinking presented no obstacle, then, to telepathic communication of symbols.

One young psychology student who was spurred on by the Duke work was J. L. Woodruff, of Tarkio College in Missouri. In his tests he introduced a new testing technique whereby a series of five target cards, one each of the five Zener symbols, was laid out for the subject to see. The subject had to match each Zener card of a deck blindly to the key card which the subject thought it matched. Sometimes, the key cards were left face downward and the subject had to perform a similar task. The purpose behind the use of this technique was that a motor response, physically placing the card on top of its target, would be automatic and less complex than trying to envision the target. Woodruff's test was successful, but no more so than the old basic GESP tests and clairvoyance (or PC—pure clairvoyance) methods.

Meanwhile, Miss Esther Bond, a schoolteacher in Sarasota, Florida, also began similar tests with mentally retarded children and achieved above average results. The use of children for ESP testing was a natural step, since it was possible that, being less sophisticated than adults, they would not bar their ESP abilities from manifesting. Among the children tested there appeared one brilliant subject, discovered by Margaret Pegram who was herself a gifted subject. Her finest results were achieved when she tested herself, since visitors or observers had a negative affect on her ESP. When she turned to testing others she discovered a young girl, Lillian, with whom she built a very close emotional bond. Lillian came from a broken home, and was living in a children's home at the time. It was in 1936 that Miss Pegram had, by chance, begun testing the children, aged six to thirteen, for ESP at the home. In order to make these tests interesting, a game was played with them: an open matching test such as the one developed for ESP by Woodruff. The higher the total scores per run, the larger the piece of candy won by the child. Lillian soon became the best subject, achieving one score of 23. One day she closed her eyes and set out the cards. Completing the run she told Miss Pegram, "I was wishing all the time that I would get twenty-five." She did, and became one of the few perfect scorers in parapsychological history. In reference to the experimental precautions outlined earlier, it should be added that Pegram was using a deck of cards that the girl had not seen before.[2] In the official report the fraud hypothesis is considered at length and justifiably rejected.

So far, the story of the development of experimental ESP has come from the United States and the foregoing material consists of only a few highlights of the successes of the Duke program and its offshoots. There were many more studies and many more projects by other experimenters which cannot be detailed here because of lack of space.*

* A complete consideration of the early Duke work and a critical evaluation of its significance was first written up by Rhine in his *Extrasensory Perception* (1934), a source which has been mentioned several times. A summary of this work and the story of further developments at Duke and other projects is outlined in Rhine's *New Frontiers of the Mind* (1937). In order to review the meanings of this work for the scientist, Rhine, Pratt, and others joined forces and in 1940 put out their *Extrasensory Perception After Sixty Years*, a technical review of the evidence for ESP and an evaluation of various criticisms against it.

When Rhine's work was published in full form in 1934, a scientific scandal followed. Rhine was criticized and in one instance was refused the right to answer his critics in a journal which was attacking him. Most of these criticisms assailed the experimental conditions and the statistical models used to evaluate the results. The criticism on statistical models was answered by the American Institute of Mathematical Statistics in 1937 when it issued a statement that Rhine's statistical applications and procedures were not in the least faulty. The arguments about experimental conditions were often irrelevant and the oft-cited "sensory cuing" theory could not explain the results. Nor can tests such as the Pearce–Pratt trials be explained away so easily.

In 1938 a symposium was held at the annual meeting of the American Psychological Association to debate the ESP issue. It became a central topic of the conference. But after the flurry of charges, claims, arguments, and even harangues were over, parapsychology had clearly become a legitimate experimental science. A year before, in 1937, Rhine had initiated the publication of the *Journal of Parapsychology* as a clearinghouse for information concerning ESP and experiments carried out, using extremely stringent criteria for the acceptance of such reports.

Even though the full story of the Duke ESP project had not yet been concluded in 1938, important developments in the search for ESP were taking place along similar lines in Great Britain.

G. N. M. Tyrrell, a telegraphic engineer and a longtime student of parapsychology, discovered a talented subject, Gertrude Johnson, in 1921 with whom he conducted some ESP tests using the suits of playing cards as targets. After Rhine's work was published, he initiated a lengthy series of novel tests using automated recording devices to check against recording error and inadvertent cues from the experimenter. In order to reach his goal, Tyrrell invented a five-box setup: five little boxes set in a row. Each box had a tiny light inside which could be lit from a distance, producing a target box. The lids to the boxes were light-proof, of course. The subject was cut off from the experimenter by a large screen behind which the experimenter also had a set of five boxes. When a decision was made by Tyrrell,

Miss Johnson was signaled by a light and then made her guess as to which box was lit. Later, a refinement was added so that all of the guesses and target decisions were automatically recorded on a mechanically operated moving band of paper.

Miss Johnson scored highly above chance but there were certain problems even with this setup. In the early experiments Tyrrell himself selected the lights to be chosen. This could cause a stacking effect, for he may have had a predilection for one special box over the others. Miss Johnson also may have had a similar habit of predominantly guessing one specific box. This coincidence could lead to above-chance scoring that had nothing to do with ESP.* So Tyrrell added a mechanical selector to combat this criticism. A curious development arose. If the selector automatically chose the lights during the experiment, Miss Johnson did not score well. If, however, the randomizer was used to set up a series of box number sequences which were then used by Tyrrell himself, Miss Johnson would score significantly above chance. This illustrates the obvious importance Tyrrell's own presence had on the experiments. In addition, he also used an automatic device called a commutator to rearrange the key connections to the lights, and by this method he could flick a switch and would himself become unaware which box would light up when a specific key was struck. Another revision was a delay-action device whereby a light would go on only after Miss Johnson opened the lid of her choice. In this way no one could argue that somehow the subject heard the light going on in the target box by hyperesthesia which could be used as a cue.

The results after using all these checks and controls were extremely significant. When the random number sequences were employed in conjunction with the commutator (which thus eliminated telepathy), the results were 3.55×10^{14} to 1. Other techniques achieved similar staggering statistics when complete randomness was used for the experiments.[3]

* One observer of the experiments, G. W. Fisk, discovered that when Tyrrell did not use a random sequence he (Fisk) could achieve above-chance results by consistently opening one box until he scored a hit, and then repeating the procedure with a different box. When a random sequence was used by Tyrrell, Fisk's method failed to achieve anything more than chance.

Another experimenter of this same period was S. G. Soal, the mathematician and longtime student of psychical research. Spurred on by Rhine's work he began a lengthy series of ESP card tests which after five years showed absolutely nothing. He had tested 160 individuals, accumulated 128,350 guesses, all in vain. Soal stopped work in 1939 and criticized Rhine for what he felt must have been methodological errors in his reportedly successful research. However, Whately Carington urged him to reconsider his data. It will be remembered that Carington had conducted picture-drawing experiments and that often his subjects would draw either the previous day's target (latent ESP) or precognize the following day's drawing. Carington suggested that Soal's data be reexamined, comparing the guesses made to the next target card (precognition) or the one immediately before (latency). By doing so, Soal did find that two subjects, Basil Shackleton and Gloria Stewart, had consistently shown the plus 1 (+ 1) and minus 1 (− 1) displacement effect.[4]

Since Mrs. Stewart became available for further experiments only after the Second World War, Soal's first project was to test Shackleton, keeping the displacement effect in mind. Using a similar method to Rhine's, random targets were chosen consisting of animal pictures instead of geometric symbols. In this case the cards were of a lion, elephant, zebra, giraffe, and pelican. The result of all the tests made with this medium was that when the test conditions permitted telepathy, Shackleton scored continually above chance on + 1 hits. When pure clairvoyance tests were run, he failed to score above chance. This was a drastic change from Rhine's results in which his gifted ESP subjects always were able to score well on both clairvoyance and telepathy tests.

The result of the Shackleton research is, unfortunately, a sad one, for it showed how experimental designs, no matter how well thought out, contain flaws. In this case certain post-hoc discoveries have cast a cold light on the validity of the experiments.

For one Shackleton experiment two rooms were used. In one room the agent was seated with an observer. In the other, the percipient and another observer. The use of double observers was to reaffirm the results and ensure that no fraud was used. One set of experiments carried out using this technique was the

Soal–Shackleton–Goldney series which was conducted with Shackleton in one room under supervision, and Soal with the agent in another room. Under these conditions Shackleton continued to score above chance. However, some years later a controversy over these experiments was ignited by C. E. M. Hansel, the arch-critic of parapsychology, who brought up two criticisms of the experiments. Firstly, Shackleton and Soal could have worked out a code. Secondly, one of the agents, Gretl Albert, claimed that while she operated as an agent she saw Soal altering the results, thus faking the experiments. Mrs. Albert was a rather eccentric woman prone to making wild charges (such as that she had been given drugged cigars or cigarettes during the experiment), and so her accusation of experimenter fraud was not taken seriously.

However, when Hansel began to promulgate these charges about Soal's work, a reconsideration had to be undertaken. Mrs. Albert's claim could easily be checked if Soal had altered the prepared-in-advance targets, as she charged, to match Shackleton's guesses. To ensure complete randomness Soal had taken his target sequences from Chambers's Logarithm Tables which would give him a list of random numbers. (Again, remember, that unless the targets are completely random, spurious ESP results may well appear.) R. G. Medhurst, hoping to vindicate Soal, compared the Shackleton records to the Chambers's Tables and found that Soal's tables *did not match the source from which he claimed to have taken them.* This incident has several interpretations. It is not clearly indicative of experimenter fraud. It does point to the unfortunate fact that Soal's written report had obvious discrepancies and that the procedures *as written* by Soal do not match the procedures actually used. Such sloppiness in reporting are not acceptable and could alone discredit any experimental work.[5]

In order to check for tampering on the score sheets, an obvious step was to find the originals and check for alterations. Here came the next blow, for Soal had declared that he had lost the sheets on board a train some years before. The final blow came when an examination of Shackleton's results showed a high amount of calls on certain targets and a deficit amount of calls on others. This could have been a normal fluke of his calling pattern, but, unfortunately, it also matched those exact targets which Mrs. Albert claimed she saw Soal altering.

None of these developments are clear indications of fraud, but they are so suspicious that one can no longer place any credence on Shackleton's work as being fraud-proof evidence for ESP even though the tests are often described as the most tightly controlled ESP tests ever undertaken. Further, it casts poor light on S. G. Soal and his work with other subjects as well. At present a critical examination is being made of all Soal's work in the hope of clarifying the matter. But, as yet, no publications have appeared from this effort at analyzing his research.

Soal's work with Mrs. Stewart followed similar experimental lines as did the Shackleton experiments. However, when the new research was carried out, Mrs. Stewart did not show the displacement factor by which she was first discovered. Instead she scored highly on direct hits. Shackleton had showed one peculiarity in his runs—if the rate of calls were increased, in other words, if Shackleton was given less time to make his call and was rushed through the test his scoring on the next card (+ 1) vanished and he jumped two cards ahead (+ 2) consistently. A similar effect was found with Mrs. Stewart in the reverse direction. If the rate of calling was doubled, she would show latent ESP (− 1), not direct hits. As with Shackleton, Mrs. Stewart failed in tests designed to eliminate telepathy.

Further tests were carried out with two agents concentrating on the same target. Mrs. Stewart would continue scoring above chance but not to any greater degree than her usual above-chance record. If the two agents opposed each other, she tended to single out one agent and score highly, while only scoring at chance with the other. ESP would apparently isolate the source of the signal. As with Shackleton, Mrs. Stewart scored highest with only certain agents (Shackleton could not function at all with some agents). One series of tests was conducted between London and Antwerp with the same high level of success. Later the ESP ability in both Stewart and Shackleton diminished and finally vanished completely.

The odd phenomenon observed when Shackleton discerned not the target card but the next card of the stack has two possible interpretations. Could it be that he clairvoyantly became aware of the entire pack and because of some quirk mixed the order? Yet, when clairvoyance tests were run, he did not score above chance at all. The other reason could be that Shackleton was displaying precognition or, more properly, precognitive ESP. This was demonstrated when his hits jumped two ahead of the target. The random sequence had not been set in advance for some experiments, and the next targets were determined randomly at the time. Shackleton's scoring was then on targets that had not yet been determined, thus true precognitive ESP was demonstrated. There have been many cases of spontaneous precognition coming in the form of precognitive dreams, impressions, and so forth. Could such a phenomenon appear in the laboratory as well as during conventional ESP testing?

The search for concrete evidence of precognition takes us back to Duke University where J. B. Rhine, well aware that precognition was a very common form of ESP, announced in his book, *New Frontiers of the Mind*, that precognition card experiments were already under way with gifted subjects. In 1938 the *Journal of Parapsychology* carried Rhine's first report on the precognition effect, "Experiments Bearing on the Precognition Hypothesis, I" (vol. 2, pp. 38–54). The experimental procedure was simple; the subject merely guessed the order in which the targets would appear before the cards were shuffled. This technique had certain merits in that no one could know the future order of the cards, so sensory cuing by the experimenter or fraudulent peeking by the subject was ruled out. However, for this study Rhine shifted from ESP in the gifted subject to a search for a mass ESP effect. As already noted, there is a philosophy that everyone has some psi ability. This ability is too negligible to show up if individuals are tested one by one. They might score slightly above chance, but not high enough to be truly significant. However, if all the subjects are tested together, their combined minute ESP will show a significant overall meaning. In his precognition experiment Rhine used forty-nine subjects and their total guesses showed 614 more hits than chance would dictate. This is a probability against chance of $<.00001$. (Remember that p. $<.01$ is significant of ESP.)

While this might be true precognition Rhine and his co-workers were not at all sure that it really was. It was possible that since the experimenters were aware of the guessing responses of the subjects, they might be using their *own* clairvoyance to stop shuffling the cards at the exact time when the position of the cards most closely matched the half-filled score sheets. Therefore, the only ESP demonstrated would be clairvoyance on the part of the experimenters.* So, a new series of experiments was undertaken with mechanically shuffled cards. Rhine published his results in another article on the precognition effect in the *Journal of Parapsychology* (vol. V, pp. 1–58), which showed results that were negligible.

Even had these experiments paid off, pure precognition was still not achieved inasmuch as psychokinesis might be the deciding factor. There has long been a school of thought in parapsychology that true precognition does not exist, but that an individual uses his PK to make a future event (seen in a dream or otherwise) take place. This issue has been much debated, but it was a very real possibility to Rhine. At that time he and his co-workers had demonstrated that by exerting conscious will a subject could make rolling dice fall in a certain manner more often than chance would allow. Mind over matter had been experimentally demonstrated. If PK could affect rolling dice, it might also affect the apparatus shuffling the target cards for precognition tests. Thus, an experiment using both ESP and PK (remembering that often these two phenomena work in conjunction) might clairvoyantly perceive a favorable sequence of cards and then use PK to rig the shuffler to stop at a favorable moment. Ergo—pseudoprecognition. All this may strike the reader as far-fetched, but these were very real issues that had to be kept in mind. After all, it had been discovered that good experimenters were often good ESP subjects as well. Secondly, it was known that much PK needs ESP to reach its target. For example, if one is given the task of making dice land on a certain face, it is hard to believe that the subject could actually see the

---

* This problem later led to a new type of ESP test called "the psychic shuffle." The subject records his guesses and then an experimenter shuffles the target cards. The subject then tells the experimenter to stop when he thinks there will be a close correspondence between his guesses and the position of the cards, or the subject himself shuffles the cards trying to match a hidden series of target cards.

die faces as they rolled, especially when long-distance PK tests were conducted where the subject was not even in the experimental area. The subject, therefore, had first to discern the die faces by ESP, then effect the fall by PK. So the theory that the experimenter uses ESP and PK to produce a precognition effect is not as outlandish as it may seem.

With this problem in mind Rhine adopted a technique whereby, after the cards were shuffled, an automatic random method was employed to cut the deck arbitrarily, upsetting the original sequence. Using this method no direct evidence of precognition was found. However, when the score sheets were analyzed, they did reveal one curious effect—a gradual decline of hits from the top to the bottom of the runs with a flourish of success at the end (salience). It was well known that a subject's ESP would gradually decline during continual testing, and it was also recognized that even during the course of a few runs the subject was likely to score better at the start of the run and then sink to chance and then pick up again by the end of the run.

Pure chance would not produce such a consistent scoring pattern which was undoubtedly due somehow to an odd feature of how ESP manifests itself in statistical tests. This exact feature was found in these new precognition tests, and so evidence was finally achieved for pure precognition.[6]

So far we have outlined the development of experimental parapsychology from the first systematic attempts to isolate the phenomena at Duke through its confirmation in Europe, and up to the confirmation of the precognition effect. Roughly this spans the era of 1930–1950. Before discussing the changes that parapsychology has undergone since then, a general consideration should be given to the concrete advances parapsychology had made up until that point. Although the major emphasis of ESP research had been on establishing the evidence for the various forms of ESP, certain characteristics of the phenomenon were beginning to reveal themselves. In September 1967 Rhine was invited to give an address before the annual convention of the American Psychological Association held in Washington, D.C. There he spoke on the topic, "Psi and Psychology: Conflict and Solution," in which he made the following summary of what experimentation in the first two decades of modern para-psychology had shown:

> The findings of this research period, both at Duke and else-where, were substantial. Broadly, parapsychology began to take definite shape as a field, to assume the outlines of an organized whole. The phenomena that were being studied began to show lawful interrelations and even a degree of unity. One by one the major claims, based originally only upon spontaneous human experiences, were subjected to labo-ratory test and experimentally verified. Independent confir-mations both in and out of the Duke center followed during this period . . .
>
> Certain general characteristics of the psi process became clear during this period. The most revealing of these is the subject's lack of conscious control over any type of psi ability, a characteristic which accounts for its elusive nature. That discovery showed the importance of learning to measure a genuinely unconscious mental process accurately and quanti-tatively. It was new methodological ground, even for psychol-ogy.
>
> Also, we were surprised to find that psi ability is wide-spread, probably even a specific human capacity rather than a capability possessed by a few rare individuals as had been the popular belief. Evidence that psi is not linked with illness or abnormality was another welcome advance . . .
>
> By 1951, as the period ended, a healthy young science was emerging. The basic claims of the field had been verified ex-perimentally and independently confirmed. These findings rested upon no single research center, or school, or profes-sion, or even country.

Parapsychology is more than just demonstrating the existence of ESP. After the initial work had survived the criticisms of the skeptics, research on paranormal modes of cognition was free to go on to the roots of its prime concern—finding out just how ESP functions and why. Since 1950 parapsychology has moved in several directions. However, certain changes were already ev-ident by the 1950s.

The most notable was the shift from studying gifted subjects to testing large masses of individuals. This change was inevita-ble. Subjects, such as Pearce, Stewart, Zirkle, and others, showed a consistent decline in their abilities until their ESP became dormant. The loss of a central subject is always a severe blow to any research, but since large groups of individuals showed a collective ESP effect, the use of group testing became a safer and easier method to employ. A typical example of how mass ESP testing can be used is illustrated by the work of Gertrude Schmeidler of the City College of the City University of New York, who wished to see if a person's attitude toward ESP affected his scoring. To do so Schmeidler tested two groups of ESP subjects—those who believed in the possibility of ESP and those who did not. These groups were called "sheep" and "goats." In the initial experiments the sheep did score better on clairvoyance tests than the goats. The tests were repeated, making sure that both groups were tested under exactly the same conditions. Again, the sheep scored slightly above chance, while the goats scored slightly below.

Schmeidler had now outlined a hypothesis that other researchers could confirm or invalidate, that is that those who believed in ESP could score better than those who rejected the idea. Working with a single subject would make it difficult to set up such hypotheses and test them. However, the shift to group ESP testing did make experimentation-confirmation a natural part of parapsychological techniques. Later sheep-goat tests have had varying results, but generally it has remained a "true" ESP characteristic.[7]

Groups of schoolchildren have also been tested for a group ESP effect by a Dutch experimenter, Van Busschbach, who showed in his reports in the *Journal of Parapsychology* between 1953 and 1961 that children score better in ESP tests when their teacher acts as agent. Margaret Anderson and Rhea White in the United States conducted a similar test with teachers whom the students liked best and teachers who were not so honored. The children scored significantly better with the popular teachers. Again in this case the shift from the gifted subject to group testing made confirmation of particular ESP characteristics possible.[8]

It is impossible to cover all the different hypotheses that have been tested in ESP research using this method, but some of them relate to what personality characteristics affect ESP, effects of distance, types of targets, conditions of the experiments, and so on. When K. Ramakrishna Rao attempted a coverage of the combined findings of experimental ESP, he was faced with over five hundred papers to summarize in his book, *Experimental Parapsychology* (1966).

A further development in ESP testing has been the use of more interesting and diversified target material. The old Zener cards have fallen from their once-dominant position because subjects had a difficult time finding anything emotionally stimulating in them. It has been found that emotion is the key in bringing out ESP during experimental sessions, so parapsychologists have tried to find targets to which the subject could respond more dramatically. Some researchers went back to picture tests, some used clock hands set at certain positions, emotionally significant names, and so forth. The list is endless.

The most important of the newer developments in ESP research has been the shift to completely automated testing procedures, using machine-chosen targets and automatic scoring. This development, which had its precedents in earlier research such as Tyrrell's and Troland's, was chiefly the work of an ingenious physicist at the Boeing Laboratories in Seattle, Dr. Helmut Schmidt. Schmidt invented a machine wherein the subject had to select one of four colored lights by pressing a button that automatically recorded his guess. The actual target was determined at that time by a process based on the decay of a radioactive fragment which throws off electrons completely at random. The interval at which these particles travel determines the actual choice of target. Thus, the test is one of precognition, since the guess is made before the target is determined. Like the guess, the target choice is recorded automatically. For his experiment Schmidt selected three gifted subjects who made a total of 63,066 trials trying to determine which light would be illuminated. Their success rate was so high as to give odds of 2000 million to 1 against chance. All told, six subjects were tested using his machine, and sometimes instead of a quantum process he used a random sequence of numbers prearranged to select the targets. This then was more a test of clairvoyance, and his subjects scored over 1 million to 1 against anything other than ESP being responsible for the success.[9]

Schmidt has developed several machines to help test for psi under fraud- and error-proof conditions. In 1972 he reported in the *Journal of Parapsychology* (vol. 36, pp. 222–31) on one machine that could test either precognition or psychokinesis. For precognition the subject had to guess which target light would be selected by a random process. However, if the experimenter flicked a switch, the machine was revised to test the subject for "willing" a certain target to be selected by PK. The real novelty of this apparatus is that the change-over can be done without the subject's knowing (normally) that the alteration had taken place. Using this machine Schmidt found that his subjects were consistently able to succeed at the psi task and display ESP and PK.

At this point one might wonder if the Schmidt machines were perhaps biased and normally would show above-chance results just from malfunction. The answer to this might come from other experimenters, such as John Beloff, a British parapsychologist, who has failed to achieve any results using Schmidt's devices. On the other hand, computer checks of the random target sequences, prepared by the machines, vindicated the apparatuses and have shown them to be unbiased.

Throughout the search for ESP many surprising discoveries about psi have been made. The importance of these findings, many of which confirmed principles governing spontaneous ESP as well, is that ESP, sporadic as it is, is guided by certain patterns and principles. These discoveries can be broken down into two sections: (1) how ESP manifests experimentally, and (2) findings on the ESP ability itself.*

The main result of ESP research is the determination that telepathy, clairvoyance, precognition, and retrocognition are all basically the same phenomenon, merely occurring under different conditions. If a subject scores well on one form of ESP test he is likely to score well on other forms. It is true that Soal's subjects did not do well on clairvoyance testing, but this was probably due primarily to their own uncertainty about their ability to succeed at such a task. Both Rhine and Tyrrell found

* Much of the following discussion is suggested by the ESP effects outlined by Robert Thouless in his *From Anecdote to Experiment in Psychical Research*. The discussions, though, are my own.

that changing the conditions of an experiment often deterred ESP until the subject became comfortable in the new situation. At that point, ESP would reappear. Schmidt's experiments suggest that not only are all ESP-based phenomena one unitary process, but that ESP and PK share a basic principle. Several fine ESP subjects have also turned out to be talented PK subjects. Lalsingh Harribance, a subject being tested at the Foundation for Research on the Nature of Man, was initially tested for ESP but was later found to score well on PK tests. Harribance's case is not rare.

The second major finding of experimental parapsychology is the "decline effect" that has been previously noted. There are three types of declines which have been observed in ESP experiments: declines within a run, within the experiment, and during the course of the subject's ESP career.

Rhine had found that Pearce scored most successfully at the beginning of an experimental run. Similarly a decline effect was discovered in group ESP testing for precognition. George Estabrooks had uncovered this feature in his experiments and commented on it in 1927. Even earlier, Ina Jephson noted that her ESP subjects scored well predominantly on the first few targets of a run and then declined. This same principle occurs during long experiments when a subject may begin by showing strong ESP and then falter. There is one modification to this rule known as "salience." During a run the subject will often decline, but will successfully score on the last few targets. The total pattern, if graphed, would produce a U curve. As has also been noted, most gifted ESP subjects generally lose their abilities completely after a slow decline.

There have been two different explanations of the decline effect. Rhine initially thought that decline stemmed from boredom. Calling Zener card after Zener card for several runs is not an especially stimulating or provocative test situation, and a subject may become bored with the individual run, the whole experiment, and even the entire experimental program. This would account for the three-way decline effect. Rhine's position regarding this is not novel. In 1885 Malcolm Guthrie, with whom Lodge conducted and witnessed successful ESP tests, wrote, "I have noticed a falling off . . . since our first great results . . . as the novelty and vivacity of our seances has departed there is not the same geniality and freshness as at the onset. The thing has become monotonous, whereas it was formerly a succession of surprises . . ." [10]

This view can explain several oddities in the history of experimental research. No doubt Rhine's enthusiasm and freshness of approach set up an ideal natural and spirit-of-discovery situation. This was a perfect setting for ESP to manifest. Yet, as discoveries were made, what was at first novel became routine and ESP failed to appear so consistently. Perhaps the subjects became bored and gradually no longer were motivated to exhibit ESP. It is also notable that never in the history of experimental parapsychology have there been so many gifted subjects to be tested as Rhine discovered in the 1930s. As the Zirkles, Ownbeys, and Pearces retired from the scene, no one came forward to take their places, and this was one of the prime reasons for the shift to group ESP testing. The decline effect might also stem from the fact that after a few years ESP research no longer was so emotionally charged as at the onset of the Duke program. Gifted subjects were no longer sufficiently motivated to prove their ESP, inasmuch as the burden of proof now rested on the skeptic. The acceptance of parapsychology might have been its most stunning blow.

A different approach to the decline effect has been offered by Robert Thouless who views ESP as being so out of the ordinary that most people are inhibited about displaying it. It is generally believed that ESP manifests so rarely in daily life because we automatically inhibit it from occurring. This is due to our cultural conditioning which is severely critical of anything supernatural, and the stigma of abnormality often brands anyone who claims ESP ability. We know that ESP is an unconscious process (the evidence for which is to be examined shortly) and that the unconscious might bar ESP from reaching consciousness. Psychoanalysis has shown how the mind can repress unpleasant memories from conscious recall or control. A similar inhibiting factor probably affects the emergence of ESP. Thouless has suggested that a subject may subconsciously feel so inhibited about demonstrating ESP that he tries to cover his tracks. Thus his declines during the run are attempts to offset his initial success.

A similar process would occur during an experiment, and finally the repression becomes so great that the subject's ESP disappears altogether.[11]

ESP does not follow typical learning patterns. Unlike any other experimental tasks, reinforcing ESP by rewards, practice, or conditioning does not improve it. This is so contrary to the nurturing of any other talent that a psychological mechanism probably underlies the faculty. Perhaps Thouless' theory of inhibition does lie at the root of this enigma.*

A third finding about ESP is that it may not overtly manifest by success at hitting a target. As the displacement effect illustrates, psi might manifest in a number of more subtle ways. So far four significant scoring manifestations are known: psi-missing, differential scoring, focusing, and variance.

1. Psi-missing is the habit of a subject (or subjects) to score consistently *below* chance. This suggests that ESP is used as a means to mitigate against success. The usually ascribed cause for psi-missing is the subject's uncomfortableness in the test situation. Once when Linzmayer was pushed too far in an experiment, he began to score negatively. The psi-miss effect may appear to be just a convenient way of explaining very inconvenient data. However, purposive psi-missing has been demonstrated in experiments. The Linzmayer example was a spontaneous occurrence when the subject became ill at ease during the experiment. He had wished to stop experimenting, but Rhine pushed him on against his will. And at that time his scores not only dropped to chance but far under. At the 1972 Parapsychological Association Convention (Edinburgh, September 1972), Charles Honorton, M. Ramsey, and C. Cabibbo described an experiment which deliberately produced psi-missing. Two groups of subjects were used; one group was treated courteously by the experimenters,

* Recently Russell Targ, a physicist at the Stanford Research Institute, has reported on an ESP self-testing apparatus by which the subject is rewarded for successful calls. By employing this machine Targ has reported a gradual increase of scoring level. This finding is contrary to what previous researchers have found. If other parapsychologists can replicate Targ's work then the commonly held notion that ESP cannot be acquired by any method of learning known to psychology will have to be revised. At present, though, Targ's work must be considered only an anomaly.

the other group was rudely dealt with to make the entire experimental situation uncomfortable. This second group psi-missed to a marked degree, while the first group did quite well. Schmidt, in his experiments, found that subjects would intentionally psi-miss when asked to do so deliberately.

2. Differential scoring is the tendency of subjects to score on one task better than on another during an experiment if two variables are employed. K. Ramakrishna Rao carried out an experiment in which the test material consisted of fifty cards, half printed with five each of five different English-language words, the others with Telugu translations of the key words. The subjects had to match these cards clairvoyantly with five key cards either in English or Telugu. He discovered a consistent ESP effect only on those cards that matched the language (no matter which) of the key cards. This phenomenon was later confirmed by Rao himself and P. Sailaja.[12] In this case two different tasks were assigned and the subjects successfully differentiated between them. The key to the differential effect is thought to be the favoring of one task over the other by the subject.

3. Focusing is the tendency for a subject to succeed on a certain target, such as a card, consistently no matter how disguised. This effect has been widely analyzed in the work of Pavel Stepanek who is one of parapsychology's modern gifted subjects. He has consistently succeeded in ESP testing for several years in conjunction with several different experimenters. It was found that Stepanek favored certain target cards during the experiments. These cards were of two different colored sides, and he had to guess the correct color over 50 percent of the time. The cards were usually presented to Stepanek in sealed containers. He has consistently made the same "call," over many tests, on certain of the card sides while only at chance with others. This tendency became so marked that it was clear that he was "focusing in" on certain targets for either psychical or psychological reasons.[13]

4. Variance is perhaps the most subtle measure and manifestation of psi. Since psi is so erratic and difficult to control, parapsychologists wondered if even though a subject's total score was not significant, could it be that he was using ESP during one portion of the test? (A chance result would be achieved

if a subject psi-hit and then psi-missed evenly during an experiment.) If a subject has a wide range of hits per run (remember that five is chance), it may not be due to just the natural ups and downs of random coincidential hits but be a manifestation of ESP occurring sporadically.

This may sound a little more confusing than it really is. If a standard twenty-five-guess ESP run is made and only chance hits appear, one could get scores such as 5, 2, 7, 6, 3, 7. If ESP is sporadically manifesting, the results might show runs of 10, 2, 0, 9, 12, 1. This is still at chance level, but the fluctuation is so great that it looks as if ESP were manifesting during some of the runs but not others, or that psi-hitting and psi-missing were operating during the same experiment.

There is now a mathematical formula to test for variance. A typical experiment showing the ESP nature of variance was carried out by Rex Stanford who followed a previous experiment by R. J. Cadoret in which a subject did best on an ESP test when exhibiting a certain brain-wave rhythm on an electroencephalograph. This rhythm, the alpha rhythm, denoted a relaxed, passive state. Cadoret's work then showed a direct relation between high amounts of alpha and success at ESP. Stanford duplicated these experiments but did not find evidence of ESP, but further analysis revealed that when alpha increased during an ESP run so did the wide variance level of the scores, and there was a wide deviation around chance scoring. During decreased shifts the runs showed an adherence toward chance. This is very subtle but unmistakable evidence of ESP working sporadically.

All of these methods of evaluation may strike the reader as labored, or attempts to read into the statistics evidence that is only coincidental. These analyses are, nevertheless, based upon commonly accepted mathematical models used in any experimental science. The appearance of variance, focusing, and differentiation have all been noted over long periods of time by different research workers. Most of these effects can be deliberately elicited by experimentation as did Honorton with psi-missing.

Another important finding of experimental parapsychology is that the experimenter is an integral part of the experiment, not merely a casual conductor or onlooker. One of the greatest problems in ESP research is that not every experimenter can motivate his subjects to exhibit psi in the laboratory. Some experimenters are able to run success after success while others are unable to get any results at all. For example, John Beloff has consistently failed to run a successful ESP test, while J. B. Rhine, J. G. Pratt, and others have a Midas touch for getting their subjects to exhibit ESP. The "experimenter effect" is what this oddity has been dubbed. Rhine has suggested that a researcher new to ESP testing should first see if he can get any results at all before going on with parapsychology as a career.

The best-known example of the experimenter effect is a classic experiment by G. W. Fisk and D. J. West. The idea of the trial was to see if subjects could call the correct time recorded on cards printed with clock faces. Thirty-two packs of twelve cards were employed, sixteen prepared by Fisk, sixteen prepared by West. When the results were tallied, it was discovered that the subjects were successful only with the decks handled by Fisk. They failed miserably with West's decks. Now, the subjects could not have known who shuffled which decks, so West, merely by handling certain decks, somehow inhibited the subjects from succeeding on the test.[14] Another experimenter, J. D. MacFarland, ran a test using two different packs of cards handled by two different experimenters—one successful, the other unsuccessful. The deck previously used by the successful experimenter did in fact continue to be successfully "called," unlike the "contaminated" deck. A further example of the experimenter effect is illustrated by an incident concerning Pavel Stepanek. Although Stepanek has been considered a gifted subject because of his phenomenally high rate of scoring success with different experimenters, he not only failed to succeed in tests with John Beloff who had gone to Czechoslovakia specifically to test him, but also for the first and only time in his career psi-missed to a significant degree.

There are two interpretations of the experimenter effect. On one hand there are most likely personality traits that certain experimenters possess which lead to a more open, cordial, enthusiastic manner of testing for ESP. Because they are able to build up a good experimental bond with their subjects, ESP more readily appears. On the other hand, it may be that ESP is a two-way channel and only agents with certain ESP abilities themselves can succeed in ESP testing. Just as there are gifted subjects, there might be gifted agents. Many of Rhine's first gifted subjects were successful as agents, such as Ownbey, Cooper, Bailey, and Stuart. Some experimenters, such as Woodruff, also proved to be good subjects. Furthermore, a few subjects can elicit strong ESP from nonpsychic subjects by "impressing" their ESP onto them. William Delmore was a high-scoring subject studied at FRNM who, during one experiment conducted by a talented but nonpsychic experimenter, B. K. Kanthamani, changed roles with the experimenter. Acting as agent he was able to elicit from Kanthamani exceptionally high ESP scoring solely due to his ability to send. Warcollier had also noted that good subjects became good agents. And Malcolm Guthrie felt his positive ESP results were not necessarily due to good psychic subjects but to his own ability as a sender of ESP impressions. Even Shackleton could only succeed with certain agents.

The possibility that an experimenter can use his own psi ability to gain success at psi testing is a crucial issue. When a mass test is run, is it true group psi manifesting, or is it the ability of the experimenter that comes into play? To demonstrate the difficulties arising from this paradox one significant experiment need only be cited. Helmut Schmidt was interested in testing to see if small animals could demonstrate psychokinesis. Cockroaches were placed on a grill that would periodically give an electric shock. Schmidt was trying to determine if the cockroaches could, by PK, cause the apparatus to give *fewer* shocks than it was designed to give. After the test was completed it was clear that PK had been demonstrated and the machine had given many *more* shocks than it should have which was explainable only by PK. It is inconceivable that small insects would deliberately submit themselves to a negative stimulus. But what about Schmidt? The experimenter admitted that he dislikes cockroaches immensely, so it is not hard to believe that Schmidt, being a good PK subject, was affecting the apparatus himself.*

* Some of this material is unpublished and stems from a seminar on experimental effects in parapsychology held at FRNM on August 23, 1973. In attendance were Helmut Schmidt, B. K. Kanthamani, Robert Morris, J. Levy, C. Akers who organized the material, and the author among others mostly of the FRNM research staff.

All this leads to the inevitable conclusion that only certain experimenters are able to achieve results, and the experimenter is likely to employ this ability to achieve ESP evidence that fits his own notions about psi. Experimenter effects are not known only in parapsychology, but also in other sciences as well. Robert Rosenthal has written a fascinating book, *Experimenter Effects in Behavioral Research*, on this touchy problem. In one celebrated experiment testers were given rats to run through mazes. They were told that certain rats were good maze subjects and that others were poor subjects. In truth the animals had been selected at random and arbitrarily assigned to one of the two groups. But sure enough, those animals designated as poor subjects did poorly and those who were designated as good maze runners did well in accordance with the tester's preconceived notions. The very way the experimenters went about the test conditioned the results they achieved. An ESP experimenter may be up against a similar problem.

The above phenomena relate to only one small element of psi—the many ways that it appears in the laboratory. These studies tell us very little about the nature of psi itself. However, a few general principles about the psi process are slowly being revealed.

The most important principle behind ESP is that it is an unconscious process. Because of this, ESP functions in two stages—the subconscious first assembles the ESP data and then transfers it to conscious awareness. There are many ways that the gap between the conscious and unconscious can be bridged—dreams, intuitions, impressions, hallucinations, and so forth—and it is just in these ways that most ESP manifests in daily life. This principle has also been uncovered and demonstrated in the laboratory. Even gifted subjects have been unable to control ESP, and most subjects cannot tell if they are doing well or poorly during conventional ESP testing. They may be able to show some awareness that certain calls are more likely to be hits than others, but all in all, they are usually guessing or relying on hunches. If ESP were a conscious process this inability would not occur.

ESP may manifest even though the subject is not conscious of it. A person may respond unconsciously to an ESP stimulus during an experiment and to demonstrate this, ESP tests using a plethysmograph have been successfully run. A plethysmograph is a psychophysiological apparatus that tests for shifts in blood volume to various parts of the body. It records those changes on a graph similar to a seismograph. When there is a sudden decrease in blood volume from an area under examination, a vasoconstriction occurs. Emotional responses also produce such constrictions. In the 1950s a Czechoslovakian experimenter, S. Figar, conducted an ESP test with sets of emotionally linked relatives. Separated by a screen, one of them would be hooked up to a plethysmograph while the other was, at one point during the experiment, given an arithmetic problem to solve. As the subject began to calculate the answer, which would normally cause a vasoconstriction as blood flowed to the brain, the other subject showed an inexplicable vasoconstriction at the same time. Figar considered this as evidence of unconscious ESP on the part of the subject.[15]

E. Douglas Dean, who was at the time working in the research division of the Parapsychology Foundation, a nonprofit organization founded in 1951 to promote scientific research and education in parapsychology, took a cue from these experiments and elaborated upon them. Two subjects were separated by a wall. One was continually monitored by the plethysmograph while the other, the agent, was given a group of cards upon which several names were written. Some of these names were emotionally significant to the subject, some emotionally meaningful to the agent only, some taken randomly from the phone book, and others were blank cards. The agent then tried to telepathically send the names to the percipient. Twenty-second intervals were used per card. After the experiment was completed, independent judges examined the plethysmograph record and measured the number and depth of the vasoconstrictions. They found that when emotionally meaningful names for the percipient were sent, the apparatus revealed greater constrictions than when neutral names or blank cards were sent.

After Dean left the Parapsychology Foundation (when the foundation discontinued its research division), he continued his experiments in conjunction with another parapsychologist, Carroll B. Nash, a biology professor at St. Joseph's College in Philadelphia. Selected subjects were used in their tests, and again names known to the percipient elicited strong unconscious physiological responses; especially strong vasoconstrictions manifested when the name of one subject's daughter was the target.

The prime discovery resulting from these experiments is that the tests can reveal unconscious ESP. Most people are totally oblivious to changes in blood supply to various parts of the body, just as they are to most automatic functions of the body. Nonetheless, the plethysmograph experiments do reveal that the unconscious mind can employ, receive, and assimilate ESP impressions without them ever coming into consciousness.[16]

Charles Tart conducted a similar test with subjects in two different rooms. The percipients were hooked up to a plethysmograph, an electroencephalograph, as well as a device to gauge their galvanic skin response. The subjects did not know an ESP test was in operation but were told to try to guess when a "subliminal stimulus" was being directed to them. Actually, the agent was periodically given a mild electric shock to which the subjects would hopefully respond. The subject's hunches did not correlate with the shocks, but their psychophysiological records showed abrupt changes and complexity when they were administered. Thus, while the subjects failed at the conscious but disguised ESP task, they did respond unconsciously and physiologically to the ESP stimulus.[17] A fuller understanding of the unconscious nature of ESP comes from studying spontaneous cases.

Because ESP is an unconscious process, the next question that parapsychologists faced was when and why does it surface at all? Since ESP is governed by psychological principles, the real issue is why some people show ESP and others do not. Some individuals may go through life regularly having psi experiences, yet others will claim never to have had even one. Since the beginnings of experimental parapsychology researchers have grappled with the task of finding certain personality factors which correlated with ESP ability. These experiments taken together point to certain laws which seem to govern psi very loosely. Experiments run to determine if psychotics or neurotics were better ESP subjects than well-adjusted persons were uniformly unsuccessful. In fact, two researchers, Betty Humphrey and H. J. Urban, independently found that disturbed individuals scored better on ESP tests only when their mental health began to improve. So far, several experimenters, including B. K. Kanthamani, Gertrude Schmeidler, and Ramakrishna Rao, compared the results of ESP performances between well-adjusted subjects and neurotic subjects and invariably found that the well-adjusted individuals scored better.[18]

Schmeidler was one of the first parapsychologists to show that the attitude shown toward ESP was a significant determinate of success. As mentioned, she discovered that believers (sheep) consistently scored higher than nonbelievers (goats). Few experiments in parapsychology have been successfully replicated, but the sheep-goat effect is one of the rarities and remains one of the few consistently confirmed (or at least partially so) predictions of ESP success. In 1971 John Palmer, now of the University of Virginia School of Medicine's division of parapsychology, reviewed all research on the sheep-goat effect and concluded (*Journal:* ASPR 65 [1971]: 401) that ". . . the data presently available support the hypothesis of a genuine SGE [sheep-goat effect], although the relationship is very slight and difficult to demonstrate with small samples."

Another psychological trait that has been confirmed as correlating with ESP success is extroversion. Persons are usually typed as either extroverted or introverted. Extroverts are more outgoing, sociable, and open, while introverts are more likely to be withdrawn. Several experimental studies have shown that extroversion is linked to ESP success. If they are pitted against introverts, the difference in their success is compounded, since introverts even have psi-missing during experimental runs. Betty Humphrey, whose specialty has been correlating personality measurements to ESP success, once wrote, "Thus far in ESP personality research, no other measure of personality has distinguished high and low ESP scores with this degree of accuracy." [19]

The story of personality measurements and ESP which lead to the differentiation between the scoring levels of introverts and extroverts has an interesting sidelight. It begins with C. E. Stuart who, as noted earlier, was both an able experimenter and subject. Stuart did not limit himself to conventional ESP testing and had attempted a replication of the picture-drawing tests so successfully employed during psychical research's earlier days. In these tests the subjects had either to clairvoyantly or tele-pathically draw target pictures, and the results were then mathe-matically scored. When Stuart gathered his data he disappoint-ingly found no evidence of psi. When Betty Humphrey started her research at Duke, her primary interest was personality fac-tors and ESP even at that time, and she was especially interested in judging those personality types labeled expansion and com-pression. These terms refer to one's ability to make contact with the outside world or tendencies toward isolation. This is a form of extroversion and introversion. These traits can be judged by examining drawings made by the subjects. Even though Stuart's subjects were attempting a clairvoyant or telepathic task, their drawings could still be considered either expansive or compres-sive. Dividing the clairvoyant drawings and reevaluating them, Humphrey found that the expansives had scored significantly higher than the compressives, but due to the latter's poor show-ing a cancellation had occurred when the drawings were jointly computed. Separating the pictures into the two groups showed that some ESP had entered into the test. After more analysis a clear picture began to form. On clairvoyant tasks the expansives scored the best, but on the telepathy tests the compressives were the ones who showed psi more overtly.

Louisa Rhine, commenting on the Stuart–Humphrey work in *ESP in Life and Lab*, suggested that expansives might feel freer in a clairvoyant test and annoyed by the possibility that another party was aiding in their attempt at telepathy. Compressives, on the other hand, may like the feeling of support during telepathy tests but are lost and confused when approached with the idea of clairvoyance. Humphrey later confirmed, during a formal exper-iment, that expansives can succeed better on clairvoyant tests than compressives. B. K. Kanthamani and K. Ramakrishna Rao also tested expansives versus compressives for clairvoyant ESP and confirmed the earlier findings. It should be mentioned though that expansive-compressive ratings are sometimes merely mood indicators and might shift day to day. A compressive, if retested another day, might become an expansive and vice versa. Humphrey found a correlation between the changes in ESP scoring with such shifts, consistent with her original findings.[20]

A further correlation to these studies again comes from Gertrude Schmeidler working with Lawrence LeShan. They tested subjects post hoc for either high or low barrier as shown on Rorschach testing. Barrier refers to how a person views his own body in relation to the world. The inverse of barrier is penetration. Simply, those who see their bodies as open to the outside world have low barrier, while those who see their bodies as closed to the outside world have high barrier. Again, those who tended toward low barrier were found to have been better subjects.[21]

All of these measurements—introversion-extroversion, compressive-expansive, high and low barrier—point in the same direction. A more open, sociable, and nonego centered personality is more conducive to psi. This is not to say that these individuals have more ESP, but that they are more likely to allow ESP to break into consciousness. However, this pattern may not hold true for gifted subjects. Pavel Stepanek, for example, is introverted, depressive, and submissive. (These measurements were made by standard psychological evaluations during his stay at the University of Virginia for research experimentation.) So, even though these measurements may be valid for the normal population, the truly gifted subject is conditioned by more complex determinates.

These few findings are merely highlights of what experimental parapsychology has told us about the psychology of ESP. Few findings in parapsychology are consistent with each other, but beyond this quagmire the fact that ESP is an unconscious process and is determined by psychological variables seems well substantiated. Yet, all these discoveries are products of the laboratory. We really have little right to say that they are also the laws that govern ESP as it occurs in daily life. Many parapsychologists are acutely aware that spontaneous ESP may not necessarily follow the same principles as laboratory ESP. A telepathic dream is a much different phenomenon in appearance than guessing cards above the level of chance. The study of spontaneous cases did not end with *Phantasms of the Living* and the *Census of Hallucinations*, but has also developed alongside the rigors of the laboratory. This realm of inquiry is now our next step—ESP in real life.

5

Spontaneous ESP

Of what use are purely anecdotal accounts of ESP experiences? Even if they can be corroborated by outside verification, how can they help us to understand the psi process? These are the two main questions raised by the study of spontaneous cases. Originally, analyzing large bodies of anecdotes was carried out for one major purpose, to prove that ESP occurs. Nonetheless, spontaneous cases can tell us a great deal about the nature of psi and they can help us understand the emotional setting that is most instrumental in causing ESP to surface to consciousness. They outline the range of forms of psychical experience, and they help us to understand themes and agent-percipient relationships most suitable for ESP.

Gertrude Schmeidler has argued that laboratory ESP is usually only inferential evidence of psi. Since ESP tests are attempts to beat chance, one cannot tell exactly when ESP is operating during a test or when chance is merely taking its just toll. The basic laboratory finding, Schmeidler argues, is that ESP is a vague, weak, elusive creature, flickering off and on sporadically. Spontaneous cases are the other side of the coin: "Spontaneous cases . . . can give a very different impression—an impression of ESP which occurs clearly and sometimes steadily and which functions like a powerful, accurate ability. It reminds one of what Freud said so many years ago, that dreams are a 'royal road to the unconscious'. Spontaneous cases seem like a royal road to ESP, while laboratory work is more like a narrow path chopped slowly through heavy underbrush." [1]

A rather opposing view of the uses of spontaneous ESP material comes from Robert Thouless. As an experimentalist, he believes that the greatest value of spontaneous case studies is that they suggest hypotheses about psi that can be tested in the laboratory. Experimentalism is primarily a method of advancing knowledge on the basis of testing theories drawn from natural observations. In this respect spontaneous cases would be considered the basis for these initial observations. [2] This view was originally suggested by Rhine. The basic difference in approach between Schmeidler's train of thought and the Rhine–Thouless view is the problem of evidence. If we wish to base our conclusions about psi on spontaneous cases, then we must be assured that the cases collected can be verified and are true illustrations of ESP. The experimentalist would be less concerned with the evidential aspects of the cases. If they merely serve to suggest theories for experimental validation, then it matters little if the original cases are valid or not. Louisa Rhine holds a center position between these two views and argues that, in a large body of reports, some cases are valid, some not corroborated at all, and some manufactured. However, counterfeits are usually based on a real prototype, and so if taken together, a large body of spontaneous cases will be representative of the range and forms of spontaneous ESP, even if one individual case is suspect.

Actually, the problem of fraud in analyzing spontaneous ESP cases appears to be a moot issue. Even the collectors of *Phantasms of the Living* came across only a very few cases of deliberate hoaxes. The same was true when C. J. Jung and Aniela Jaffé assembled their collection of apparitional and precognitive experiences. Those relatively few falsified stories were easily spotted. They were atypical, complicated, and exaggerated.

The atypicality of some reports can be considered a valid criterion for suspicion. As collectors of spontaneous cases have noted, patterns gradually emerge from these incidents, and by analyzing large bodies of cases, patterns, characteristics of content, form of the experience, and other factors emerge into a stereotype. If a single case is drastically contrary to this stereotype, suspicion is justified.

More important than the amassing of representative examples of spontaneous psi are several questions they pose: what types of psi (telepathy, clairvoyance, and so forth) are employed, in what forms do they manifest, and in what state of mind are the percipients during the experience? Parapsychology does have some statistics on these queries. We will use the following collections of spontaneous cases upon which to base our considerations of these problems:

1. An analysis of a thousand cases collected in Germany by G. Sannwald and published in the *Zeitschrift für Parapsychologie und Grenzgebiete der Psychologie* in 1959 (vol. 3, pp. 57–71).

2. A collection of three hundred English cases analyzed by Celia Green and published as "Analysis of Spontaneous Cases" (*Proceedings:* SPR 53 [1960]: 97–161).

3. A survey by Louisa Rhine of a total collection of 3290 cases sent to Duke University Parapsychology Laboratory and to her personally as published in a paper "Frequency of Types of Experiences in Spontaneous Precognition" (*Journal of Parapsychology* 18 [1954]: 93–123). Also used in Mrs. Rhine's "Subjective Forms of Spontaneous Psi Experiences," *Journal of Parapsychology* 17 (1953): 79–114.

4. A study of spontaneous ESP in school children carried out in India by J. Prasad and Ian Stevenson, "A Survey of Spontaneous Psychical Experiences in School Children of Uttar Pradesh, India," *International Journal of Parapsychology* 10 (1968): 241–61.

To the first question as to what types of ESP are experienced, these can be roughly designated as either contemporary (telepathic or clairvoyant) or precognitive. By far, the largest *single* classification of spontaneous cases were precognitive: of the four studies cited above, the figures are respectively, 52 percent, 34 percent, 40 percent, 40 percent. This signifies that precognitive experiences are more common than might be generally believed.

What forms do these cases take? Louisa Rhine has broken these experiences down into four major classifications. Dreams are a major media for psi experiences, being either realistic dreams in which the subject sees an actual representation of a clairvoyantly, telepathically, or precognitively cognized event, or unrealistic dreams which are symbolic representations of the stimulus event. Waking spontaneous ESP consists of either intuitions or impressions and full-blown hallucinations. The former range from vague feelings or apprehension coinciding with such an event as death or accident, to complete sudden "awareness" of a foreign event. Mrs. Rhine also includes spontaneous psychokinesis as a form of spontaneous ESP. This is based on a large block of cases where physical manifestations, such as inexplicable clock stoppings, are concurrent to a death or accident. She argues that the percipient first employs the naturally unconscious ESP to become aware of a death or similar occurrence, then uses PK to carry out a symbolic physical act to bring this knowledge to consciousness. Thus, a physical act is employed instead of an intuition or dream. Spontaneous PK will not be discussed here, but deferred until the chapter on physical phenomena. All these forms of psi once again illustrate the basic unconscious nature of ESP; dreams, intuitions, and hallucinations are unconscious processes and are the main carriers of ESP impressions.

Comparing the aforementioned four major studies of spontaneous ESP, the following chart represents how collections of ESP cases compare cross-culturally * when breaking down the cases of type of impression.

Series	Dreams	Waking Hallucinations	Waking Impressions	Intermediate
American	58.0%	6.1%	28.7%	7.2%
German	63.0%	10.3%	26.7%	—
English	37.0%	39.0%	15.0%	9.0%
Indian	52.4%	15.7%	31.9%	—

There are only two irregularities breaking the overall pattern of these cases. Firstly, the English survey shows more waking hallucinations than should have been expected by the results of the other surveys. This may be due to the fact that the English survey was based on a much smaller group of cases than the others. This might, then, be a biased sample. Secondly, the Indian cases show a disproportionately large amount of waking im-

* This chart is adapted from a similar one graphed in the Prasad-Stevenson study.

pression cases. This quirk might actually be a key to understanding the rarity of psi. As stated earlier, one theory about why psi so rarely surfaces to consciousness is a censoring mechanism in the mind. We know that the mind can only accept a certain range of outside stimuli at one time and censors unnecessary stimuli from cluttering the consciousness. For example, as we walk we do not perceive every sight and sound as equally stimulating. Our brain only processes that which is necessary for us to function. In fact, it has been independently suggested that drug-induced hallucinatory and psychedelic impressions, as well as schizophrenic states, are caused by a malfunction in our ability to censor unwanted sensory stimuli. Naturally this ability to censor would cancel out oncoming ESP impressions for two reasons: (1) except when bringing very vivid impressions, they are unwarranted and unneeded, and (2) psi experiences in Western society are culturally nonacceptable due to our general scientific and mechanistic culture pattern which prejudices against them.

These points lead to a view of Louisa Rhine's that even though psi is rare in our culture because of our deep-seated prejudices against it, a culture more accepting of psi would show a higher frequency of cases. The Indian study points in that direction. Although we have no statistics on whether cultures foreign to our own have a more common incidence of psi, the Indian study does show that their culture does have a higher percentage of waking impression cases. During our waking hours we would probably be the least susceptible to ESP impressions due to unconscious censoring. This is the reason why dreams, a mediating point between the conscious and unconscious, are so typically the media for psi. In India, with a culture more accepting of psi, we find a high incidence of waking ESP experiences. This might represent less of a cultural barrier for having spontaneous ESP. In any event, a cross-cultural analysis of spontaneous ESP narratives is consistent with the Rhine culture-mediated view.

Keeping the preceding discussion in mind, several types of spontaneous cases will be examined. By far the most conspicuous form of ESP experiences are waking intuition or impression cases. Louisa Rhine has written that such cases represent a block to prevent the ESP message from popping fully and directly into consciousness. The most in-depth analysis of such cases has been made by Ian Stevenson,[3] who, in surveying the published literature on impression cases, has found the following traits to be typical: the largest proportion of cases occurs between members of the same family; the most predominent cause for the impression is death followed by serious accident; impression cases occur rarely in sleep but predominantly manifest during waking hours; there is a slight tendency for the percipients to be with others when the impression surfaces. Stevenson's excellent analysis of cases is accompanied by thirty-five new cases, all of which are strongly evidential. In the following case from his study the impression was strongly focused. That is, although the actual impression was not visual, the percipient immediately was able to focus on the likely agent and interpret her experience correctly.

> When my five-year-old daughter came home from a birthday party, she was disappointed to find that her father and brother had gone to the Walt Disney movie without her. The Rivoli Theater is a block and a half away on the main street (Washington Ave.) which runs parallel with Portland Avenue, our home address. I told Joicey that her father expected her to join them there, so she waved goodbye and skipped toward the corner.
>
> I returned to the dinner dishes still unwashed in the kitchen sink. Quite suddenly while I held a plate in my hand an awesome feeling came over me. I dropped the plate, turned my eyes towards heaven and prayed aloud, "Oh, God, don't let her get killed!"
>
> For some unexplainable reason I knew Joicey had been hit by a car or was going to be. I was quite conscious of her involvement in an accident.

Mrs. Hurth, the percipient, called the theater, and the manager there verified that Joicey had indeed been hit by a car but not injured. Both Joicey and Mrs. Hurth sent in corroborating statements.

In this case the impression was vivid and there can be no doubt that Mrs. Hurth's experience was extrasensory. It is typical of many such cases—it is concise, brings with it certain conviction, and is highly emotional. However, impression cases are often not nearly so well-defined, consisting only of little more than an abrupt shift in mood correlating with a concordant event in the life of an emotionally binding friend or relative. Louisa Rhine offers a fairly representative case of a vague but unmistakable impression in her *ESP in Life and Lab* (abbreviated for the purposes of this book):

> My husband and I were living in Youngstown, Ohio. I was pregnant with our second child. Our first was in a home for retarded children in Dayton, Ohio. He was ten months old, and I had seen him only twice. From that time neither my husband nor I saw nor heard of him.
>
> My second pregnancy was a very happy one. I didn't have a blue day and was happy as a lark. That is why when one night in March during my sixth month the terrible gloom that descended upon me was so unexpected. We had been out to dinner, arrived home early and were getting ready for bed when this heavy unhappy feeling began filling my heart. I tried analyzing myself as I do when something is bothering me, but try as I might, I could not find the answer. That night was a mixture of tears, tossing and turning. When the morning finally came that horrible heavy feeling was still with me. My husband was reluctant to leave me and made me promise to get out of the house and be with someone . . . At 2 in the afternoon I dragged myself to the grocery store to buy food I didn't need. I remember vividly standing by the meat counter when all of a sudden a glorious feeling as though a great weight had been lifted from my shoulders. It was exactly 3 P.M.
>
> That evening I told my husband everything. We had just finished eating when we received a long-distance phone call. It was from the home our baby was in in Dayton. Our baby had been very sick the night before and had passed away that afternoon at 3 P.M.
>
> This certainly was not an earth shaking experience, but every word is true.

In this case the only impression was that of mood and emotion. Although undoubtedly the unconscious had received a more accurate ESP impression, only a vague and then a heightened affectation of mood filtered gradually into consciousness.

In this type of case it is hard to judge paranormality, since no veridical piece of data is delivered during the experience. However, the main points by which such cases can be validated is based on the dual factors of (1) timing the mood with the incident and (2) the large amount of case material involving effects of mood. As Mrs. Rhine adds, ". . . it would not seem unreasonable to suppose that the emotion would be more penetrating than the idea. Many persons can testify to moods without ideas; even when the cause is some well known and easily traced memory or physiological state."

Full-form waking hallucinations are rarer than impression cases, and unlike dream ESP these visions are not as prone to symbolic distortion or representation. The hallucinations are often visual, but may affect other senses as well. One case, originally collected by the early SPR investigators, reported that a woman had awaken from sleep feeling as if a swift and powerful blow had been delivered to her mouth. She also tasted blood. These two pseudosensory experiences correlated to an accident occurring to her husband at the same time while he was out sailing. He had accidentally been hit by a tiller and had bled profusely from his mouth. In another SPR case, a woman and her daughter both heard the voice of their son/brother crying out, "Mama. Mama." Yet he was at sea at the time. Their collective experience did relate however to a frightening, though harmless, incident on board the ship. The boy had been accidentally knocked overboard and in his fright had called out, "Mama! Mama!" much to the amusement of his shipmates. These two experiences represent waking audile, tactile, and taste hallucinations.

Visual hallucinations are the most vivid form of ESP occurrence, as witness the following case verified and published by Dr. G. Dupré in the *Annales des Sciences Psychiques* (vol. 1, pp. 324–25).

I had just been visiting a patient, and was coming downstairs, when suddenly I had the impression that my little girl of four years old had fallen down the stone stairs of my house and hurt herself.

Then gradually after the first impression, as though a curtain which hid the sight from me were slowly drawn back, I saw my child lying in front of the stairs, with her chin bleeding, but I had no impression of hearing her cries.

The vision was blotted out suddenly, but the memory of it remained with me. I took note of the hour—10:30 A.M.—and continued my professional rounds.

When I got home I much astonished my family by giving a description of the accident and naming the hour when it occurred.

This anecdote, verified by Mme Dupré, illustrates a number of characteristics inherent in a waking ESP vision. Firstly, it brought with it utter conviction of its veracity. Secondly, the percipient had no control over the vision which, although never becoming a hallucination, remained a visual experience. Thirdly, the case began as a typical impression case. Comparing this report to the previously cited impression cases, this one shows the typical mechanics of a waking ESP intuition as it emerges from unconsciousness to consciousness. First only a vague impression surfaced and then slowly it broke into full consciousness after a gestation period. Had the impression not been able to break into a visionary experience, it would likely have remained only an impression case.

However, other cases of spontaneous waking ESP can become fully conscious in an instant and manifest as an all-engulfing hallucinatory experience. The following famous case is from *Phantasms of the Living* and occurred while the percipient was a child. This rather dramatic case is so celebrated since good corroborating testimony for it was given by the still-living parents:

> I was walking in a country lane at A., the place where my parents resided. I was reading geometry as I walked along, a subject little likely to produce fancies or morbid phenomena of any kind, when, in a moment, I saw a bedroom known as the White Room in my home, and upon the floor lay my mother, to all appearances dead. The vision must have remained some minutes during which time my real surroundings appeared to pale and die out; but as the vision faded, actual surroundings came back, at first dimly, and then clearly.
>
> I could not doubt that what I had seen was real, so, instead of going home, I went at once to the house of our medical man and found him at home. He at once set out with me for

my home, on the way putting questions I could not answer, as my mother was to all appearances well when I left home.

I led the doctor straight to the White Room, where we found my mother actually lying as in my vision. This was true even to minute details. She had been seized suddenly by an attack at the heart, and would soon have breathed her last but for the doctor's timely advent.

This case also represents the difficulty in distinguishing between telepathy and clairvoyance. Although all psi phenomena represent a unified process, there is still the possibility that the mechanics of spontaneous ESP rest either with the agent who sends a telepathic impression or with the clairvoyance of the percipient who through constant scanning discovers grave circumstances and jolts them into consciousness. Louisa Rhine, in her analysis of spontaneous ESP cases, reached the conclusion that it is often the percipient who is the active partner in the ESP experience. This would radically upset the commonly held notion of a pure agent-who-sends, percipient-who-receives, active-passive relationship. Mrs. Rhine further argues that telepathy might be an active dynamic process wherein both the partners mutually build up the ESP impression. Ian Stevenson in his study of telepathic impressions has argued that either the percipient or the agent might be the active party in spontaneous ESP. The active nature of the percipient also suggests more of a clairvoyant process than a telepathic one. But again, such distinctions are of purely academic interest.

Although waking visual impressions are the most vivid forms of spontaneous psi, they are apparently no more common than auditory or tactile hallucinations as represented by unaccountable physical sensations related to a distant accident (as in the case of the wife who felt a blow to her mouth when her husband was hurt), or hearing cries for help (as in the case of the lad who fell overboard). As illustration of this Mrs. Rhine presented the following breakdown in 1956 based on cases she had collected.*

Dreams have long been known as the major vehicle of psi, and as Mrs. Rhine has noted, ESP may manifest within them either

* From Louisa Rhine's "Hallucinatory Psi Experiences—I: An Introductory Survey," *Journal of Parapsychology* 20 (1956): 233–56.

SENSE MODALITIES

	Visual	Auditory	Olfactory	Somatic	Total
Telepathy	81	244	0	106	431
Clairvoyance	9	46	11	0	66
Precognition	12	32	8	8	60
GESP	129	113	17	9	268
	231	435	36	123	825

by realistic or symbolic representation. Since dreams are primarily a vehicle of the unconscious, symbolic distortions might be expected to play a part even in realistic dreams. The following is an example of a realistic ESP dream taken from Tyrrell's *Science and Psychical Phenomena:*

> I was in an overhead signal-box, extending over a railway-line I had never seen before. It was night, and I saw approaching what I knew was an excursion train, full of people returning from some big function. I knew it was my duty to signal this train through, which I did, but at the same time I had a feeling that the train was doomed. . . .
>
> In my dream I seemed to hover in the air, and follow the express as it slowed to round a loop line. As it approached a station I saw, to my horror, another small train on the same line. Although they seemed both travelling slowly, they met with terrible impact. I saw the express and its coaches pitch and twist in the air, and the noise was terrible.
>
> Afterwards, I walked beside the wreckage in the dim light of dawn viewing with a feeling of terror the huge overturned engine and smashed coaches. I was now amid an indescribable scene of horror, with dead and injured people, and rescue workers everywhere. . . .

Later that day, the narrator discovered an identical description of a similar accident in the evening paper.

Most ESP-type dreams are rarely so clear, but are often subject to distortion, either symbolic disguising or intrusions from the dreamer's own unconscious. The former again appears to be a type of censoring mechanism as a final attempt to block the impression. In the following case from Mrs. Rhine's collection, while the event is correctly portrayed, the setting is altered into a less anxiety-provoking symbolic representation:

> I grew up with one of the toughest, meanest, most unpredictable horses that any youngster ever tried to handle. . . . We called him Brown.
>
> In December 1918 I was returning home from the Army. No one was expecting me. At about 4:15 A.M. the train I was riding derailed and there was a terrible wreck. I was unhurt. I reached home after dark some fifteen hours later. The first greeting from my mother was, "Where were you at 4:15 this morning?" I tried to keep a straight face and asked why such a question. She told me that in a dream Brown and I had been in one of our acts which had been unusually violent. Brown had come out of it clear—not a piece of leather left on him— but nothing was clear as to what had become of me. Then she awoke and the clock stood at 4:15; she had been worrying about me all day. Then, of course, I told her about the wreck.

Considerable light on the nature of these symbolic distortions have been uncovered by psychoanalytic theory. Some psychiatrists and psychologists have observed ESP dreaming in their patients, and since dream theory and interpretation are of key concern in traditional psychoanalytically oriented therapy, several cogent views on the nature of psi dreaming have been put forth. Freud, for example, offers a typical example of a symbolic ESP dream. The subject had dreamed that his wife gave birth to twins. This occurred on the same night that his daughter actually gave birth to twins. The case showed, to Freud, how telepathic dreaming did not necessarily affect his own concept of dream symbolism. In this case the dream, on one level, represented the man's own incestful desires toward his daughter. In order to sublimate this unwanted and socially unacceptable position, his wife was substituted in the dream for his daughter. Yet, the key catalyst to the dream was an ESP stimulus. From such cases Freud came to the conclusion that symbolic distortions in a telepathic dream can become so complex and subliminated that only a psychoanalytical interpretation could reveal the dream's psi nature.

Soon after the birth of the psychoanalytical movement, other therapists began to find examples of ESP in the dreams of their patients. Sandor Ferenczi tried telepathically to impress a psychic he knew by concentrating on an elephant. He felt the experiment was a failure but soon afterward another friend called to report a dream he had of Ferenczi fighting off wild animals including an elephant.[4] Ferenczi experienced other ESP transfers between himself and his patients. Another of Freud's early followers, Wilhelm Stekel, wrote a book on telepathic dreaming, and Helene Deutsch also wrote upon the subject. Geraldine Pederson-Krag noted that as she delved into her patients' lives, they in turn might telepathically tune in on hers and reveal dreams, often symbolic, concerning private and intimate details of her own life. The patients rarely identified the dreams as telepathic and they would have remained inexplicable had not the therapist been able to interpret the dreams and identify them as containing an element of psi. She reported the following incident as an example: She was giving a dinner party but was worried about having enough silverware. At the same time one of her patients dreamed of having company for dinner and being worried about not having enough silver. The entire dream took place under the scornful eye of a male figure. In the dream the male figure represented a threat in her relationship to her father. This threat was part of the transference from her father to the therapist. The transference had catalyzed the dream.[5]

Jule Eisenbud, the contemporary psychoanalyst, has argued a step further—that ESP may form into a network between a therapist and various unrelated patients.

It is certain that psychoanalytic theory can be of immense value in helping us understand the meaning of symbolic distortion in dream ESP and even of the emotional factors which cause the phenomena. Nonetheless, there are two differing ways of viewing the role psychoanalytic theory plays in the understanding of spontaneous ESP cases. First there is the view that the psychoanalytic setting is a free setting and that the manifestation of psi during psychoanalysis is a true representation of how ESP works in daily life. Psychoanalytical findings on the nature of such ESP cases are therefore valid as characteristic of all spontaneous ESP which is also usually conditioned by a deep emotional involvement with the other party in the ESP transfer and disguised by symbolic distortion. (By far the greatest number of spontaneous ESP reports are between close relations or friends.) Emilio Servadio, an Italian psycholanalyst, has theorized that in daily life we build up relations with others based on transference and countertransference. Therefore, spontaneous ESP even in daily life is analogous to the therapeutic session.

Another approach has been outlined by Dr. Jan Ehrenwald in an excellent presentation, "The Telepathy Hypothesis and Doctrinal Compliance in Psychotherapy," which originally appeared in the *American Journal of Psychotherapy* (1957). Briefly, Ehrenwald's theory is similar to the previously outlined discussion of the experimenter effect, in which the experimenter can mold the results he gets. He believes the same problem can arise in therapy where the therapist can unintentionally suggest to the patient the types of dreams he wishes to get, or the patient can use ESP to help satisfy and please the analyst by producing ESP dreams consistent with his theoretical ideas. Similarly, dream ESP can manifest as a joint endeavor between patient and therapist to produce those types of dreams that fit into the therapist's notions about psi and even the therapy itself. In defense of this view it has been noted that therapists who shift their theoretical orientation often find a sudden and unaccountable and similar reorientation in the dreams of their patients. This is suggestive of ESP. Another point is that apparently only therapists open to the possibility of psi report patient-therapist ESP. Thus, Eisenbud, Ehrenwald, Ferenczi, and others observed extrasensory processes in their clinical experience to a great extent, while on the other hand skeptics such as Alfred Adler and Albert Ellis report no such occurrences in their practices. Like most issues in parapsychology, the psychoanalytic approach to spontaneous ESP can be argued either way.*

Spontaneous precognition is the final major type of spontaneous ESP. Like contemporary ESP, precognition may occur during either waking or in dreams. However, a vast majority of precognitive ESP cases are reported during the dreaming state.

---

* A complete appraisal of psychiatry's contribution to parapsychology can be found in Jule Eisenbud's paper, "Psychiatric Contributions to Parapsychology: A Review," *Journal of Parapsychology* 13 (1949): 247–62. A more contemporary anecdotal and abbreviated overview of the situation may be found in a chapter "ESP on the Couch" in the Ullman, Krippner, and Vaughan *Dream Telepathy*.

Mrs. Sidgwick found that 66 percent of her cases were dream precognitions (*Proceedings:* SPR 5 [1888–1889]: 288–354). Another survey by Celia Green showed a similar percentile of 68.8 percent (*Proceedings:* SPR 53 [1960]: 96–161). Sannwald's cases of dream precognition showed 60 percent and Mrs. Rhine's revealed 68 percent. Again, the only exception was the Prasad-Stevenson Indian survey where there was an equal ratio of dream to waking precognition. This once again suggests a cultural openness to the phenomenon. Louisa Rhine has broken down precognitive experiences into intuitive, hallucinatory, and dream types similar to her analysis of contemporary cases. Oddly, precognition conforms to a different pattern than GESP cases as the following analysis shows.* (As with experimental research, GESP represents "general extrasensory perception" where one cannot differentiate between telepathic condition or clairvoyant condition ESP.)

	Precognitive	Contemporaneous	Total Cases
Intuitive	19.0%	35.0%	943
Hallucinatory	6.0%	25.0%	570
Dreaming— Realistic	15.0%	21.0%	619
Dreaming— Unrealistic	60.0%	19.0%	1158

Phenomenologically, precognitive experiences manifest similarly to contemporaneous ESP experiences. In impression cases the feeling may either be vague or focused, although the actual ESP stimulus only occurs later than the initial intuition. Sometimes these cases can be dramatic. The following two cases are taken from Aniela Jaffé's *Apparitions and Precognition* (1963) and represent two different forms of premonitory experiences. The first is only a vague impression, the second is more focused:

(1)
  It was in February, 1948, early in the morning, and I was getting ready to take my little boy of seven for a long-promised ski-outing. Everything was ready and we were just

---

* Reference, Louisa E. Rhine, "Frequency of Types of Experience in Spontaneous Precognition," *Journal of Parapsychology* 18 (1954): 93–123.

about to leave the house when a feeling came over me—hard to describe, but increasingly strong—that we must not go. At first I did not want to give in to it, but in the end we decided to stay at home, in spite of the good weather reports and disappointed faces. In the evening we heard on the radio the news of the terrible railway accident at Wadenswil. For quite a time afterwards I lived in a constant state of terror, for we would almost certainly have come home by that train and perhaps met our death.

(2)

I have been an invalid for many years, so I lie down for a little every day around noon. One morning, when I woke up, I had an uncomfortable feeling. I couldn't get any peace no matter where I was or what I did. I went to see my neighbor, but she could give me no advice. Then I lay down on a sofa. A picture was hanging on the wall—a beautiful landscape. I had been resting for about a quarter of an hour when I heard the voice of my inmost self; it cried: "Get up!" and again "Get up." I jumped up and looked around, but there was nothing to be seen. Full of uneasiness I went into the kitchen to make some tea. I had hardly been out there two minutes when I heard a dull bang. First I looked out into the street, but there was nothing to be seen there. But when I opened the door of the sitting-room I froze with terror: The picture had fallen from the wall straight onto the sofa. If I had still been lying there the glass might have cut my face to pieces.

These two cases illustrate the expectedly common feature of an unconscious basis of precognition conforming to ESP in general. In the first instance only an impression surfaced just as in telepathic cases. In the second illustration not only was an initial impression felt, but finally a subconscious compulsion brought the experience to a climax. These features again point to the laboratory finding that precognition is only one component of an overall ESP process. That precognition appears in symbolic dreams at a vastly higher rate than GESP also betrays our natural barrier. While many people can readily accept that one mind can affect another mind (telepathy), fewer would admit that the mind can perceive a future event. Precognitive experiences are thus even more of a threat than GESP. The high amount of symbolism in spontaneous precognitive dreams may stem from two sources: firstly, the continuous mechanism to repress the stimulus from consciousness; secondly, to disguise the psi event when it does reach consciousness. This second possibility needs some explanation. Both the above-cited cases related to tragedy and accident. By far the most consistent precognized events are of an anxiety-provoking nature. In the Prasad–Stevenson study of Indian children, over 50 percent of reported premonitions related to either death or accident. The large amount of symbolism occurring in precognitive experiences may represent the mind's own wish to soften the impact of the premonition. The following two cases represent procognitive dreams, one realistic, the other symbolic. Both are taken from the cases of Louisa Rhine:

(1)
I dreamed I was downtown on Main Street and stopped to look in the window of a dress shop. Just inside the shop an old school chum of mine came out dressed in a black coat. I said, "I am sorry to hear about your mother's death, Helen." A few weeks later Helen's mother did die, and one day as I was downtown in the same spot of my dream, the whole thing happened exactly as dreamed.

(2)
I awoke one night to find our baby in convulsions. We took her to the hospital at 2 A.M. on Sunday morning. We had no idea she was so ill. The next day I received a letter from my mother a thousand miles away. She said, "Be careful with the baby. Dad dreamed about her this week. He was quite disturbed because although he kept reaching and reaching for her, she kept slipping away from him until she was gone." Our baby died on March 1. She never regained consciousness from February 25.

The fact that precognition occurs so often during dreams has lead some experimenters to keep detailed records of their own dreams in order to discover whether or not precognition manifests in them and, if so, the frequency of it. The most celebrated of these dream records was made by a brilliant aeronautical engineer, J. W. Dunne, who had gradually become aware that some of his dreams predicted events in his life, often within the next few days. Since most people forget their dreaming soon after waking, Dunne kept pencil and paper at hand in order to jot down all his dreams before losing grasp of them after he awoke. These he kept in record books and carefully noted any future occurrences that bore any resemblance to them. Dunne's dream records, published in 1927 as *An Experiment with Time*, reveal several ostensibly paranormal dreams. Sometimes, the dreams were realized the next day or soon afterward, but others took several months before the predictions came to pass. Often the dreams were distorted. In one dream record Dunne wrote that he was walking down a path between two fields, each bordered by high iron railings. To his left he spotted a terrifying horse, kicking and plunging in heated rage. Looking around to assure himself that the horse could not get loose, he continued on his way. By chance he again looked back and to his horror saw that the horse had escaped and was charging directly at him. Dunne fled in terror toward some wooden steps and awoke. The next day Dunne and his brother decided to spend some leisure time fishing. During their expedition his brother called attention to a wild-looking horse in a nearby open field. Sure enough, Dunne recognized the scene, railings and all, as fulfilling his previous night's dream. The dream was distorted since many minor details of the scene were different from the dream setting; but even the wooden steps were in front of him leading to a bridge crossing a river. Dunne began to relate his dream to his brother when the horse jumped the fence and charged them, plunging into the river in its attack. As Dunne continues, "The end was tame, for, on emerging from the water on our side, the animal merely looked at us, snorted, and galloped off down a road."

In another of Dunne's prolific dreams the catalyzing event was not actualized for several months. He dreamed of a high railway embankment by Forth Bridge in Scotland. In the dream a train had fallen over the embankment. He reported the dream to his sister and stated that it probably forecasted an event several months away. Indeed several months later the Flying Scotsman, a famous train of its day, jumped the tracks and fell over an embankment fifteen miles north of Forth Bridge.

The large body of premonitions recorded by Dunne revealed quite a bit about the nature of precognition. His most important observation was that precognitive dreams follow the typical construct of normal dreams which are rehashes of recent experiences, reconstituted into symbolic presentations. Yet, normal dream elements are not new constructs, but merely assorted life experiences reworked for the purpose of the dream. Dunne found this same pattern with precognitive dreams. Even premonitory dreams are made up from residue of daily experiences though reconstructed into a premonition. This was not necessarily an idiosyncrasy of Dunne's psychic dreams. In 1966 Rosalind Heywood and Ian Stevenson presented an in-depth analysis of a precognitive dream in which they showed that its foundation elements were based upon the subject's previous experiences but remodeled into a vehicle for precognition.[6]

Because Dunne had found that dream precognition occurred so regularly, he was able to formulate a theory to account for them. Although he was familiar with psychical research, he disdained the idea that dream premonitions had anything to do with ESP. Since he denied being psychic, he preferred to believe that precognition was a normal function of time, and so he devised the theory of "serial time." This vague and hard to comprehend concept boils down to a form of "conditional predestination." At any point in time some future events are determined by the past and present, and the mind can become aware of these incidents. (Dunne came suspiciously close to postulating clairvoyance at this point.)

Dunne's theory could be put to a crucial test, for he felt that anybody might be able to record his dreams and prove the naturalness of precognition. Theodore Besterman, then investigations officer for the Society for Psychical Research, took Dunne to task and organized a research project of several volunteers who recorded their dreams and posted them to Besterman. By analyzing all these reports it was shown that Dunne's theory just did not hold water, for outside of a few scattered dreams and validations suggestive of precognition, no profuse or systematic evidence for the phenomenon was observed in the group of experimental subjects. Whatever gift Dunne had, it was obviously semi-unique. Dunne himself participated with Besterman, but failed to achieve the amount of success expected from his earlier claims, although he did obtain some scattered hits.[7]

One point does stand out in Dunne's records: the triviality of many precognitions. We usually think of precognition as being stimulated by a powerfully emotional catalyst such as death or accident. Indeed these catalysts might help us to understand when and why precognition surfaces. But, in a rough way, Dunne might have been correct in viewing precognitive dreaming as a perfectly normal function of sleep and an ability that all people possess. Even if psi seems to surface only rarely, there is presently sufficient evidence to indicate that our minds are constantly bombarded by psi impressions that remain repressed and subliminated.

Some dream precognitions seem to be little more than irregular intrusions of precognitive ESP into consciousness. In the following case from Louisa Rhine's collection, there is no emotional content and it is difficult to reason why the event should serve in a paranormal dream at all. Instead it looks more like an accidental leakage filtering through the unconscious mind's ESP censor.

> I dreamed I was driving past a very old school or church with a large bell over the door to be pulled by a rope. A family were living there. This building was very close to a fence. The next afternoon my sister and her husband stopped in and asked me if I could drive with them as he had to go to see someone on business. To my surprise I saw the people with the children as we passed the identical spot that I had dreamed.

Evidence pointing in the direction of an ever-recurring ESP-precognitive ability stems from the study of mass precognition of disasters. Certain highly publicized events have often been the theme of precognitive experiences in totally disinterested parties. Most precognition occurs between individuals who are strongly linked emotionally, but some disasters have ignited precognitive experiences in a large group of independent individuals who have no emotional tie with the event or anyone involved in it.

Two such studies concern the famous sinking of the *Titanic* and the Aberfan disaster. Ian Stevenson has collected nineteen paranormal experiences related to the *Titanic*'s sinking taken from both published and unpublished sources. Of these, six were precognitive.[8] A similar study was made of the events surrounding the Aberfan disaster in which a mountain of coal refuse collapsed, burying a school and killing many children. J. C. Barker was able to collect thirty-six premonitions of which twenty-five were dream premonitions. His cases fit a basic pattern of mass precognition, that is the closer the time to the tragedy, the more frequent the number of independent premonitions: *

Time of Premonition	Number	Waking	Realistic Dream	Symbolic Dream
1 week	16	1	2	13
1–2 weeks	7	0	3	4
2–4 weeks	2	1	0	1
1 month or longer	6	1	1	4

Few of the Aberfan cases were experienced by people who had children in the school. In his *Titanic* survey Stevenson found a similar clustering of paranormal events closer in time to the actual tragedy. This could be caused either by some principle through which precognition operates, or by the fact that people might be more prone to report premonitions when they are realized shortly afterward. When the stimulus event finally transpired, long-term dream precognitions might be forgotten or dismissed as coincidental and unrelated. Dr. John Orme analyzed Mrs. Rhine's spontaneous cases and also discovered a systematic decline between the number of short-term and long-term precognitive psi. (A paper delivered at the 21st Conference of the Parapsychology Foundation, Amsterdam, 1972.)

In these studies it is indicated that precognition, like its sister phenomena GESP, probably occurs more often than is realized. Plethysmograph ESP experiments have demonstrated not only that ESP is an unconscious phenomenon, but that one can react subconsciously to an ESP stimulus. A similar principle was found by W. F. Cox in his study of the spontaneous precognition of disasters. Cox accumulated passenger statistics for

* This chart was graphed by the present author from thirty-one cases presented in J. C. Barker's "Premonitions of the Aberfan Disaster," *Journal:* SPR 44 (1967): 169–80.

twenty-eight railway accidents and then compared the number traveling on the trains on the fateful days to the seven days preceding the accident and a few days after the accident. On the target days there was a noticeable decline of passengers. This suggested to Cox that somehow masses of potential travelers were aware of the oncoming tragedy but that most likely it was a subconscious psi awareness.[9]

J. W. Dunne was not the only experimenter to record his dreams to evaluate their paranormal content. A similar record has been made by Alan Vaughan whose main interest is the role of symbolism in spontaneous precognition. By constant introspection he has been able to extract some of the working principles causing the distortions. The symbolic distortion is often based on past events as Dunne suggested. In these cases a dream remembrance of a past event triggers a precognition of a similar future event. This led Vaughan to postulate that precognitive dreams have double catalysts which work hand in hand; that is, material drawn from both the past and the present is combined. Since realistic dreams are scarce and even these are rarely exactly fulfilled, he believes that the future event does not really catalyze the dream, but that the mind when constructing the dream draws not only from the past but may partake of the future as well. As he states, "In precognitive dreaming one finds exactly the same sort of symbolism, condensation, substitution, and metaphor as one finds in ordinary dreams. The only difference is that the precognitive dream draws its material from the future while the ordinary dream draws its material from the past." [10]

Just as it was hard for J. B. Rhine and his co-workers to prove the precognitive hypothesis, true spontaneous precognition is also hard to prove. Stevenson and many others have suggested that what we call precognition is really a global form of clairvoyance. The mind, scanning by unconscious ESP, makes rational deductions about the future from clairvoyantly gathered data. These deductions are then presented to the mind via a premonition. Of course, an ESP process is the root of the phenomenon, but the ESP is of the clairvoyance type, not true precognition. The main evidence for this theory rests on the short- to long-term ratio found in spontaneous cases. Short-term premonitions would be more profuse and more within the capability of the mind's ESP scanning. This whole concept in turn is based upon a principle of subliminal perception. In 1911 Theodore Flournoy, in his book, *Spiritism and Psychology*, showed that many alleged premonitions were just rational deductions based on subliminally perceived information subconsciously processed. For example, if a person dreams of the rear tire of his car blowing, this may be due to his own unconscious perception that the tire is worn and ready to blow anyway. However, the dream would be mistakenly interpreted as paranormal cognition of a future event if the tire actually did blow. Stevenson and others have suggested that a similar process of deduction may account for precognition. They argue that the mind is contantly gathering data by ESP. The unconscious mind then assimilates various bits of this data and makes predictions from them. For example, a parapsychological explanation of the above incident might be constructed as follows. The percipient may not have been aware of the worn tire but his ESP ability might have clairvoyantly perceived it. Based on this knowledge, the unconscious then built up the dream of the tire's blowing as a warning to the driver. This is a case of a precognitive dream, but the dream is really based on clairvoyant perception, not true precognition of a future event. It is hard to find specific evidence for this theory, but some verification of it comes from the research of Eugene Osty.

Eugene Osty, a French physician, after studying many gifted psychics, came to the conclusion that every individual is aware of his own future so that when one precognizes about another person a form of ESP transfer has occurred due to one's own knowledge of predestined events. Osty did not accept pure precognition of a nonexistent event, but believed it was telepathy from a party already subconsciously cognizant of his own preordained future. Osty was led to this opinion by his discovery that his subjects could not predict nonpersonal events or world happenings. Alan Vaughan has postulated a similar theory.

Despite these provocative concepts and theories, certain cases of precognition do seem explainable only as the pure premonition of a future event. A classic example was originally reported by Dunne:

I seemed to be standing on high ground—the upper slopes of some spur of a hill or mountain. The ground was a curious white formation. Here and there in this were little fissures, and from these jets of vapour were spouting upward. In my dream I recognized the place as an island of which I had dreamed before—an island which was in imminent peril from a volcano. And, when I saw the vapour spouting from the ground, I gasped: "It's the island! Good Lord, the whole thing is going to *blow up!*" For I had memories of reading about Krakatoa, where the sea, making its way into the heart of a volcano through a submarine crevice, flashed into steam, and blew the whole mountain to pieces. Forthwith I was seized with a frantic desire to save the four thousand (I knew the number) unsuspecting inhabitants. Obviously, there was only one way of doing this, and that was to take them off in ships. There followed a most distressing nightmare, in which I was at a neighboring island, trying to get the incredulous *French* authorities to despatch vessels of every and any description to remove the inhabitants of the threatened island. . . . All through the dream the number of the people in danger obsessed my mind. I repeated it to everyone I met, and, at the moment of waking I was shouting . . . "Listen! Four thousand people will be killed unless . . ."

Soon afterward Dunne read in the *Daily Telegraph:* "Volcano Disaster in Martinique—town swept away—an avalanche of flame—probable loss of over 40,000 lives—British steamer burnt!" Dunne at first misread 40,000 for 4000 and only years later discovered his error. However, the true fatality figures had no relation to either 4000 or 40,000. The logical inference was that Dunne had not predicted the actual event, but the headlines. This would indicate true precognition since there was no telepathic agent. Theoretically, Dunne suggested that the case might have been telepathically received from a newspaper writer working on the story. But in answer to this possibility, one may turn to the experiments of C. Drayton Thomas with the gifted psychic Gladys Osborne Leonard. Mrs. Leonard would enter a trance state during which a control (an alleged discarnate) would take possession of her. In some of the experiments the controls would be asked to describe passages from the following day's newspapers. The experiments were timed in such a way that the type would not yet have been set up or determined. Any success would have to be true precognition. Several of the experiments were strikingly successful.[11] Dunne's dream also recalls Vaughan's analysis of how the mind pulls material from either the past or present to produce a paranormal dream. Dunne wrote of the Martinique dream, "Indeed, the more I thought of the two episodes the clearer it became that, in each case, the dream had been precisely the sort of thing I might have expected to have experienced after reading the printed report—a perfectly ordinary dream based upon the personal experience of reading. . . ."

Another interpretation of precognition which maneuvers around the concept of true precognition is similar to the possibility Rhine confronted—that the experimenter might use his own PK (unconsciously or consciously) to make a predicted result occur. Jule Eisenbud, W. G. Roll, and most notably A. Tanagras in his *Le Destin et La Chance* (translated and republished as *Psychophysical Elements in Parapsychological Traditions*, 1967) favor or promote the theory that true precognition does not exist, but that the subject uses his own PK to fulfill his premonition. A dream concerning a fatal car accident could be realized by the subject's utilizing PK to cause the accident. However, in response to this, G. F. Dalton has pointed out that the large amount of correctly precognized natural phenomena, such as volcanic eruptions and earthquakes, are inexplicable by the PK theory.

A phenomenon that may be related to precognition is *déjà vu*. *Déjà vu* may range from a vague familiarity that a present predicament has been experienced before, to cases in which the experiencer can actually predict a future event from an unfocused memory. The former cases cannot serve as evidence of psi, since they offer no veridical details. However, reports of the latter do represent a rather unique form of psi:

> Some miles after leaving camp, I remarked to my mate, "I have been here before". He said, "Don't be stupid. This is our first time". He laughed. I said, "I know what's around that bend". I described a cottage, two steps to the door, white curtains on the left window, three jars in the right—I cannot hazard a guess how I knew.[12]

In this case the percipient could relate veridical information based on a memory recall, although the source of this memory could not be isolated. The tie-in with precognition comes when trying to explain this phenomenon. F. W. H. Myers, Louisa Rhine, and C. T. K. Chari have all interpreted *déjà vu* to have a basis in *forgotten* precognitive dreams. The stimulus event brings back a vague memory of the dream's content, but not the dream. The percipient relates only to a repressed memory. This theory is corroborated by cases of *déjà vu* wherein the percipient is able to cite a previous dream as the source as in the following case reported by Rhea White.[13]

> One such example came to me recently from a 21-year-old college student with whom I work. "About seven years ago . . . I had a recurring dream which I remember until this day. I was running away from somebody. As I was running and running, I ran over a bridge and to the right was a square house with a bumpy roof. Straight ahead was the end of the road. It met at a T-type junction. Straight ahead was a hill or bank that went straight up. I took the right turn."
>
> Several nights later her uncle, with whom she has always felt close, visited her family. Later they drove him to his recently acquired apartment where neither the percipient nor her parents had been. She continues: "In fact, I had never been to the section of New York where his apartment was at all. While we were driving, I had a strange feeling that I'd been there before. The feeling was so strong, I was scared and started to cry. We did pass over a cement bridge that crossed over some railroad and old trolley tracks. There was a square building on the right with a bumpy roof (probably a train station of some sort). The road did come to an end at a T-type junction. There was a hill in front of us (with a cemetery on it) and we did take the right."

Although most cases of spontaneous ESP relate either to contemporary or future events, there is another form of spontaneous ESP in which a long-past event is cognized as though it existed in the present. Such cases of retrocognition seem rarer either because of their nature or because parapsychologists have not given them as much attention as other forms of spontaneous psi. Retrocognition may either manifest visually or auditorily. In each case the experiencer feels himself to be completely engrossed within the experience and, in fact, often mistakes it as reality until some inconsistency jolts him into the realization that he is witnessing something paranormal. Sometimes this realization does not occur until after the experience has been completed, and often the discovery is accidental. The following case is taken from the *Journal:* ASPR 60 (1966): 306–20 and represents a well-documented case of visual retrocognition which occurred in a building at Nebraska Wesleyan University in October 1963. The percipient, Mrs. Coleen Baterbaugh, was running an errand for Dean Sam Dahl:

As I first walked into the room everything was quite normal. About four steps into the room was when the odor hit me. When I say strong odor, I mean the kind that simply stops you in your tracks and almost chokes you. I was looking down at the floor, as one often does when walking, and as soon as that odor stopped me I felt that there was someone in the room with me. It was then that I was aware that there were no noises out in the hall. Everything was deathly quiet. I looked up and something drew my eyes to the cabinet along the wall in the next room. I looked up and there she was. She had her back to me, reaching up into one of the shelves of the cabinet with her right hand, and standing perfectly still. She wasn't at all aware of my presence. While I was watching her she never moved. She was not transparent and yet I knew she wasn't real. While I was looking at her she just faded away—not parts of her body at one time, but her whole body all at once.

Up until the time she faded away, I was not aware of anyone else being in the suite of rooms, but just about the time of her fading out I felt as though I was not alone. To my left was a desk and I had a feeling there was a man sitting at that desk. I turned around and saw no one, but I still felt his presence. When the feeling of his presence left I have no idea because it was then, when I looked out the window behind the desk, that I got frightened and left the room. I am not sure whether I ran or walked out of the room . . . When I looked out that window there wasn't one modern thing out there. The street (Madison Street), which is less than a half block away from the building, was not even there and neither was the new Willard House. That was when *I realized that these people were not in my time, but that I was back in their time.*

It was not until I was back in the hall that I again heard familiar noises. This must have all taken place in a few seconds because the girls going into the orientation class as I entered the rooms were still going in and someone was still playing the marimba.

The value of this case is that a firsthand investigation was launched by Dr. Gardner Murphy and Dr. Herbert L. Klemme, who made a complete psychiatric examination of the percipient. Hypnotic probing failed to reveal any inconsistency in Mrs. Baterbaugh's report. Further historical research revealed that a former employee who fitted Mrs. Baterbaugh's description had died in a nearby room of the university in 1936.

This experience has several characteristics which are typical of retrocognition, but not of any other type of spontaneous psi: (1) Although such experiences are classified as visual, all the senses respond simultaneously to the paranormal stimulus: sight, hearing, and smell. (2) These paranormal cognitions block off normal sense perception completely and the subject takes an active role in the total hallucination. (3) Time is distorted for the duration of the experience. (4) There is little recognition at first that an ESP experience is taking place.

The pattern of these rare and puzzling cases can also be seen in the Dieppe Raid case in which the retrocognition was basically auditory. The main percipients were Dorothy and Agnes Norton (pseudonyms for purposes of publication in the *Journal* of the SPR in 1952). The two women had arrived in Puys, France, on the English Channel in 1951. They lodged in a second-story room overlooking the sea. On the morning of Monday, July 30, Dorothy Norton was awakened by the sounds of gunfire, planes, cries, and finally singing. On Saturday, August 4, both women heard the sounds, even when one left the room. The hour was clocked at 4:20 A.M. By this time the gunfire and voices had been augmented by sounds of dive bombers, violent shelling, and other noises which sounded like a long-distance radio broadcast. The sounds abruptly terminated at 4:50 A.M. and resumed at 5:05 A.M. When daylight arrived the women could not see anything to account for the noises which continued from 5:40 to 5:50 and 6:20 to 6:55. They suspected that something paranormal might be the cause of the acoustical displays which apparently only they had heard. No one else in the lodging house heard or at least mentioned anything unusual. However, on August 19, 1942, the area had been the scene of the Dieppe Raid by the Canadian Army landing on German-occupied territory. When an analysis was made of the actual timing and battle periods of the raid, it matched closely those time intervals reported by the two women. However, this concordance was not exact, but too close to be merely coincidental.

Retrocognition is one form of psi experience that seems to be related more to a certain physical area than with the individual's own ESP. Although there is no doubt that ESP is employed by the percipient, the actual stimulus may be the locale as in a haunting. One of the most famous of all retrocognition cases is the experiences of two women, Miss Moberly and Miss Jourdain, during a visit to Versailles. While sight-seeing, both women felt a certain "unreality" about the Petit Trianon. Later, upon visiting there again, they were amazed to see different sights than they had witnessed before and eventually came to believe that they had seen the sights and sounds of prerevolutionary Versailles. When they published their account in a little book, *An Adventure,* a fierce debate ensued as to whether they had really experienced retrocognition or whether they had suggestionized themselves into misperceiving perfectly normal events. What is of considerable interest is that further analysis of the Versailles mystery has turned up several other cases of retrocognition by independent witnesses at or around the Petit Trianon. *An Adventure* concerned the women's experience in 1901 and Miss Jourdain had a further manifestation there in 1902. Other witnesses have reported odd retrocognitory occurrences at the same place in 1908, 1928, and 1955.

A significant feature of retrocognition is that although the experience is taken as "reality," the verbal reports often show a vague awareness that something "isn't quite right" with the scene. The Dieppe Raid noises were heard as a radio broadcast and both women heard the sounds coming in peculiar waves of audibility. Similarly, Miss Jourdain described her visual impressions during her experience as "unnatural, unpleasant," "flat and lifeless," "no effect of light and shade," "the impression of a stage set." And of her auditory experiences, "eerie and oppressive, diminished in tone, compared to a phonograph."

Retrocognition is so rare and so hard to evaluate that parapsychologists have not given much attention to the phenomenon. Louisa Rhine makes no substantial reference to it in her writings, and aside from the Versailles case, which became a mild *cause célèbre* in psychical research when it was first reported, little mention of spontaneous retrocognition is made in general surveys of psychical phenomena. Unlike precognitive experiences, a case of retrocognition is difficult to verify, nor is it very testable in the laboratory. All in all spontaneous retrocognition seems just an anomaly of psychical phenomena. The only serious discussion of it has been made not by a parapsychologist, but by a writer, Gracia-Fay Ellwood,[14] who has traced spontaneous retrocognition cases back to 1642. Unfortunately, trying to explain retrocognition usually boils down to such theories as the telepathic pickup of memory traces or the eternal now concept (that all actions exist somewhere in space and can be grasped clairvoyantly). This theory can neither be tested experimentally nor validated by observation and analysis.

Since certain personality characteristics are related to success at laboratory ESP tasks, a natural query is, "What type of person experiences spontaneous ESP?" From surveys of this type of occurrence it is fairly clear that such factors as age, sex, and religion have little bearing on whether or not an individual will be subject to spontaneous ESP. Further, the real determinates are most likely subtle psychological factors. This is, of course, if there are any such determinates at all. Survey reports also point to the fact that, although a great many people in a given poll will have had some ostensible experience of psi, these experiences are rare in their lives. The most notable search for personality variables linked to spontaneous ESP has been made by Jan Kappers and R. P. Greiner,[15] who sent out an ESP questionnaire to eight thousand adults in the city of Amsterdam. Of these, 1329 replied. A third reported ESP experiences. From this rich collection, twenty-one individuals were evaluated with standard psychological tests which were then matched to two control groups, one of individuals who did not report psi experiences, and a random group who had not been questioned at all. The finding showed no differences among the three groups.

In one way the Kappers–Greiner study is disappointing, for it did not offer any insight into "the psychic personality." Nonetheless, as William Crookes once said, an interesting failure might be more revealing than a success. Kappers has actually verified an initial concept of the ESP experience that originated during the Duke years—that ESP is so natural and common that anybody is likely to experience it.

6

ESP Research with Gifted Subjects

The fact that ESP is so elusive is one of the reasons it is so challenging to science. Two different ways in which ESP manifests itself have so far been presented. Firstly, there is the laboratory evidence of ESP where subjects try to outguess chance, although the ESP impression may never break into consciousness. Secondly, there are full-fledged cases of spontaneous ESP where the psi process breaches the barriers of the unconscious and is manifested in a waking or sleeping message. These two adaptations of the psi process could not be more different in their emotional and psychological content. Laboratory ESP is rarely dramatic to most of the subjects participating in an experiment, whereas spontaneous ESP is vivid, emotionally charged, and may even alter the world view of its experiencer. Subjects in ESP tests are rarely aware that they are scoring well or badly. Spontaneous ESP brings with it a certain conviction of what the participant has experienced.

There is a third major form of ESP which is a midpoint between these extremes. Before parapsychology shifted to group ESP testing, most research centered on gifted subjects who were able to control partially or continually exhibit ESP. Craig Sinclair, several of René Warcollier's subjects, and Gilbert Murray were all individuals whose ESP abilities showed a curious mixture of an almost spontaneous ability that could be tested under controlled conditions. These subjects did not guess at the targets but were able to bring the ESP impression directly into consciousness. Emotionally or psychologically meaningful targets were the greatest stimulus. Yet, if set in an experimental situation, they might still function and react to neutral targets such as simple drawings as did Hubert Pearce and Miss Ownbey who would visualize and force the Zener card symbols into their conscious minds. The study of the gifted subject was one of parapsychology's first concerns, and the search for such psychics has long been one of its main preoccupations.

In this chapter a survey will be made on the various ways that ESP manifests in the gifted subject, or sensitive, spontaneously, in qualitative experiments and in quantitative testing. Like most forms of ESP, the history of research into gifted subjects begins with the evidence they have produced and the range of psychic phenomena they exhibited, that is, their potentials and limits. Secondly comes more practical and process-oriented research. How can we evaluate this material and what facts seem to enhance or limit this ability? Finally comes the search for well-designed experimental research adopting the sensitive's unique form of psi into a series of experiments that will (1) offer evidence for the subject's ESP ability and (2) tell us about its nature.

During the first decades of psychical research the study of sensitives was mainly anecdotal. The research was basically oriented to proving ESP and only incidentally did the early parapsychologists discover certain principles by which it manifested. Nonetheless, these early studies have contributed to our knowledge of the psi process.

Stephan Ossowiecki was a Polish engineer born in 1877, whose abilities encompassed both ESP and PK. The latter phenomena gradually diminished and disappeared when he was thirty-five, as he concentrated more on the development of ESP. He soon came to the attention of several top European parapsychologists, including Charles Richet and Gustave Geley, and his first series of experiments with Geley were carried out in April and May of 1921. In the first trial Ossowiecki was handed an envelope with a letter inside and asked to describe clairvoyantly either the letter's contents or its writer. At first he described the writer as "a refined man of feminine type," an interesting appraisal since the writer was actually a woman. He correctly stated that the signature had nine letters and was able to give the first five. George Lange, also in attendance during the experiment, then handed him a folded piece of paper. The only impression received was that the message was written in English.

A second experiment was carried out by Richet who had written on a piece of paper, "Jamais la mer ne paraît plus grande que lorsqu'elle est calme. Ses colères la rapetissent." Ossowiecki made the following comments after holding the paper in his hand: "I see much water. It is something rather difficult. It is not a question; it is an idea that you have taken. La mer n'était jamais tellement grand que . . . I can't put it together. La mer est tellement grand qu'a côté de ses mouvements."

Although the exact inscription was not read, Ossowiecki was able to get the correct impressions of water, several ideas such as movements and "never so splendid," all contained in Richet's message. In this type of experiment it is difficult to isolate whether telepathy or clairvoyance is the operating factor. In order to offset the telepathic theory, proxy tests were sometimes carried out wherein one experimenter would choose the target but another would present it to the subject. Richet had given Ossowiecki a sealed letter to decipher but no veridical impressions were forthcoming. Since Richet was leaving the next day, the target was turned over to Geley who presented it to Ossowiecki. He immediately stated that the letter was about a lady named Berger, that it was an invitation, that the woman was thirty-three years old and married, and that the message was written sloppily and unreadable. When Geley opened the packet, all of these impressions were found to be correct. Ossowiecki had made only one error and that was in stating that the letter came from "near the sea" when it had really come from Berlin.

Another form of experimentation carried out with Ossowiecki was to test his ability to describe written-down thoughts or drawings sealed in envelopes. The following is taken from one of Geley's tests. A sealed envelope was prepared with a numbered list of the following written ideas: (1) An Oriental landscape with camels; (2) drawing of a fish including an illustration;

(3) a peal of bells; (4) the perfume of mimosa; (5) *Vive la Pologne!* After handling the target Ossowiecki gave the following impressions:

> This is long. It is written by a man. It is a chaos. It is so chaotic that I cannot grasp it. These are four or five ideas. What a hash. Something big. Something that swims. I see work on a fish which is like a certain large Polish fish. It is not writing but there is a fish. What relation is there between the fish and Poland?
>
> I cannot understand. There is an exclamation: Vive la Pologne!
>
> I sense perfume, delicious perfume. There is also something of Nature.
>
> There is something else, these things in this mixture. I see the fish and will draw it. [Draws a similar illustration.]
>
> Why perfumes? Why Poland? There are numbers—1, 2, 3, 4, 5. After 2 there is nothing written. Something of Nature.
>
> I can see no more.

The experiment was revealing in that it cast light on how Ossowiecki's psi worked. First, Ossowiecki grasped most of the impressions as a gestalt and then had to isolate its constituents. Only after getting a general feeling for the total message could he isolate various components and details. For example, the impression of Poland came before he was able to grasp the inscription *Vive la Pologne*. This suggests that the subject responds first to the entire target and only afterward can he pull the impressions into a logical order.

These early experiments were constructed mainly to prove Ossowiecki's ability, and the following two experiments are typical of the type of fraud-proof tests incorporated in testing gifted subjects. The concept of the first of these experiments was initiated by Count Guy du Bourg de Bozas who had a 1¼-inch-thick lead tube made especially for the experiment. A friend penned an illustration and message, giving it to a third party who placed it in the tube which was then soldered shut. Ossowiecki made two trials on the message. After an unsatisfactory first trial, the experiment was repeated two days later at which time he was able to give the following impressions: (1) A powerful man; (2) A great man of the century; (3) The target was a drawing and a message; (4) The drawing was of a man with a heavy moustache, eyebrows, no nose and is in uniform; (5) The figure represented Marshal Pilsudski; (6) The writing was in French which Ossowiecki deciphered as: "Cet homme il n'a peur de rien, comme un chevalier."

The tube was then sawed open revealing a caricature of Pilsudski (sans nose) and the words, "Le chevalier sans peur et sans reproche." Again, Ossowiecki's first impressions were global and then later became refined and detailed.

A second fraud-proof experiment was conducted as part of an international conference on psychical research held in Warsaw in 1923. Eric Dingwall, in England, had made up a special envelope consisting of three separate envelopes with the target in the third. For the target he sketched a flag with a bottle etched in its upper-left-hand corner. The date, August 22, 1923, was written below. Dingwall sent the target to Baron Albert von Schrenck-Notzing, a famous pathologist of his day; René Sudre; and Geley to present to Ossowiecki. The contents were not known to any of the experimenters and Dingwall remained in England. Ossowiecki's impressions were as follows: (1) That Schrenck-Notzing had not written the message; (2) The letter consisted of several envelopes; (3) Something greenish—cardboard. After some confusion he went on, adding (4) A little bottle; (5) (There followed a detailed description of Schrenck's study which although correct had nothing to do with the stimulus target); (6) A square in one corner of the drawing. At this point, in a very agitated manner, Ossowiecki grabbed a pen and drew an almost identical replica of the target. He also wrote the year 1923 and stated that something was written before it but he could not tell what it was.

Geley ultimately was able to discover certain principles (strengths and limitations) of Ossowiecki's abilities, and after several series of experiments he was able to state that the psi ability was not hampered by shielding—envelopes, lead tubes, paper of different weight did not appreciably affect Ossowiecki's functioning. Whether the target was prepared in his presence or by proxy made no difference. Knowledge of the target by the experimenters was also irrelevant. Geley made two further findings which have an important bearing on the psi process as it occurs in the gifted subject—that sometimes the target will excite only a vague form or idea and that *any* object given to Ossowiecki could carry psi impressions. The main weakness that Geley found was that Ossowiecki could not respond to typewritten messages, only to handwritten ones.[1]

The fact that an object may be a carrier or vehicle for ESP was first demonstrated by J. Rodes Buchanon who published his findings in 1849. Using nonprofessional subjects the Ohio physician found that they could identify different medicines hidden in sealed envelopes. After his initial discovery, subjects were given handwritten letters from which they were able to often give accurate descriptions of the writers. Buchanan subsequently coined the word *psychometry* to describe the phenomenon.*

One of the most in-depth investigations into clairvoyance and psychometry was made by a German physician living in Mexico, Gustav Pagenstecher with a selected subject, Senora Maria Reyes de Zierold.[2] Pagenstecher accidentally discovered that this patient, who had come to him complaining of insomnia, was unusually gifted with ESP. He had used hypnosis as part of his clinical approach to Senora Zierold's complaints, and one day the entranced woman suddenly told him that his daughter was eavesdropping in the next room. Incredulous, he investigated and found the girl outside the door just as described. Realizing that hypnosis might be a key to ESP, Pagenstecher began a long training project with Senora Zierold using hypnotic visualization techniques. She was trained to visualize the room and the doctor until eventually she could perceive hidden targets. During the initial training Senora Zierold became extremely sensitive to Pagenstecher as would be expected from their strong rapport, conditioned by constant hypnotic induction. In her introspective report, Senora Zierold records the typical community of sensation that Elliotson had encountered with his hypnotized subjects:

* Literally, psychometry means "measure of the soul." The phrase has become a common label for the phenomena, though the technical term now used is *token object reading*. The verbal impressions given by the sensitive are "free response material" contrasted to *forced-choice* testing as in conventional ESP experiments.

When in deep hypnotic trance all my senses are blocked and not only blocked, but transferred to the hypnotist to such an extent that I feel the pricking of *his* ears, I taste the sugar or salt put on *his* tongue, and I hear the watch put in the vicinity of *his* ears, I also feel the burning sensation whenever a match is brought near to his fingers.

Research with Senora Zierold fell into three categories. First were target studies in which she was asked to give impressions of several objects especially conditioned for the test. Second were more conventional free-response tests with token objects, and third were attempts by outside investigators to confirm Zierold's abilities.

A typical experiment with specially prepared targets was made before a committee of Pagenstecher's colleagues. Four pieces of pumice were presented to the subject. Each had been treated in a curious fashion which hopefully she would be able to decipher extrasensorily. The four fragments had been treated in the following manner: (1) soaked in tincture of gentian and asafetida; (2) shut up near a clock for three weeks; (3) rolled in saccharin and sugar; (4) heated by burning sulfur. Under hypnosis, Senora Zierold gave the following impressions of the targets: (1) taste sensation, (2) rhythmic sounds, (3) sweetness, (4) heat and smell of sulfur.

In order to explain more fully the range of the subject's ESP, token objects were given to Senora Zierold to see what type of impressions they would elicit. In such tasks she would see vivid scenes and images ignited by the tactile stimulation of the object. In the following example Senora Zierold was given a piece of string that originally had been attached to some dog tags worn by a German soldier:

> It is intensely cold and the day is foggy . . . I am in a battlefield, it smells of gun powder. In front of me a tall man standing, with a gray overcoat on, which reaches to his feet. Behind him I see three other men standing likewise. They talk German, or better said, they shout. In front of them and lying on the snow, behind an earthwork, I see lines of soldiers keeping up a continuous rifle fire. Some five meters back of the fire line there are two groups of men plainly to be seen, one consisting of about five to six men, and another about

twelve to fifteen men. Quite of a sudden I see coming through the air and moving with great rapidity a big red ball of fire . . . which drops just in the middle of the fifteen men tearing them to pieces.

Senora Zierold's impression was a reenactment of a war scene experienced by the soldier whose string she held, and who described the scene as "the first great impression I received of the war."

A major attempt by an outside investigator to test Senora Zierold was made by W. F. Prince, research officer for the ASPR. Prince traveled to Mexico specifically to determine whether or not he could elicit ESP from the subject and to try to prove clairvoyance as opposed to telepathy as her main ability. It should be remembered that during the pre-Duke years telepathy, clairvoyance, precognition, and other ESP effects were not seen as a unitary process but rather as all different types of phenomena. The work with Ossowiecki and Senora Zierold was more often directed at discovering what *type* of ESP was being displayed than in learning anything about the mechanics of the phenomenon.

Prince brought with him fourteen target objects. During one experiment two boxes were used, each enclosing identical pieces of silk ribbon. One came from an altar; the other came directly from the manufacturer. Prince mixed the two boxes so that even he did not know which was which and handed them to Senora Zierold. Responding to the first closed box she saw a Mexican church scene with dancing Indians; to the second target she described a French ribbon factory. This suggested to Prince that the ESP was primarily clairvoyance not telepathy. Pagenstecher was forced to concur in this theory by a sudden and unexpected turn of events when a garment once worn by a murdered farmer was used as the target object. The only impression received was of a mundane clothing factory. But when her fingers touched a bloodstain, she immediately gave a detailed description of the murder. The facts were far beyond the vague details Pagenstecher knew of the case, but his subsequent investigation of the history of the case verified Senora Zierold's impressions.

Often when targets were presented to Senora Zierold, only scenes associated with them were transferred by ESP. In these instances the experimenters held in mind certain connections with the object which they expected the subject to relate. However, different sets of associations would be offered which could only be verified by retracing the object's history. Prince wrote of one such puzzling incident in his report:

> One fact which turned out quite other than I expected at the time, related to an object which I picked up on the beach at Vera Cruz. I had owned one like it for several years, given me under the name of "sea-bean". I am no botanist, and when I found a duplicate among the seaweed on the beach, I was then more confirmed in the supposition that it was the large seed of a marine plant. But the entranced lady, holding the object rigidly between the tips of her fingers, talked of seeing tall tropical trees growing in a forest near some water. After the sitting was over I told Dr. Pagenstecher that I thought the vision in error, and he responded: "With my experience, I bet on her horse rather than yours." The seed or nut was taken to two professional botanists, a German and a Mexican both unhesitatingly declared it to be from such a tree as the medium had described, and said that the nut often falls into a river or is washed into it by freshets and at length turns up on an ocean beach.[3]

Data such as this indicate that the subject is responding to the object and not to the experimenter, and concordantly that the associations are often not based on human memories or emotions. The above test is not very strong evidence for ESP, but a similar illustration can be taken from an experiment made by Pagenstecher's wife. Mrs. Pagenstecher had in her possession a shell which she gave to the subject, expecting her to describe a scene at Vera Cruz bay where she had found it. Senora Zierold instead offered an underwater scene. Pagenstecher instructed her to remember the scene after waking, and when the hypnotic session was over, she was given a book of fish illustrations and asked to pinpoint those fish she saw in her images. Those chosen by the subject were all appropriate to the marine life where the shell had been found.

A modern reassessment of Pagenstecher's work has been made by W. G. Roll in an attempt to discover what principles Senora Zierold's ESP followed. In analyzing the psychometric readings given by the subject, Roll found that certain laws of association operated. The primary feature was that the first or earliest events in the history of an object were more likely to be impressed onto the subject than other, later events. Vivid events in the history of the object and relatively recent occurrences were the next likely impressions.[4]

The principle of the primary impression being based on an early occurrence in an object's history bears significantly on a curious incident in Ossowiecki's career. While giving a reading on a sealed envelope, he saw the impression of a French franc. The envelope's wax seal had originally been stamped with a French franc but had later been opened and resealed with a Babylonian coin. Ossowiecki saw the original but nonexistent impression and not the later one.

Both this incident with Ossowiecki and Pagenstecher's research point to a similar conclusion—that while the token object serves as the stimulus for the ESP, the subject is not actually responding to the physical object but is directed to the source of the information by it. Eugene Osty had worked with several sensitives, primarily psychometrists, and set down certain premises about the function of the token object. He also came to the conclusion that the object serves only as a pointer to the source of the information and is not the source itself:

1. The token object helps guide the subject to extrasensory contact with its owner.

2. Any person who has been in physical contact with the inductor may also become accessible to the subject's psi ability.

3. Persons even *associated* with someone who has handled the object are likewise accessible.

4. The psychic is not dependent on the token object for this information and can work independently of it.

5. After contact is made, the original object may be destroyed without affecting the psychic's rapport.

6. The past, present, or future of these persons is accessible to the psychic.

7. The physical or chemical constitution of the object is of no importance.

8. The amount of data received about an individual is not determined by length of contact with the object.

9. The time elapsed since contact with the token is irrelevant.

10. If token objects are in mutual contact, the subject will not confuse impressions between them.

11. Initial erroneous impressions are likely to be reported during subsequent sessions.

By the time Osty's *Supernormal Faculties in Man* was published, he had determined that psychometry could manifest as telepathic, clairvoyant, or precognitive. He viewed psychometry as basically an induced form of telepathy wherein the token object guides the psychic's ESP to the likely agent. It was this interpretation that lead Osty to his views on precognition. Since he did not believe that the object itself was the generator of psi impressions but only a catalyst to telepathy, true precognition was a cumbersome burden for interpretation. As pointed out in the previous chapter, Osty initially resolved this issue by theorizing that every individual is unconsciously aware of his own future, and the sensitive can tap this unconscious material by telepathy.

Since ESP is a unitary process, reasoning such as Osty's has become antiquated. G. N. M. Tyrrell offered the suggestion that psychometry catalyzed a curious mixture of both telepathy and clairvoyance. However, it was W. G. Roll who tried to tie in the various principles functioning in psychometry as an outgrowth of a total ESP process, and who suggested a general theory for all psi phenomena which he has termed the "psi field." [5] According to Roll all objects and individuals have psi fields around them which are the carriers of psi impressions. A psychic can "read" these impressions when an object's psi field interacts with the psychic's own personal psi field. Since any contact between two such fields will leave an impression, a token object can carry with it impressions from its own history, the history of its handlers, or people associated with them. Further, these psi fields can impress and affect physical fields. By employing the model of the psi field, telepathy, clairvoyance, and even PK are made into different aspects of one unitary process. The psi field explains why in psychometry some of the evidence (as in Pagenstecher's work) points to the object as the source of the impressions, while in other work (Osty's), psychometry appears to be merely a form of telepathy. The token would actually serve as a physical carrier of intermingled information-packed psi fields which can exist independently of the object should it be damaged or destroyed. In Osty's work, the subjects often began to discuss details about Osty himself before focusing on the object or its owner. With a British psychic, Mrs. Warren Elliott, the subject would often begin with a description of the SPR office where the tokens had been kept, or of the SPR's secretary who prepared them for the tests. In these two cases the object served initially to give impressions from its most recent past which might be expected, since these would be the "freshest" on the object's psi field.

The full range of ESP as it manifests in a gifted subject can best be illustrated by the case of Gerard Croiset, a contemporaneous Dutch psychic. Croiset's abilities encompass both psychometry and clairvoyance as well as precognition. The major research done with him has primarily been the work of Professor W. H. C. Tenhaeff at the University of Utrecht. One of the most unusual features of Croiset's ESP is his ability to succeed at chair tests. In this form of precognition, a seat is randomly selected in a hall and Croiset is asked to give his impressions of the occupant of the chair at a certain future date. Sometimes the experimenter picks the target, but on other occasions Croiset himself chooses the target chair. On January 6, 1957, in Utrecht, Croiset, accompanied by Tenhaeff and two colleagues, was shown a floor plan of an assembly hall in The Hague. Croiset pinpointed one area on the plan and gave a series of impressions about the individual who would occupy that space during a meeting that would be held twenty-five days in the future.

In order to offset any charge of collusion between Croiset and an accomplice, the guests at the assembly had to draw lots for their seat numbers. The following table is a point-by-point comparison of Croiset's impressions and their validation:

Impressions	*Comments*
1. At the fixed time on February 1, 1957, on Chair No. 9 there will be sitting a merry middle-aged woman. She takes much interest in the care of children.	1. The woman was forty-two and admitted a great interest in caring for children.

Impressions	*Comments*
2. In the years 1928–1930 she was several times near the spa building in Schoveningh.	2. True, she often visited the city.
3. In her early childhood she was often in a district where cheese was produced. I can see a burning farm. Some animals are burned alive.	3. True, but the product chiefly manufactured was butter. The farm and cattle were destroyed by fire.
4. I can see three boys. One of them works somewhere overseas; it seems to be a British dominion.	4. The lady's husband had two brothers; one had been overseas.
5. Was not the woman strongly excited when seeing the opera *Falstaff*? Is that not the first opera she has ever seen?	5. The subject was an opera singer. *Falstaff* was the first opera she *sang* and she fell in love with the chief tenor singing in the opera.
6. Did her father get a gold medal for rendered services?	6. He had received an inscribed gold cigarette case.
7. She went to the dentist as a little girl. And did this visit cause a lot of excitement? [6]	7. This had occurred a short time before the meeting.

While several of Croiset's impressions were correct in this test, they were often subject to slight inaccuracies or distortions. A gold case became a gold medal, and to Croiset the first opera the subject had sung became the first opera she had seen. These distortions illustrate the difficulty in controlling psi impressions as they reach consciousness. Several transatlantic chair tests have been conducted in order to determine the range of Croiset's prognostications. A pioneering test was carried out between Utrecht and Rockland State Hospital, New York, on June 12, 1968. Croiset was approached by Dr. A. Esser with the idea for an experiment in which he would try to predict something about a person in a seat of his own choosing to be occupied during an assembly scheduled for June 21. Croiset was videotaped in his home giving his impressions. Records and films of this reading were subsequently sent to the director of research at the hospital, Nathan S. Kline, who would not be attending the meeting. After the meeting, Kline's records would be given over to Esser to compare with the verification offered by the target. The following table summarizes the results:

Impressions	*Comments*
1. In the middle row, third chair from the left, there will be a gentleman, middle-aged, firmly built, his white shirt clearly visible, and he has sparse bristly hair.	1. The subject was 33, 210 pounds, a muscular man wearing a white shirt. His hair was wavy and long, but he admitted that he used to wear a crew cut.
2. Has he tried one of these days to pry loose a string from a package with his fingers and has he hurt his finger doing this?	2. Incorrect.
3. Has he tried to open with a pen a piece of copper tubing that was plugged?	3. This was incorrect, but the woman sitting directly behind the target chair had done so.
4. Has he tried to bury a piece of paper or to attach it to a fence in the garden . . . with emotion . . . something special that he would not do otherwise?	4. Again, incorrect, but directly applicable to the woman behind him as before.
5. If he is home . . . does he see [from his window] a street corner with a shop with an awning?	5. No.
6. . . . lives with three persons, but also with seven persons at home?	6. The subject does live with three roommates and is eldest of seven children.
7. Has he recently a severe pain in his right shin?	7. Subject suffers from a slipped disk which specifically affects his right shin.

Impressions

Comments

8. Has he recently laughed heartily about a drum band in which a fellow with the big drum made a funny movement?

8. Correct.

9. I see at the moment a kind of Chinese house . . . he has entered and had to remove his shoes, which has occasioned some commotion. It is like a temple with two pillars . . . an Oriental home . . . he did not like to do this.

9. A true incident that had recently occurred to the subject while visiting the apartment of an Indian doctor.

10. Had he, in an emotional upset, torn up a map? This was a present of a lady behind a desk . . . in a kind of study where on the side two gentlemen were seated.

10. Incorrect.

11. This gentleman is too old to build sand castles, but has he put sand in a pot . . . I do not understand it.

11. Vaguely reminiscent of an act carried out by the subject.

12. Has he recently been involved with a person where between the toes a sharp object had come . . . one toe was hurt and had to be bandaged?

12. Correct.

13. I see momentarily a street, people, a man with a briefcase and another person tries to tear the briefcase loose . . . Had this happened to him personally or will this story be related to him . . . which can happen between this moment and the time of the chair test?

13. Not applicable to the subject. After the test another guest did tell Esser of a similar incident told him during the week by his father.

This experiment is notable both for its successes and its confusions. Several of the impressions exactly suited the target person. The themes of these impressions are similar to those Roll found in evaluating Pagenstecher's work. The best hits were either vivid or impressive to the subject, or actions recently carried out. In addition, the impressions that missed the mark focused on another individual in close physical proximity to the target.[7]

Another of Croiset's abilities is using ESP in drowning cases, and to track missing persons, especially children. His success at this type of task reveals a prime factor about his ESP. Croiset himself almost drowned as a child and Tenhaeff believes that he, as well as other paragnosts, are especially adept at using ESP in cases where there is a close identification between the object of concern and the psychic.

When considerable confusion arises during a free-response session, the natural problem is how to evaluate the material. Could these hits be coincidental? Or could the sitter overinterpret only vague impressions as more applicable than they really are? The shift in contemporary parapsychology has been away from purely anecdotal and value-judgment assessments. Even with free-response material the trend has been to quantify the material. Both J. G. Pratt, working with W. R. Birge, and Robert Morris have outlined complex mathematical methods for appraising free-response material. Simpler methods have been suggested by H. F. Saltmarsh and Ian Stevenson.

Saltmarsh developed his method of evaluation during experiments with Mrs. Warren Elliott in which token objects were used. In several of the tests the object's owner was not present at the sessions which were held by proxy. After the experiments a typed copy of all impressions offered by Mrs. Elliott in trance were sent to the owners for comment and validation. However, the evaluation was carried out by Saltmarsh as an independent judge. First he went through all the readings and filtered out those impressions which were repeated very frequently during independent sittings. These impressions were probably stock clichés and thus carried less weight should they be cited as hits by those participating in the experiment. Each impression was given a numerical rating indicating if it were categorized as vague, definite, or characteristic. These differentiations were based on the premise that a vague impression would, by its nature, apply to a great many people; a definite impression to some people; and a characteristic impression, one that would apply only to the target of the session. The numerical values were 1, 5, and 20 respectively. A hypothetical maximum was calculated by supposing that *all* the impressions given were accurate. This was then compared against the actual score of the session. False statements received no value, and if a session offered only a few definite or characteristic statements, an automatic deduction of 10 percent was made.

In order to check for a bias in overapplying generalities himself, Saltmarsh sent copies of several sessions to various participants, asking that they be annotated. The scorers did not contribute the token object used, but had to annotate the records as though the impressions were directed at each of them. Saltmarsh could then check to see if the actual target person's scores were substantially higher than the control scores. For one experiment, most of the impressions concerned an airman killed in action. For this aggregate of fifty-three records, Saltmarsh sent the impressions to six independent individuals who had lost a relative in the war. The total scores based on the target's annotations were 4107 (there was more than one target subject to whom the records were directed). The total score for the pseudotargets was only 452. Since the total possible score was 5642, the percentage ratio was 72.8 percent to 8 percent accuracy.[8]

A slight variation in this method was employed by Gertrude Schmeidler during proxy experiments with a psychic, Mrs. Caroline Chapman. Sixteen sessions were conducted using four sitters (proxy experimenters) and four target individuals. Each of the participants had to annotate all of the sixteen records without knowing which applied to himself. Schmeidler then scored the records mathematically and compared the scores for each of the sets of applicable sessions to the control sessions.[9]

Ian Stevenson's method of evaluation is chiefly dependent on differentiating between objective and subjective impressions. Objective items such as proper names, occupation of the target person, and physical characteristics would apply to fewer individuals than subjective impressions such as "he has an amiable nature," which calls for value judgments by the recorder. "O" items would therefore carry more weight. The records of a session are given to three independent judges who then rate each impression offered during the session as either "O" or "S." Ian Stevenson used this technique in experiments with a French psychic, Yvonne Nomine, and he acted as the target as well as the experimenter. After evaluating his results, he calculated that 70 percent of the "O" items were correct and 73 percent of the "S" items were accurate. Some of the "O" items were impressions such as: "Your mother is still living," "You have lost a young brother," "There was a river near where you grew up." In checking over the records, both the independent scorers, Charles Tart and J. G. Pratt, were more liberal in designating "O" as against "S" impressions than was Stevenson.[10]

There are distinct advantages in using these methods of evaluation. Firstly, it keeps potential bias in check. Secondly, it gives a specific statistical appraisal by which a session can be evaluated. In this way the experimenter can be assured that the level of success is not a combination of merely shrewd guesswork or vague generalities. Thirdly, a comparison can be made between high- and low-scoring experiments to discover what leads to success during an ESP session. Older methods of appraisal were inexact and could not isolate a comparative level of success for a session. Lastly, complex statistical analyses can be made which can give an exact mathematical value against probability and chance accounting for various hits. In the Pratt–Birge method all the verbal material was eventually reduced to probability ratings just as are conventional ESP tests.

To give an idea how qualitative material can be quantified for research purposes, experiments with Lalsingh Harribance are typical. Harribance, originally from Trinidad, was brought to the United States by a Trinidad psychologist who felt that his abilities needed proper sophisticated evaluation. Most of the research carried out with Harribance has been conducted at the Psychical Research Foundation in Durham, North Carolina. In 1969 an experiment was arranged with Harribance using the following methods: Two series were run, one of ten target men and another of ten target women. During each test he knew only the sex of the sitter. The sitter was photographed and asked to write out a personal problem for which he would like aid. This card and the photograph were placed in an opaque envelope along with a bit of the target's hair to be used as a token object. The envelopes were then given to Harribance as inductors for his ESP impressions. Throughout the session he never actually saw the participant. After this procedure was completed for all ten in each group, the participants were given *all* the records and asked to choose the one that applied to him. By chance this would give a 10 to 1 probability. When all the subjects had chosen the record most closely pertaining to them, it was clear that Harribance had demonstrated ESP, since his impressions were often specific and so apropos that several of the participants could identify their own records. Both sessions (for men and for women) were significant. Afterward another experimenter, Jacqueline Damgaard, analyzed the content of the impressions and found that Harribance's greatest successes were in describing the targets' physical appearance, family life, and emotional attachments (a euphemism for love life!).

Since Harribance liked to use photographs, several experiments have been run to see if he can successfully differentiate between sealed envelopes carrying pictures of men and those of women. Although anyone should normally succeed 50 percent of the time, Harribance has consistently scored above that level.

The most recent research with Harribance has been to see if his level of success is correlated to specific states of consciousness as recorded by an electroencephalograph. R. J. Cadoret, as mentioned in a previous chapter, demonstrated in one experiment that there is a connection between ESP success and alpha, a specific brain rhythm signifying a passive, relaxed state of mind. To check for this possibility, a series of tests were run in which Harribance had to call whether an envelope contained a picture of a male or female. All during the test his brain waves were monitored. After the conclusion of the tests, the experimenter merely had to compare the score records to see if each run of guesses was accompanied by more or less alpha. The results confirmed Cadoret's theory—success at ESP was found to correlate with shifts in the production of the alpha rhythm.[11]

Like most areas of parapsychology the study of the gifted subject has shifted from anecdote to experiment. Yet, pure experimentation does have its drawbacks, since this type of research seems more directed at "proof" than how the psi process actually functions. The psychology of the gifted subject can best be studied by analyzing the actual records of his impressions, sorting out what type of statements seem most likely to be hits, and discovering why errors so often crop up. With Harribance, themes of love are often predominant. Alan Vaughan has noted that impressions from his own mind often disrupt his psi impressions. Croiset succeeds best when young children are involved. Understanding the whys and hows for these characteristics of ESP is the basic promise held out by the study of gifted subjects.

One approach to this problem has been studied by Rhea White who was interested in a fundamental question facing parapsychologists—why were the subjects of parapsychology's infancy so much more striking in their success than experimental subjects today? Parapsychology today has a notable lack of Craig Sinclairs, René Warcolliers, and Gertrude Johnsons, whose staggering and somewhat consistent successes were much more dramatic than most of the modern gifted subjects such as Harribance or Pavel Stepanek tested in the laboratory. In order to grapple with this problem White began searching the autobiographical reports of gifted subjects of the past and was able to extrapolate from their introspective records just how they responded to the ESP target. She was able to map out certain principles they often shared in common when responding to the target by ESP.

White based her search on the fact that subjects today, stemming from the Duke work, seem only to "guess" at the target quickly and unthinkingly, hoping that their intuitions might reveal an unconscious ESP compulsion. Nonetheless, their only mental function is one of "guessing," and White felt that perhaps this approach by the participant is in error:

> Apparently some very different assumptions were in the minds of the earliest psychical researchers. It seems clear from their reports that they assumed there was much the participant had to do before he could expect to attain a state of mind in which it would be possible for him to obtain paranormal knowledge of the target; that if he could attain this state of

mind, then he would be far more likely to get a correct impression than if he simply grasped the first thing that presented itself to consciousness. Therefore these pioneer investigators encouraged their subjects not only to respond to the target, but to attain the proper state of mind for doing so.

This principle was also used during the early Duke years. Linzmayer and Pearce often appeared dazed during their guessing. Miss Bailey entered into a light trance and after a long period of testing so did Pearce. Miss Ownbey even perceived the Zener card figures by subjective visions.

After plunging into the historical records of gifted subjects, White discovered that several set procedures were used by the subjects to gain access to ESP impressions which were labeled as: (1) relaxing; (2) engaging the conscious mind; (2a) the demand; (3) the waiting, the tension, and the release; (4) the way the response enters consciousness.

The first procedure included deliberate attempts to relax the mind and body by physical techniques and clearing the mind until blankness occurred. The second step, to engage the conscious mind, seems a technique to shift attention to a neutral stimulus so that unconscious material might more easily surface. Several gifted subjects used such methods as concentrating on a mental image, or making the mind a total blank, or creating and holding a blank screen before the shut eyes. The demand is a corollary which appears in the reports of only a few sensitives and is a subjective command for the ESP impression to pop into consciousness. However, most psychics go through a period of waiting, tension, and release. The waiting is a passive period as the psychic engages the conscious mind and merely waits for the ESP impression to surface. Often several minutes pass during this period. This waiting leads to a period of passive tension after which an image or thought comes into the subject's mind, which is reported as the ESP impression.* This actual appearance of the impression is the fourth step of the overall process.

White has pointed out not only differences in the method of

---

* Of course these are only basic principles used by gifted subjects surveyed by White and are not necessarily indicative of all psychics. Ossowiecki's whole psi process was characterized by fierce mental effort to "drag" the impressions into consciousness.

responding to the ESP target between gifted subjects of the past and those of the present, but also a contrast in the sense of conviction that the experiment brings. Subjects today rarely can evaluate whether or not they are doing well, and are almost emotionally neutral during their responses. The gifted subjects of parapsychology's infancy often were cognizant that they had succeeded and based their verbal responses on this very conviction. In this manner, they were not really "guessing" at all. The earlier subjects also spent considerable time before making a response which is in striking contrast to the quickness with which modern ESP experiments are conducted. White has suggested that if modern subjects would try to emulate such gifted subjects as Sinclair, Johnson, and others, parapsychology might once again find a key to success which seems to have been lost in the post-Duke years.[12]

Despite the fact that sensitives go through an intensely introspective process while demonstrating ESP, errors do habitually distort the evidence. In the before-mentioned chair tests with Croiset, some of his impressions were wrong, misdirected, or slightly distorted. Why? The problem of what disturbs the ESP process in the gifted subject led W. H. C. Tenhaeff to give special consideration to this question. Tenhaeff, working with Croiset as well as with over thirty other sensitives during his career, uncovered several sources of error that can affect a psychic's ability. Firstly, when a token object is used, the object itself may bring certain associations to the mind of the sensitive which are mistaken for ESP impressions. By sheer logical association, a knife, by its very nature, might suggest to the psychic a murder by stabbing. Secondly, the psychic might be disturbed by telepathic interference from the target person. In some cases the paragnosts may quote material the subject *would like to receive* regardless of its accuracy. In other instances peripheral thoughts in the target's mind might be picked up and confused with impressions from a token object. The third major source of confusion may be nonpsychic subconscious images which surface during the ESP process which the psychic mistakenly focuses upon, believing them to be psi impressions.

A final area of consideration is the psychological makeup and characteristics of the gifted subject. Kappers and Greiner demonstrated that spontaneous ESP is not experienced by persons with any set psychological traits. But what of the psychic? The full-fledged ESP ability of the gifted subject is so striking that certain psychological concomitants might be expected to accompany it. Tenhaeff, Sannwald, and Hans Bender have also made psychological evaluations of gifted subjects, and all three surveys point to similar personality patterns. Chief among these was the tendency toward more extroversion than would be found in a normal control group of nonpsychics; but on the other hand, there was less adjustment to reality and more imagination, and a sensitiveness to external stimuli. They could "identify" with persons around them easily, but tended toward dissociation (mental abstraction and disintegration). In examining the life of the well-known psychic, Mrs. Eileen Garrett, Dr. Jan Ehrenwald noted a similar tendency toward dissociation and unbalance which generally resolved into the development of her psi ability. Ehrenwald notes in his discussion of Mrs. Garrett in his *Telepathy and Medical Psychology* (1947) that it is hard to make a clear distinction between tendencies toward eliciting psi impressions and betraying symptoms of mental unbalance, and that the two might even intertwine in a gifted subject.

These studies do offer a rather global, but representative, portrait of the gifted psychic—extroverted, with tendencies toward hysteria, dissociation, sensitive to the psychological environment, and highly field-dependent. Nonetheless, another investigator, Dr. O. L. Trick of Duke University, psychologically analyzed two gifted subjects studied by W. G. Roll and found both to be normal in every respect.[13]

Although there is a trend toward some similarity in the personality patterns of gifted subjects, this is not to say that the psi ability is necessarily psychologically determined. There is still the possibility that hereditary factors might contribute to the development of the gifted subject as well. This thinking, once much in vogue in European parapsychology, is based on the fact that ESP and PK abilities usually run in families. The Jones boys studied by S. G. Soal were cousins. Mrs. Verrall and her daughter, Helen Verrall, were gifted sensitives. Willie and Rudi Schneider, both outstanding PK mediums, were brothers, and of course there is good evidence that at least two of the three

Fox sisters had similar abilities. Gustave Geley once wrote that "in all cases of the great mediums I have studied right up to the present [1922], and among them there were ESP subjects as well as those specializing in physical phenomena, I came across heredity. The heredity could be in direct line, or could be traced to ancestors or collaterals." [14] Unfortunately, there has been no direct study of genetic factors in ESP. The issue thus comes down to the age-old heredity versus environment controversy in academic psychology. Is a trait hereditary or does the possessor of a trait raise his children in such a way that a similar trait develops? We simply do not know.

Whatever lies at the heart of the ESP ability as it develops in the gifted subject, the key factors have either eluded us or we have, as yet, no tools by which to discover or measure them.

7

Mind, Space, and Matter
— Telekinesis

One can interpret telepathy various ways. Perhaps the percipient's mind constantly scans through space and time, carefully selecting what to impress upon his conscious mind. On the other hand, perhaps the agent causes some impression to be planted in the mind, or even directly into the brain of the percipient. ESP may not represent only one single process but may use different mechanics under different conditions when it is called into action. Robert Thouless and B. P. Weisner have argued that there might be, in the case of telepathy, two different forms: one in which the agent's mind might directly affect the percipient's brain, and another type in which the percipient's mind could initiate rapport with the agent's. These two types of telepathy are called respectively kappa telepathy and gamma telepathy, but it would be hard to differentiate between them. The old conception of telepathy was that of a sender-receiver phenomenon, but spontaneous case material suggests that the percipient often activates the transference.

If one mind can directly affect another mind or brain, we might be faced with something measurable, such as a force or field, at the heart of ESP. If a mind can directly affect a brain, it is conceivable that it can affect an object as well. And it is here that the study of mind over matter becomes critical to the study of the paranormal. Like the study of ESP, research into mind

over matter was a gradual evolution from anecdotal and spontaneous observations to controlled experimentation.

The spontaneous movement of objects and similar phenomena
were prolifically recorded during parapsychology's early years.
However, as research became more oriented toward ESP, physical phenomena diminished and almost vanished from the parapsychological scene. Nonetheless, instances of spontaneous telekinesis continue to be reported, and like most spontaneous ESP
cases, spontaneous telekinesis most often occurs during an emotional situation as in the following experience:

> My father and I are living in Isere. One of our friends was
> seriously ill, and each day we expected to see him die.
>
> One evening, after having paid him a visit, we had gone to
> bed, fairly tired (for he lived three or four kilometers from our
> home.) Scarcely were we in bed when a violent blow was
> struck on the head of the bed, and the curtains were set in
> motion by an inexplicable puff of air. My father leaped out of
> bed, saying, "He is dead!". He looked at the time, and
> dressed himself hastily, that he might go back to his friend.
>
> The latter had died at the moment when we had heard the
> blow and felt the puff of air.[1]

How can one interpret cases such as these? Crisis telekinesis
can manifest in various forms: objects topple; odd sounds may
be heard; and, commonly, clocks stop. Usually, the timing is coincidental to a death or accident. One of the earliest interpretations for such cases was offered by a French parapsychologist,
Paul Joire, who suggested that the experience was actually a hallucination. He believed that the percipient became aware of a
death or accident by ESP and that the unconscious, instead of
creating a visual or auditory hallucination to bring the impression to consciousness, hallucinated the percipient into believing
he had witnessed a physical act. This interpretation has difficulty explaining collective cases as quoted above, and is impossible to put forth in cases where objects are seen to move or
break and remain so after the experience is over.

A similar approach to telekinesis was presented by Louisa
Rhine who also argues that it is the percipient who generates the
phenomenon. She found, while surveying spontaneous crisis
ESP cases, that the percipient was more often the initiator of

ESP than was the agent undergoing the crisis. Mrs. Rhine felt that in transfering the ESP impression from the unconscious to the conscious, the mind might use psychokinesis to carry out a symbolic act, such as inexplicably stopping a clock at the moment of death instead of in a more conventional or auditory psi hallucination. This explanation does explain certain patterns of spontaneous PK when a similar physical phenomena repeats itself during several different crises. One Illinois woman wrote Mrs. Rhine that at the exact time of her mother's death, an antique clock suddenly stopped. The clock stopped at the same time the next day. Three years later it stopped again, signifying the birth of a grandchild, and a fourth time when another child was married. In this case it does seem that the woman herself was able to use her PK ability to carry out a symbolic act to bring an ESP impression to consciousness. This type of case illustrates some fundamental unity between ESP and PK.

Despite percipient-induced spontaneous telekinesis, there are two other types which suggest that an outside agency, such as the person undergoing the crisis, perpetrates the physical phenomena himself by projecting some physical force which, like ESP, is not bound by the laws of time or space. The first of these are cases in which the telekinesis repeats itself until the percipient is finally able to interpret the message. In such instances it looks as though an outside intelligence directs the telekinesis. Since percipient-induced PK necessitates a mixture of both ESP and PK, there is little reason for the percipient to fail to realize that the effect is paranormal until it is repeated, or not immediately comprehend what the action signifies. Usually when the percipient correctly interprets the event, the phenomenon stops:

> One evening, at about nine o'clock, while the whole family was at prayers, an extraordinary noise made itself heard in the office, as though the heavy counter had been violently shaken, making the scales and everything upon it resound noisily. All rushed into the room to learn the reason for this unusual noise, to their great stupefication, they found everything in place and nothing unnatural could be discovered. When the interrupted prayer had been resumed, there was another noise, absolutely like the first: in the face of the general rest-

lessness my great-grandfather told them not to move, and added that this noise must have been made by the soul of a member of the family who had just died; he went on to say that it was probably his mother, who lived at Charavines and he said a *de profundis*. Now, that same night a special messenger from Charavines, seventeen kilometers away, confirmed my great-grandfather's prevision by announcing that his mother had just died: the hour of her death coincided exactly with the hour at which the noises of the evening had been itself heard.[2]

In other cases the sounds remain inexplicable until the announcement of a death clears up the mystery. In a few rare instances these physical displays occur in the presence of the dying agent, and these seem unexplainable on the Rhine ESP-con-PK hypothesis.

Despite the problem of who acts as the PK agent, spontaneous telekinesis indicates that the human organism has some ability to affect physical matter. Further, spontaneous PK follows similar principles to spontaneous ESP: (1) it most often occurs at the moment of a crisis; (2) it may be caused by either agent or percipient; and (3) it often manifests in a symbolic form. This close similarity would support a further contention of Thouless and Wiesner that ESP and PK are two sides of the same coin, one manifestation affecting the senses, the other affecting matter.

ESP is often used, subconsciously, by an individual for various purposes—to scan or focus on a target (as in the case of patient-therapist ESP), or to gain access to normally inaccessible information. Can PK be used for similar purposes? New light has been shed on this question by the study of the poltergeist.

For ages there have been tales of houses haunted by some force which manifests by recurrent displays of telekinesis—objects thrown about, crockery smashed, and missiles hurled at onlookers. Such hauntings were distinguished from more conventional haunted houses by the fact that they were short-lived, violently physical, and centered about a certain individual residing in the disturbed dwelling. Conventional hauntings usually go on for years, manifesting by the appearance of apparitions or auditory phenomena, and are independent of its residents, often outlasting several tenancies. In a poltergeist, the phenomena may "follow" a family or individual if he moves from the focus of its attention: The term poltergeist (from the German, meaning noisy ghost) was popularized when Harry Price, an English investigator, adopted the term in his writings to account for this type of haunting. A more descriptive term, recurrent spontaneous psychokinesis (RSPK), has also been suggested.

Unlike ESP which manifests in four tightly related forms (telepathy, clairvoyance, precognition, and retrocognition), RSPK phenomena have an incredibly diversified range of effects: rapping (strong percussive noises); movements of objects including levitation, breakage, hurling, and shifting position; teleportation (the inexplicable appearance and disappearance of objects from sealed rooms or containers); diverse forms of noises; fire igniting; biting (appearance of bites and welts on the human body); such ghostly phenomena as apparitions and voices; and stone-throwing (where a house, either its interior or exterior, will be subject to a barrage of missiles, usually stones, thrown from an undefinable or indiscernible source).

The phenomenon of the poltergeist is age old. In 1951 Hereward Carrington presented a historical survey of poltergeist cases and found five of them recorded before A.D. 1000, including such phenomena as raps, showers of stones, fires, and telekinesis.[3] Between A.D. 1000 and the advent of modern parapsychology (1882), Carrington found and described 130 cases predominantly recorded in Great Britain, France, the United States, and Germany. However, the worldwide pattern of the poltergeist has been substantiated by historical and modern examples occurring in Scandinavia, Africa, Jamaica, China, Java, South America, Haiti, and so forth. A typical example of a historical poltergeist can be found in the Drummer of Tedworth case described earlier in the book.

The story of the scientific study of the poltergeist ranges from well-witnessed cases during parapsychology's infancy to the first attempt at studying a poltergeist in the laboratory by Harry Price in the 1920s, and finally psychological and physical analyses of well-investigated cases today, chiefly by W. G. Roll in the United States and Hans Bender in Germany.

RSPK outbreaks were witnessed by Sir William Barrett and

Cesare Lombroso during their careers as psychical investigators. The observation of these bizarre events by scientifically trained men was one of the chief reasons for the ultimate acceptance of the poltergeist as a topic for serious attention by the first parapsychologists. In his book, *After Death—What?* (1909), Lombroso recorded how he had been called in to investigate a haunting in a Turin wine cellar whose proprietor complained that bottles would move by themselves, shatter and break, pop their corks, and cause considerable damage. Kitchen utensils and furniture also behaved erratically. In order to observe these incidents firsthand, Lombroso ventured into the wine cellar and reported:

> There was a deep wine cellar, access to which was obtained by means of a long stairway and a passageway. The people informed me that they noticed that whenever anyone entered the cellar the bottles began to be broken. I entered at first in the dark, and, sure enough, I heard the breaking of glasses, and the rolling of bottles under my feet. I there-upon lit up the place. The bottles were massed together upon five shelves, one over the other. In the middle of the room was a rude table. I had six lighted candles placed upon this, on the supposition that the spiritualist phenomena would cease in bright light. On the contrary, I saw three empty bottles, which stood upright on the floor, spin along as if twirled by a finger and break to pieces near the table. To avoid a possible trick I carefully examined by the light of a large candle, and touched with my hand all the full bottles standing on the shelves and ascertained that there were no wires or strings that might explain the movements. After a few minutes two bottles, then four, and later others on the second and third shelves separated themselves from the rest and fell to the floor without any violent motion, but rather as if they had been lifted down by someone; and after the descent, rather than fall, six burst upon the wet floor (already drenched with wine) and two remained intact. A quarter of an hour afterwards three others from the last compartment fell and were broken on the floor. Then I turned to leave the cellar. As I was on the point of going out, I heard the breaking of another bottle on the floor. When the door was shut, all again became quiet.

Lombroso saw that the series of events was disturbing the psychological well-being of the proprietor's wife and suggested that she vacate the premises. During her absence no odd phenomena were recorded nor did any accompany the woman to Nole where she resided in the interim. However, her return heralded the return of the poltergeist. A second departure did not restrict the poltergeist which persisted despite her absence. However, when two young waiters were dismissed, all the phenomena stopped.

Even to the first serious students of the poltergeist, the study of historical cases revealed a pattern—poltergeists usually erupted in a family which contained a child near the age of puberty and about whom the events focused. The first to enunciate this pattern was Frank Podmore in 1908. He found that in more cases than not the focus of attention was a young girl. Since fraud had previously been discovered in many poltergeist cases where youngsters were caught throwing objects or pounding on walls to create raps, he believed that the conspicuous presence of children indicated that poltergeists were invariably hoaxes generated by them. The years since Podmore's writings have brought forth better-witnessed cases which have confirmed the pattern of children as the focus of the poltergeist in a large percentage of cases. This led John Layard to suggest that the poltergeist represents a "force" projected unconsciously by some children to express hostility which could not be expressed in a more conventional way. The hostility is projected by breaking objects or hurling them by PK instead of the child carrying out his frustrations normally.[4] A psychoanalyst, Nandor Fodor, suggested that the close tie between RSPK and puberty shows that the hostilities and frustrations are sexually based.[5]

The first attempt to study the poltergeist-agent in a scientific setting was made by Harry Price with a Romanian girl, Eleanore Zugun, whose poltergeist attack had ostracized her from her own family. Luckily the case came to the attention of a capable researcher, Fritz Grunewald, who was able to place the unfortunate girl under the protection of the Countess Zoe Wassilko-Serecki, a patroness of psychical research in Vienna. Both Grunewald and the countess witnessed phenomena such as telekinesis and sudden biting marks appearing on the girl's flesh. In 1926 Price observed some of the events himself, including the inexplicable flight of a letter opener, and brought Eleanore

Zugun to England to be studied at his own National Laboratory of Psychical Research, one of the most sophisticated for its kind in Europe. The investigation was made not so much to test the girl, but to witness further PK under more controlled conditions. Price was not disappointed. Soon he was able to witness the sudden appearance of an enameled notice-board letter (used for spelling out announcements on an encased bulletin board) which dropped on Eleanore as she played, and later saw more complex displays of spontaneous telekinesis. Finally, under controlled conditions, Price and his associates saw the appearance of bites and welts. Newspaper reporters covering the case for the popular press also saw the sudden appearance of the marks. One student of parapsychology, Dr. R. J. Tillyard, had an object spontaneously teleported directly into his own pocket.

These observations demonstrated that careful scrutiny could be used to verify the manifestations. Eleanore went back to Vienna. Shortly afterward her menstruation began for the first time and this was accompanied by the abrupt cessation of the RSPK outbreak.[6]

A further analysis of RSPK phenomena has been the product of several years of investigation by W. G. Roll who has been singularly fortunate to be able to observe and make detailed notes of several poltergeist cases. In 1958 he and J. G. Pratt investigated a home in Seaford, New York, plagued by popping bottles, breaking glassware, and rapping sounds. Roll questioned the Hermanns who resided in the house with their two children, Lucille and Jimmy. A chief witness was a police lieutenant who had been called in to get at the heart of the matter and who had observed the RSPK incidents under conditions where the children could not have caused this disturbance. Roll and Pratt tried to find normal explanations for the events (bad plumbing, sonic booms, underground river currents, and so forth). However, in analyzing the total of sixty-seven incidents reported by the Hermanns, it became apparent that the great majority of them occurred when Jimmy was present and awake. However, the poltergeist ceased just as the investigators arrived.

In 1961 Roll was called in to investigate a rampaging poltergeist which was disturbing a black family in Newark, New Jersey. In this case objects were being hurled around the room or displaced—all seemingly centered on the tenant's thirteen-year-old grandson, Ernie. The incidents were still active when Roll arrived on the scene, and arrangements were made for Ernie and his grandmother to go to Durham, North Carolina. RSPK outbreaks resumed in the hotel where they were staying, but under careful observation Ernie was seen to hurl some objects deliberately and then blame it on the poltergeist. Nonetheless, several earlier incidents suggested that Ernie was not normally responsible for the moving objects but only fell to faking incidents later on in the course of events.

Another difficult case cropped up in 1962, a "biting poltergeist" in Indianapolis. Tiny punctures appeared on the flesh of the family members as well as manifestations such as raps and telekinesis. Roll himself witnessed one event—a vase flew from a kitchen table, made a detonating sound, but rolled innocuously at his feet. Unfortunately, the case was ruined when one member of the family became hysterical and started throwing objects about during a paroxysm. Nevertheless, the family did include a teen-age girl.

The breakthrough in the study of the poltergeist came when Roll and Pratt were able to control directly the conditions under which RSPK took place in a warehouse in Miami. Inexplicable breakage had occurred, and the events seemed to center on a nineteen-year-old Cuban refugee, Julio, who worked there. The site was a large facility with tiers of shelves containing curios and novelty items which would fling themselves from the shelves, often breaking when they fell. Several witnesses had observed the odd motions which eventually totaled 224 incidents. After interviewing the witnesses, Roll and Pratt began a systematic study in which they attempted to induce the RSPK. Several guards patrolled the aisles, and certain objects were chosen as targets, but as soon as attention was shifted from one certain area to another, and even though all present were under surveillance, an object would mysteriously fall from the shelves. In one instance this occurred even though Pratt and Julio were all alone in the building, and the RSPK continued its same particular pattern—an object apparently would be pushed off the shelf by an invisible force.

Roll persuaded Julio to come to Durham to be examined scientifically. There he would be tested for conventional PK in which the subject tries to influence the fall of dice. Nothing significant occurred during these experiments, but oddly the machine kept malfunctioning—the bottom of the automatic dice holder kept falling out.* This happened on several throws and usually was accompanied by success at the PK task. Therefore, it looks as if Julio was PK-ing both the dice and the apparatus. During a break in the experiments, a vase in the hallway of the Foundation for Research on the Nature of Man laboratory suddenly shattered. When Julio took ESP tests he failed to succeed. No further incidents were recorded.

Roll had his chance personally to observe a poltergeist in action in 1968 when he investigated an outbreak in Olive Hill, Kentucky. Again objects were displaced and the events had followed the Callihan family even when they changed residences. John Stump, sent to take charge of the proceedings until Roll could arrive, saw three bottles slide on the sink when no one was near them. When Roll came, he was able to see a table jet up into the air, swirl around, and drop back. Unfortunately the Callihans objected to the investigation, which therefore had to be aborted. Again a twelve-year-old child was present during the outbreak.

All of these cases represent the diversity of the poltergeist. Luckily, Roll has had an assortment of poltergeist-agents to study psychologically. Verifying the cases was, however, only the first step in probing the mystery of the poltergeist. The next step was to study the agent and find out what caused the manifestations. After psychological evaluations were made by his colleagues, Roll found a certain recurring pattern, much in keeping with John Layard's theory of projected repression. The agents seemed to harbor pent-up hostilities which usually did not surface, but were being repressed or denied. The hostility was a subconscious vortex. Correlated to this was the low verbal ability of the agents which would indicate that they could not express frustrations and hostilities usually caused by stressful interfamily relations.

---

* The dice holder throws the dice and the subject has to attempt to influence the faces upon which the dice will then land.

Based on this setting, the psychological mechanics of RSPK outbreaks become fairly clear. The agent finds himself in a situation wherein he is faced with frustrations and tensions which he either cannot or will not express normally by speech or physical acts. The pressure is relieved by the PK ability which suddenly begins to carry out destructive acts. This is probably the reason poltergeist disturbances are so brief. The agent may not know he is the agent, since the psychological tensions as well as the PK ability are manipulated subconsciously. This is aggravated by the fact that the agent is usually suppressing these tensions from consciousness.[7]

Confirmation for this psychodynamic interpretation of the poltergeist comes independently from a German parapsychologist, Professor Hans Bender, who has also been able to substantiate several RSPK cases and make similar psychological evaluations of the probable agents.

In November 1967 several Bavarian newspapers reported an odd series of events plaguing a law office in Rosenheim. Neon lights flickered on and off inexplicably and even unscrewed themselves from their sockets, raps were heard, telephone bills showed nonexistent phone calls, and so on. Electrical disturbances or malfunction were at first blamed, but employees from the local power company found nothing wrong with the wiring or equipment even though during their investigation they recorded mysterious electrical discharges. Finally, after light bulbs began to explode, Bender arrived to investigate personally the events which only occurred during office hours and centered upon a nineteen-year-old employee, Annemarie. Witnesses saw overhead lights swing, bulbs explode, and objects thrown in her direction. Her telephone also was singled out as subject to a conspicuous amount of malfunction. In December a visiting physicist saw a four-hundred-pound storage filing cabinet slide away from the wall. Paintings on the wall would often rotate. This phenomenon was caught on videotape during a documentary filming. Witnesses saw a misty armlike appendage appear and strike a painting which gyrated on its axis. The camera was able to catch the painting in motion. After Annemarie left her position with the law firm no further incidents occurred there, although some peripheral PK occurred both at her new place of employment and at her home.

Bender has made psychodiagnostic evaluations of several agents in cases that he has investigated and has found that they are often the center of unmanageable frustrations, overuse of defense mechanisms, and that PK is used to resolve their conflicts.[8]

This discussion of the poltergeist began with a question, can PK be used by the individual to carry out goals? Research into the poltergeist indicates that it can. But like ESP, the direction of PK is subconsciously determined, sporadic, and usually uncontrollable—except with a few gifted PK subjects. Again, there seems to be a close relationship between ESP and PK, for they function similarly as a means of subconscious expression and it is not rare for poltergeist agents to be good ESP subjects. Although Julio failed to show conventional ESP when tested, Heiner, a fifteen-year-old apprentice from Bremen, tested by Hans Bender as a poltergeist victim, scored exceptionally high on both telepathy and clairvoyance tests even though he failed on PK tests.

It might be noted that Bender has also witnessed some of the more bizarre aspects of the poltergeist, including teleportation. Once, during an investigation, when he had come to visit an infested house, he hung up his coat upon entering a room and, turning to it only a few moments later, found it gone. It was soon discovered outside the house, folded on the snow-covered yard with no footsteps around it. The brief duration of the incident ruled out any chance fraud on the part of the household which would not had time to stage the incident.

There is yet another field of inquiry prompted by RSPK—its physical aspects. What is the PK force? How is it generated? What is its nature or mechanics? Research into the poltergeist has produced more concrete evidence about the psychological nature of RSPK than about how it actually functions. However, Roll has carefully mapped out the exact trajectories of moved objects in the hope of shedding a little more light on the physics of the poltergeist. He has found certain principles to be present: objects closest to the agent are most often moved. When objects are displaced, they often follow a pattern of either a clockwise or counterclockwise motion. The number of objects moved falls off with distance, which would indicate that the poltergeist tries to conserve energy similar to the principles that govern physical energy. Objects closest to the agent move short distances and objects farther away move longer distances (at least Roll found this to be true in the Miami case).

To explain these characteristics (also more or less confirmed in Bender's cases), Roll once again employed his concept of a psi field, a moving force field generating from the agent that can move physical objects. The field would then shift, carrying with it selected objects. If the psi field were a circular vortex around the agent, several features of the poltergeist could be explained. In a vortex, peripheral objects are moved farther than are centrally positioned objects—as Roll had found in several of his cases. Since telekinetically moved objects have a tendency to move in a unified direction, the concept of the psi field as a vortex is a satisfactory explanatory mode.[9]

The study of the poltergeist, though, is not such a cut-and-dried matter, and several of its anomalies do not fit into the psychologically engendered vortex theory. Such phenomena as apparitions, voices, disappearance and reappearance of objects point to a more complex mechanism. Before the advent of modern psychology, the poltergeist was seen as either due to a ghost or to fraud. Supposition that the PK force might stem from an external agency such as a deceased person is still considered a working hypothesis by Raymond Bayless [10] and Ian Stevenson who in 1972 undertook a reevaluation of the nature of RSPK intelligence and confirmed the well-known observation that objects are often moved not haphazardly but are levitated, move slowly with complex trajectories, turn corners, and carry out further operations as though they were being *deliberately* performed. Stevenson also outlined two cases in which the poltergeist showed deliberate intent and personality, and he questioned how PK from the living agent could account for these movements.[11] (Remember how the Rochester rappings answered questions and showed the ability to be conscious of the thoughts of the questioners.)

Although these observations are cogent and imply that an external intelligence might be the source of the RSPK outbreak, PK from a living source might just as well be able to build itself into an almost independent personality or be directed by a subconscious secondary personality of the agent. The issue is a complex one. It could be argued that the psychodynamics serve only as a "setting" in which the poltergeist could erupt, but are not the actual cause, and children are not *always* involved in poltergeist outbreaks. A significant pattern of recent validated RSPK cases does point to a living agent using PK to carry out subconsciously determined goals and expressions. However, there might be more than one type of poltergeist, and we really do not know the range of the PK force (remember that a four-hundred-pound file was moved in the Rosenheim case), so the issue that an outside intelligence engenders the poltergeist or uses the agent's PK ability is a moot point.

From the poltergeist it is only a short step to the study of physical mediumship. During an RSPK outbreak the agent uses his PK ability to carry out physical acts. Usually, though, he is not aware that he is responsible for the phenomena. In physical mediumship, however, the agent is perfectly cognizant of his own unique abilities (although often ascribing them to an outside agency such as a discarnate), and can use them to demonstrate telekinesis experimentally. Such individuals are very rare and the entire history of this type of phenomena is engulfed in fraud. While physical manifestations were commonly recorded during the early days of Spiritualism, few mediums of the time could stand up under rigorous observation. Fraud was rampant, and the exposure of several prominent mediums dulled the SPR's interest in this area of research. Nonetheless, gifted physical mediums, such as D. D. Home, have appeared on the scene and have consistently demonstrated physical phenomena under controlled conditions.*

Eusapia Palladino was a semi-illiterate Italian peasant whose remarkable telekinetic abilities first drew the attention of Professor Chiaia of Naples. In 1888 he publically challenged Cesare Lombroso to investigate her abilities. Lombroso was at the time a skeptic but agreed to take up the challenge in 1891. In his experiments Eusapia would sit in a darkened room, usually in front of a cabinet, or a partitioned corner of a room, while her hands and feet were held by the investigators or bound by

* Remember throughout the following discussions on physical mediums that the seances were usually held in darkened rooms, making observation difficult.

ropes. Eusapia and her investigators would usually be seated around a table. She would enter trance, a personality claiming to be John King would appear through her, and telekinesis could spontaneously occur in the seance room, usually affecting small objects or a table that was also used there. If this all sounds like vaudeville, read the following extract taken from the initial report of the first controlled experiments:

> The light was extinguished, and the experimenters began again. While in response to the unanimous wish, the little bell was beginning again its tinkling, and its mysterious aerial circuits [telekinetic movements], M. Ascensi, taking his cue unknown to us, from M. Tambourini, went (unperceived, owing to the darkness) and stood at the right side of the medium, and at once, with a single scratch lighted a match, so successfully, as he declared, that he could see the little bell *while it was vibrating in the air,* and suddenly fall upon a bed about six feet and a half behind Mme. Palladino.

Later in the seance a table began to rock, and even though Ascensi tried to hold it steady, it ripped from his grasp and rolled across the floor. During a second seance Palladino was bound by ropes but similar phenomena were still produced.

Several commissions studied Palladino after Lombroso had publicly avowed his belief in her genuineness. In 1892 a committee of several scientists, including Giovanni Virginio, Schiaparelli, Charles Richet, and Baron du Prel, conducted seventeen seances with her and in full light observed total levitations of the seance table, and even though Palladino was tightly controlled, the curtains of the room billowed out, the experimenters were touched by unseen hands, and telekinesis was observed.

By 1895 a glittering array of phenomena had been recorded, including luminous phenomena, materializations (the sudden appearances of physical structures such as phantom hands), levitations, and assorted feats of telekinesis. In addition, Palladino could deliberately invoke PK to affect a small scale or move objects in light. The attention of the SPR was quickly aroused, and in 1894 Charles Richet invited Oliver Lodge and F. W. H. Myers to his privately owned island, Île Roubaud, to study Palladino. A minute-by-minute record was taken of the phenomena they witnessed. The following is an extract from Lodge's report:

> 12:49: A small cigar box fell onto our table, and a sound was heard in the air as of something rapping. R. [Richet] was holding head and right hand; M. [Myers] holding left hand, raised it in the air, holding it lightly by the tips of his fingers, but with part of his own hand free. A saucer containing small shot, from another part of the room, was then put into the hand of M. in the air. A covered wire of the electric battery came onto the table and wrapped itself round R's and E's [Eusapia] hands and was pulled until E. called out . . .
>
> 12:57: The accordian, which was on the round table, got onto the floor, somehow, and began to play single notes. Bellier (the stenographer) counted twenty-six of them, and then ceased counting. While the accordian played, E's fingers made movements on the hands of both M. and L. in accord with the notes, as if she were playing them at the distance with difficulty.

During these brilliant manifestations Palladino was kept under manual control and the objects appeared to move, literally, by themselves. In the following incident Professor Julien Ochorowicz was outside the room, guarding the entrance to the experimental area, while Myers, Richet, and Lodge controlled the medium inside:

> Noise, as of key being fumbled in the door and Ochorowicz, from outside, asked who was unlocking the door. Eusapia's hands were well held, and no one was near the door. The clear space of several feet, near the door, was plainly enough visible. Blows occurred on the door. The key then arrived on the table, and was felt there by L. It disappeared again, and was heard to be replacing itself in the door, with a sound as if the door was being locked (or unlocked), then the key came again onto the table, into Richet's hand, and stayed there.
>
> Richet saw an indistinct, black, square looking object, which seemed to prolong the key when it was brought toward his hand. There was light enough to see the position of everybody's normal hands all the time on this occasion, and we were sitting some four or five feet distant from the door.
>
> Richet next saw something detached, like a bird in the air

and going to M's head. At the instant he saw it touch, M. called out that he was touched on the head.

L., R. and M. then all saw the curious imitation hand, and feather fingers, stretched horizontally over the vertical gap between the half-open shutters; a thing which L. had several times seen before.

M. was seized from behind while standing, and vigorously pulled and shaken about, while all four were standing holding hands around the table . . . A loaf, and other objects, from the buffet, hard by, arrived on the table, and a pile of five plates. . .

Both Myers and Lodge were deeply impressed by Palladino's abilities and made arrangements to bring her to England. Unfortunately her seances in Cambridge deteriorated into chaos. Several of the SPR officials were determined to brand Palladino a cheap fake even though she had convinced several continental authorities. The French, Italian, Polish, and German parapsychologists had much more experience sitting with physical mediums, and had countless times warned potential experimenters that she would cheat if she could. Thus, she had to be kept under complete control. Sometimes the fakery would be deliberate, but at other times carried out unconsciously while in trance. Despite these warnings the Cambridge experiments were loosely run, and Richard Hodgson, who had returned from the United States in order to sit with Palladino, deliberately held her hands in such a way that she could escape control. Palladino took full advantage of this and began to use her hands and feet to produce movements of the table and objects. The faking was overt, easily detected, and the SPR, having ignored the warnings of earlier researchers and commissions, branded her a fake and sent her back to Italy.

Despite this unfortunate affair, research with Palladino continued in Europe, and, during some experiments in Naples in 1895, telekinesis was observed in full light. Several of the phenomena, as in the past, were successfully photographed. In 1898 Camille Flammarion directed a series of remarkable experiments in his own salon. Palladino was always searched before and after the seances and then tightly held during the sittings. An incredible array of phenomena was recorded. During one sitting she became extremely irritable and the telekinesis actually became destructive:

> The sofa came forward when she looked at it, then recoiled before her breath; all the instruments were thrown pell mell upon the table; the tambourine rose almost to the height of the ceiling; the cushions took part in the sport, overturning everything on the table; M.M. was thrown from his chair. This chair—a heavy dining-room chair of black walnut, with stuffed seat—rose into the air, came up on the table with a great clatter, then pushed off . . .

The support given Palladino by such savants as Professors Venzano and Morselli (who calculated that Palladino's phenomena included thirty-nine different physical effects, including levitation, billowing of the seance-room curtains, wind in the seance room, raps, voices, apports, impressions in plastic molds,* and materializations), ultimately forced the SPR to reassess its hasty 1895 report. And a new commission was formed to study Palladino. It consisted of Everard Feilding, an experienced investigator and amateur conjuror, W. W. Baggally, another well-known investigator and one fully versed in the methods of fraud, and Hereward Carrington. Carrington, one of the most experienced psychical researchers of his day, was not only an able magician but had written a devastating textbook on mediumistic fraud, *The Physical Phenomena of Spiritualism*, shortly before the 1908 experiments were to take place. Feilding, Carrington, and Baggally all had three qualifications in common: they had investigated mediums for many years, all were well versed in methods of fraud, and all stated that they had never, so far, encountered a genuine physical medium.

The choice of these three experimenters was not accidental. The SPR wanted to send their most critical researchers to reevaluate Palladino, and they could not have chosen better. Unlike several earlier committees, this SPR commission planned in

* These molds are unique. A soft putty-like material would be placed in a basin during the experiments and Palladino would try to "impress" it. After the sittings, although she never left her seat, the putty would show an impression, usually of Palladino's own face, although no putty would be found on her. Obviously a PK force had been projected and carried out the act.

advance the exact battle plan they wished to follow. Their hope was either to expose Palladino once and for all or to verify her abilities irrefutably. To carry out this goal, stenographic records were kept during the seances. If any phenomena took place, each experimenter would have to call out his exact position and his control of the medium. A minute-by-minute log was kept, for the committee hoped to answer the criticism leveled at earlier investigative work with Palladino. Carrington was especially dissatisfied with the fact that many records only stated that the medium was "securely held," but did not state the exact position of each hand and foot or how the experimenters kept track of them. The committee members also brought with them a special device to test the table levitations. In a darkened room it is relatively easy to use a foot to prop up a leg of the table to simulate a levitation. To guard against this the SPR commission introduced what they called "the stocks." This was a flat, square wooden frame containing protrusions at each corner into which the legs of the table could be set. The medium would then have nothing to prop up, since each leg of the table would be encaged in a socket connected to the frame connecting all the other legs.

Despite these severe controls, phenomena often came rapidly during the eleven sittings, including the levitation of the table. Palladino sat in front of a cabinet which consisted of a large open wooden frame with a curtain covering the entrance. She and her sitters would be seated around a table. Musical tops and other small objects were either placed on or with a small table in the cabinet. The little table was once brought out of the cabinet telekinetically and levitated by the medium. The following is an extract from one of the sittings showing the detailed method of reporting: *

> C. Small table is coming out from under the curtain [of the cabinet] on my right, legs first. One leg of the table has climbed upon my chair.
> M. I can see everything very clearly.
> F. So can I.
> C. So can I.
> Noises follow gestures made by F.

* The initials represent: C.—Carrington, F.—Feilding, M.—Morselli, who took part in some of the sittings.

C. The small table attempts to climb on to the seance table and falls back.

M. I can see all the hands over and away from the table and her feet.

Things in the cabinet move about violently and with great commotion.

F. Feet are all right. [That is, seemingly held.]

11:51

C. In good light I can see the small table moving toward me, the result of my making movements toward it with my right hand. The medium's left hand holding my right hand and clearly visible. She is pressing on my right foot with her left foot.

F. Her right foot firmly fixed on mine. I have just verified with my hands the division of the toes.

Medium asked C. to lift up the small table and put it upright.

11:53

Complete levitation of the small table.

C. My right hand being on the surface, her left hand being upon mine, her left foot pressing strongly on mine.

The table is raised about a foot in the air.

F. Her right foot pressing on mine.

11:57

C. She puts her left hand on my right, which rests flat on the top of the small table and the table again rises a foot in the air. Her foot is still strongly pressing on my right.

F. Her right foot is still pressing on mine; her right hand is visible close to me, in mine.

C. I now ascertain that there is no string or connection between the medium and the small table. The distance behind the small table and the dress of the medium appears to me to be about a foot.

It was not only such controlled incidents that impressed the experimenters, but also spontaneous telekinesis. Often, after the seances were over, while the medium was in a state of near collapse, objects would still move about in perfectly normal light. By the end of the series of sittings, Carrington, Feilding, and Baggally had witnessed levitations, telekinesis, luminous manifestations (lights darting about the seance room), and artificially formed hands which melted in their grasps. All three experimenters reversed their negative opinions about physical mediumship and admitted their conversion to belief in Palladino's abilities.[12]

Despite moments of brilliance during the 1908 seances, Palladino's abilities were obviously on the wane. Carrington brought her to the United States, and here again her sitters were not trained in psychical research and were interested only in exposing her. Palladino's phenomena were present but relatively meager. Charges of fraud were made by some of the sitters, and all in all there was a repeat of the Cambridge fiasco. Palladino returned to Italy and died soon afterward, having convinced several of Europe's top psychical researchers that beneath or hidden in the fraud engulfing the Spiritualist movement, some genuine physical phenomena existed.

The investigations of Palladino have been cited, since it was the first substantial case in early parapsychology where a physical medium was thoroughly tested under controlled conditions. It also represents the difficulties inherent in studying physical mediumship—the difficulties in observation, control, the mixture of fraud and genuineness, and all. However, the investigations did show that even this problem-ridden area of research could be approached scientifically. Palladino's case achieved one major goal—it demonstrated the existence of physical phenomena. It was up to future experimenters to determine the nature of the force at work.

Carrington had a hard time believing that Palladino's own mind was responsible for much of the phenomena. In his critical discussion on the nature of her abilities in his *Eusapia Palladino and Her Phenomena* he compared various theories about the telekinetic force. Lombroso, Flammarion, and others thought that, just as Palladino claimed, spirits of the dead directed the manifestations. This was primarily based on certain acts carried out during the seances which echoed acts typical of once-living agents known to the experimenters. For example, Professor Venzano touched a materialized head during one sitting which resembled the contour of a dead friend's. Lombroso heard an independent voice which he recognized as identical to his once-living mother's. Other investigators such as Morselli, though, felt that the medium alone directed the phenomena subconsciously while in trance, and Joseph Maxwell argued that a medium generates a power taken from herself and her sitters which together forms an artificial intelligence that directs the phenomena. Carrington amalgamated all these different theories into a hypothesis that the medium innately possesses a semimaterial structure within her organism that can be projected by either the medium or by a discarnate in order to move objects, and which might even become visible, building itself in to a semisolid form.

Certain biological and physiological correlates to the phenomena were observed. After Palladino's seances she would weigh considerably less, suffer from exhaustion, and often become hysterical. During the production of the phenomena she would be in obvious pain, coughing, and bodily spasms would become violent. Clearly, whatever the PK force was, the medium's organism hid the mystery.

A major attempt to understand how telekinesis is dependent on the human organism was undertaken by Dr. W. J. Crawford with Kathleen Goligher between 1914 and 1920. Crawford was a professor of mechanical engineering and was interested in the physical mechanics of the Goligher phenomena, which consisted of table levitations and minor telekinesis. Historically, the case is hard to evaluate, since the phenomena occurred during sittings in which the entire Goligher family participated. To exclude fraud, Crawford would have had to supervise six independent possible confederates. Crawford was the sole major experimenter, and it did not aid his credibility when he committed suicide in 1920, even though his death had nothing to do with the experiments. During the sittings the family would darken the room and sing softly until the table around which they sat levitated. It was Crawford's chore to observe the levitations under a dim red light. A later experimenter, Fournier d'Albe, investigated the Golighers and, although witnessing no fraud, accused the family of collusion and of using an unspecified mechanical apparatus to move the table. Even the SPR realized that D'Albe's claims had no basis or evidence and did not publish his report. On the other hand, the Golighers were under Crawford's supervision for six years, and outside investigators such as William Barrett did verify the phenomena. After Crawford's death and Kathleen Goligher's marriage, a few independent experiments were conducted to the satisfaction of the different investigators.

Goligher's phenomena were not nearly so rich as Palladino's, consisting mainly of table levitations. Nonetheless, Crawford was able to outline certain principles about telekinesis from these demonstrations. When the table levitated, the medium's weight increased in proportion. Her total weight would then equal the weight of her own body and the weight of the table combined with a variance of 5 percent. When the table was levitated, one could press down upon it and feel an elastic resistance, although the table could not be pushed back to the floor. The movement of the table was linked to the medium by an invisible field. If Crawford placed his hand at certain points between the medium and the table, the table would fall back to the floor. This force could be felt as clammy and cold. Added weight applied to the table did not add weight to the medium or topple her forward. Alternately, the table could be made so heavy by the medium's ability that no one could lift it from its position on the floor. It would be as if it were nailed down.

From these observations, Crawford developed his cantilever theory which presumed that a projected PK force extrudes from the medium, angles to the floor, and then rises under the table and levitates it. He further speculated that the force would mold itself into rods which moved objects about. To demonstrate his theory he often placed colored matter such as powder between the medium and the table, and a trail of the material would be left as the psychic rods left the medium's body, crossed the floor, and moved toward the table. Often the substance would be found within the medium's clothing after the seances. When raps occurred, the medium's body would jerk (also witnessed with Palladino) and after the sittings it was found that all the sitters had lost a small amount of weight. Ultimately, Crawford photographed some of these extrusions. Despite the obvious difficulties he found—the mysterious evaporation of the sitters' weight and some of the motions of the table (to become heavy or light on demand) would be hard to explain normally. However, it must also be kept in mind that just as we have seen in the experimenter effect in laboratory experiments, the Goligher phenomena may have been molded by Crawford's own views on how he *expected* it to function.[13]

Similar experiments, which are easier to evaluate, were made earlier by Julien Ochorowicz with Stanislawa Tomczyk, a young Polish medium he had discovered. Unlike other mediums, Tomczyk did not display her abilities in formal seances, but mainly during private experiments. During the experiments she would be hypnotized by Ochorowicz. Her chief phenomena were the movement of small objects, and her abilities were witnessed by many independent researchers in full light. She could levitate small objects by placing her hands on either side of them (but not touching them), and as she moved her hands upward the objects would follow. Luckily, photographs were taken of these levitations. Ochorowicz observed that slender threads, which he called "rigid rays," extended from the medium's fingers. These were obviously not physical threads, since Ochorowicz could move his hand right through the ray without breaking it or disrupting the levitation.

During the sittings, spontaneous telekinesis would also occur. A cooking pot several feet from the medium, which was too hot to touch, was once seen to levitate and remain suspended in the air. Raps often broke out and apports dropped into the room. The apports were usually objects from other rooms or from outside and fell suddenly into the seance room while Tomczyk was still hypnotized and under full control.* Ultimately, Tomczyk married Everard Fielding, gave up her mediumship, and is still living in Great Britain.[14]

A further advance in the study of physical mediumship was due to Harry Price and his experiments with two mediums. The first of these was given the pseudonym of Stella C. Since Price had his own well-equipped laboratory in which to test his subjects, the use of fraud-proof devices and mechanical apparatuses to monitor the phenomena could be successfully employed during the darkened seances.

---

* An attempt to photograph the materialization of apports was made by Major Mowbray with T. Lynn at the British College of Psychic Science and a report was included in his pamphlet *Transition* (1936). The results were successful, and objects were photographed hovering in front of Lynn, often linked to the medium by a tiny ray identical to those photographed with Tomczyk.

Stella C. met Harry Price on a train when a casual conversation turned to psychical research. Since Stella C. reported experiences with spontaneous telekinesis, Price hastened to get her into his laboratory. For the experiments he constructed several gadgets which if manipulated by Stella C. would prove the genuineness of the phenomena. Chief among these was a table with gauze placed all the way around the legs and connected to the table top. The bottom was then sealed so that the table's underside was completely enclosed as a cage. Objects were placed inside the cage and since they were completely enclosed only a telekinetic force could move them. Despite the control, the objects did move and musical instruments were struck or played upon. Another table used for levitation displays was completely ripped apart by the invisible force before the eyes of the researchers:

> The sitters and medium having formed themselves into a circle around the table with only the tips of their fingers touching the table top, great power was quickly developed, and movements of the table rapidly followed. The table was then completely levitated several times, remaining in the air for several seconds upon each occasion. Once the table rose completely above the heads of the sitters, some of whom had to rise in order to keep contact with it. . . . The sitters then moved their hands from the table, only the finger tips of the medium remaining upon it. Movements of the table still continued. The sitters again placed their fingers on the table top, when still further power was developed with increasing violence, two of the legs breaking away from the table with a percussive-like noise as the fracture occurred. At this juncture Mr. Pugh excused himself and the seance continued without him. Colonel Hardwick, Mrs. Pratt, and Mr. Price still retained their fingers upon the top of the table, which was resting on the remaining leg. Suddenly, without warning, and with a violent snap, the table top broke into two pieces; at the same time the remaining leg and other supports of the table crumpled up, the whole being reduced to what is little more than matchwood. . . .

Another device invented by Price was a bell jar in which a telegraph-like key was placed, around which was blown a stable soap bubble. If the key were depressed a signal would activate. Even with these restraints, Stella C.'s telekinetic force was able to get into the jar, through the bubble, and generate enough force to push the contact key without disturbing the bubble which completely surrounded it.

Shifts in temperature within the seance room was one phenomena prolifically occurring in the Stella C. experiments. Usually the room would become abnormally cold. Price installed thermometers and periodically photographed them, verifying that the phenomenon was not an illusion and that the temperature did mysteriously lower during the seances. Sometimes these shifts would be over ten degrees. This phenomenon had been known to occur with other mediums but Price was the first to verify it objectively. This phenomenon might be a key to understanding the PK ability, since it has been noted in poltergeist outbreaks as well. When air is cooled, energy is given off. For example, if one cubic foot of air is cooled one degree Fahrenheit, fifteen foot-pounds of energy is lost. It might be that a medium somehow uses PK to lower the temperature of an area and the PK force uses the lost energy by redirecting it into telekinesis.

Further phenomena observed with Stella C. were lights, odd semiphysical masses, and conventional raps and telekinesis. One apport was observed when a branch fell into the seance room, and during one sitting while in trance, Stella C. predicted a cover picture of the *London Daily Mail* which appeared five weeks later.[15]

This last incident is representative of the association between PK and ESP. Palladino and Tomczyk both had mental phenomena as well as the PK upon which the investigations centered. Stella C. also falls into this pattern. In fact, most mental mediums also have PK. In reviewing the gifted subjects discussed in the last chapter, Ossowiecki had PK abilities which he demonstrated by consciously moving heavy objects without contact, but gave up the ability to develop his ESP more fully. Lalsingh Harribance has been successful not only at ESP tasks but in PK tests as well. Spontaneous PK occurred with Croiset on at least one occasion.

The other gifted subject Price was able to study under ideal conditions was Rudi Schneider. Rudi's older brother Willi was also tested by Baron Albert von Schrenck-Notzing. When Willi decided on a more conventional career, Rudi, who had already developed similar abilities, came into the limelight. Rudi Schneider's phenomena were similar to those of other physical mediums—telekinesis, materializations, raps, and so forth. Like most, Rudi underwent a trance state during which a new personality would manifest to direct the phenomena. When Rudi came to Price's attention, the British investigator decided on a foolproof method of experimentation. He brought Rudi to England in 1929 and sittings were held with *all* the participants under control. All the sitters and Rudi were required to sit with hands and feet in special gloves. If anyone shifted his feet or let go of his neighbor's hand during the sittings, a signal light would immediately indicate that someone had broken the control. The signal system was developed so that the culprit would be immediately isolated. Despite this unprecedented method of control, phenomena were displayed as usual. Several telekinetic effects were recorded (and later photographed) including whitish handlike formations. The seance room curtains would billow and some force would touch, jerk, and pull at the sitters. Small objects frequently moved as in the following incident. ("Olga" is the medium's guide speaking through him.)

> Waste-paper basket slowly and very evenly lifts to a height of about six feet, remains suspended for a second or two and the curtains blow right out and knock the basket toward the sitters. It falls to the ground. Curtains blow out very violently, right up to the ceiling seemingly, and in falling back brush against the sitters' heads. Olga says Mrs. Mars has very good power . . . Olga says, "Sh-sh" and as we listen the table falls over with a crash. It is then heard to rap fifteen times. Rudi's head has fallen forward on to Mr. Price's chest. Hand-bell rings.

Price noted specific physiological quirks about Rudi's mediumship. During the sittings his respirations increased until he was hyperventilating at an unbelievable rate. He also rhythmically stroked the sitters' legs. New light was shed on this oddity when Eugene Osty tested Rudi in France. Osty designed his experiments so that target objects for Rudi's telekinesis were guarded by an infrared beam which if interrupted would set off a camera flash. If Rudi tried to touch the objects manually, he would be photographed in the act. Osty employed this method to control Rudi but inadvertently made a rather surprising discovery. The beam was often intercepted and the cameras activated, but Rudi was always found to be still in his chair controlled manually by his experimenters. The beam had been activated by Rudi's PK ability. It was also discovered at that time that something penetrated the beam and oscillated it as though a force was rhythmically obstructing it. The rhythm of the oscillations was continually shown to be *exactly* double Rudi's respiration rate, and this was further evidence that the telekinetic force was closely linked to the medium's own organism.

The only unfortunate incident in Rudi's career came when he returned to England for another series of tests with Price who hoped to photograph his phenomena. Price secured a photograph revealing Rudi's arm free enough from control to fake a PK phenomena. Rudi denied the charge. The original photograph has recently been found again after having been carefully concealed by Price before his death. The photograph is a clear double exposure which vindicates Rudi Schneider from any charges of fraud. Rudi married shortly after these tests, became an auto mechanic, and in 1957 died at his home in Germany.[16]

All through this discussion of mediumship, mention has been made of semiphysical bodies that suddenly appear and disappear with mediums such as Palladino, Stella C., and Schneider. Sometimes these forms built up into hands. Carrington once held such a hand that manifested with Palladino but it melted in his grasp. This was one of the phenomena which led Carrington and others to postulate that the medium possessed some semiphysical organic substance that could be projected and molded into forms, or remain invisible and move objects. Sometimes these forms would extrude out of the medium's body and if disturbed shoot back elastically into the body. The nature of this substance occupied a great deal of attention in continental parapsychology during the 1920s and 1930s, and is the basis of a fascinating controversy. Several physical mediums specialized in this phenomena, such as Eva C. who was tested by Gustave Geley, Charles Richet, and the Baron von Schrenck-Notzing. During Eva C.'s productions, masses of white material extruded from her mouth, vagina, and other orifices, building into flat faces or figures. Richet coined the term "ectoplasm" for this sub-stance and the forms were called materializations. A clear evalu-ation of Eva C. is hard to make since her whole career was steeped in controversy and the possibility of fraud could not be dispelled by the method of control used with her. Nonetheless, the usual explanation was that Eva merely swallowed gauze or chewed-up paper which she then regurgitated. This explanation does fit some of the conditions. Eva would first be searched and then placed inside the medium's cabinet hidden by a curtain. (Remember that Palladino always sat *in front* of the curtain.) The experimenter was told when to pull back the curtain, re-vealing her draped in ectoplasm, or miniature faces extruding around her head. The seances were usually held in semidark-ness. On the positive side, though, Eva C. was never caught de-liberately faking. Sources of her "ectoplasm," if fake, were never found during the pre- and post-sitting searches. In addition, she would be forced to swallow dyes to color her stomach's con-tents. Despite this, ectoplasm would extrude from her mouth with no hint of dye or stain.

The greatest controversy surrounding Eva C. was caused by photographs of her materializations. As stated, these had a flat, two-dimensional appearance. When stereoscopic pictures were taken during Schrenck-Notzing's experiments, the back view of one such form showed letters identifying that the faces were cut-outs from the paper, *Le Miroir*. To the critics this was obviously fakery—Eva cut out the pictures and hooked them to her head, and unfortunately was caught when she allowed the back of the picture carrying the printed title *Le Miroir* to be photographed. However, the pictures, although they did *represent* faces which had appeared in the paper, did not correlate with them. Even as critical an investigator as Everard Feilding showed that the pho-tographs of the materializations showed differences in dimension to the *Le Miroir* photos. Next the critics argued that Eva had made up sketches from the paper. But would she have written the name of the paper on the back? Believers argued that per-haps Eva C. had been subconsciously impressed by the pictures which served as the "topics" for her materializations.[17]

And there the case rests. Although several top psychical re-searchers believed in Eva C., no definite or fraud-proof test was carried out. Eva C. gave sittings to the SPR during which several faces materialized and whitish extrusions were witnessed and photographed. The SPR commission could not arrive at a decision, and although it did not find any cause for suspicion it would not endorse her either. The report was rather negative and Eric Dingwall, an extremely critical researcher, would not sign his name to it. Geley's work with Eva C. was later discredited when it was found that his written reports did not coincide with his photographs. Evidence was uncovered that Eva's patron may have been faking the results, and recently discovered unpublished photographs reveal suspicious appendages hooking the materializations to her hair. Despite this, no actual fraud was ever found. The main problem with Eva C.'s materializations is that they looked so unpalatably ridiculous. Yet, since we do not know what ectoplasm is supposed to look like, we really cannot say that something does *not* look like it!

A little better evidence for the existence of ectoplasm comes from another medium, Stanislawa P. Although later in her career she was caught trying to fake telekinesis with a hand that had escaped control, some earlier photographs of her materializations are difficult to dismiss so easily. Chief among these are a group of frame-by-frame photographs of her ectoplasm extruding from her mouth and then reentering it. For control purposes, Stanislawa P. had to wear a gauze garment completely covering her head. (A similar control was used with Eva C.) Ectoplasm was seen and photographed leaving the medium's mouth, passing through the gauze, to continue forming on the other side. Any type of physical matter could not pass through the fabric which invalidates the regurgitation theory. Unfortunately, the frame-by-frame photos of the substance leaving and reentering her mouth were taken during an experiment when the gauze shield was not used. Stanislawa P.'s "substance" looked similar to Eva C.'s.

Whatever ectoplasm is or is not, the phenomenon seems so rare and draped in so much controversy that few American or British parapsychologists have given much stock to reports of it. The problem is only aggravated by the fact that the phenomenon of ectoplasmic materializations has not been witnessed since the 1930s. Nonetheless, careful students of the history of the subject cannot so quickly dismiss the possibility of a semiphysical *organic* structure as extruded by physical mediums.

Schrenck-Notzing, during his experiments, secured a specimen of the substance and analyzed it biologically. He found it to be composed mostly of common organic material.

More convincing evidence for materializations came from experiments with Franek Kluski in Warsaw. Kluski's main productions during his well-controlled darkened seances were luminous manifestations. These glowing masses would mold into pillars, appendages, and into fully formed phantoms (successfully photographed) that would pace and float about the room. Telekinesis was common. However, Kluski's uniqueness lies in his "hand molds," a phenomenon for which no one has ever been able to find a normal explanation. During the sittings a bowl of paraffin was regularly introduced into the room. The "forms" would be asked to dip into the hot paraffin and leave a cast of their often invisible appendages. Splashing would be heard and, after the completion of the sitting, molds representing very human-looking hands would be found. Some of these molds were interlacing hands, or large hands with only very small wrist openings. The molds were also paper thin. No normal way to produce them has ever been found except by the theory that whatever formed them dissolved *within* the mold. Any attempt to remove a normal hand from the mold would either break it or stretch the opening. The molds were so detailed that even ridges in the skin were reproduced. Colored dyes were sometimes secretly placed in the paraffin to offset the theory that Kluski brought the casts with him and introduced them by sleight of hand. These hand molds represent the best evidence psychical research can offer that some semimaterial substance can be produced by rare mediums which can build into semblances of organic structures. Clearly, the hand molds were formed by a structure, such as the white phantom hands seen with Palladino and Schneider, which, completing their tasks, merely dissolved without damaging the mold. Kluski also could produce mental phenomena and warned his chief investigator, Gustave Geley, not to take a plane which ultimately crashed, killing the pioneer French parapsychologist.[18]

Despite the controversy, scandal, and difficulty in the investigation of spontaneous telekinesis, poltergeists, and physical mediums, a slender line of cohesion does unite these diverse phenomena. They all show a peculiar mixture of PK and ESP, are subconsciously produced (most physical mediums enter trance before producing any phenomena), share similar types of phenomena and are dependent on the physical organism of the principle agent. Unfortunately, the universality of the poltergeist has not been matched by a similar proliferation of good physical mediums. The type of brilliant displays recorded in this chapter have not been observed for several decades. The logical argument is that the earlier parapsychologists were either duped or malobservation existed at the seances. The records, however, do not support this view.

There is a possible interpretation, however, and it is similar to the problem of the experimenter effect. Most of these mediums were a product of continental European parapsychology, not of British or American research. This might be a key. The founders of the SPR who laid the basis for the British-American parapsychological tradition were philosophers and psychologists interested in proving that man might survive bodily death, and they then turned to the study of the ESP abilities of the human mind. However, continental parapsychology was organized by biologically oriented researchers. Richet and Geley were physiologists, Hans Driesch, a biologist, and Schrenck-Notzing, a physician. They were more interested in the physical phenomena of parapsychology. Since ESP and PK are related phenomena, often manifesting side by side in a gifted subject, it is not hard to believe that parapsychological tradition gave rise to ESP subjects in England, yet good PK subjects in continental Europe. Whatever the underlying force behind both ESP and PK, the ability controlled by the subconscious mind may be molded by the cultural and parapsychological needs and wishes of a given era. In other words, British and American researchers expected their gifted subjects to demonstrate ESP, while continental investigators were searching for PK. Each received exactly what he wanted, and the ESP-PK ability merely assumed the form that was expected or sought.*

* The only major American case of this period was the investigation of Mrs. Mina Crandon or "Margery." The case, because of its scandal, is almost impossible to evaluate, although Hereward Carrington accepted the genuineness of some of the phenomena. See T. R. Tietze's *Margery*, (1973).

This is, of course, only a suggestion for the historical anomaly of why physical mediums vanished. But it is consistent with the more recent history of parapsychology. When Rhine opened a bold new frontier of statistical ESP testing, world parapsychology followed suit, and from that time no great physical mediums have appeared. Recently, however, parapsychology is shifting away from the strict psychologically oriented research approach to a framework in which biology and physics can more readily contribute, and as parapsychology becomes more "physically" oriented, PK research has begun once again to unveil gifted PK subjects. In the Soviet Union, where parapsychology is seen as a biological science and ESP as a physical-biological phenomenon, there are now reports of PK mediums whose phenomena are very reminiscent of the old-time physical mediums.

When parapsychology became an experimental science, it began by exclusively studying ESP. However, just as the older anecdotal literature had prompted a new approach to studying ESP, the older claims of physical phenomena also hold a similar promise. However, the study of telekinesis is no longer to be a darkened seance room, cops-and-robbers affair, but an exact experimental study. The study of deliberate attempts by subjects consciously to exhibit psychokinesis in the laboratory opens the next chapter in the story of mind over matter.

8

Mind, Space, and Matter
—PK in the Laboratory

It was shortly after Rhine began his ESP research at Duke University that his attention turned to the possibility that mind over matter might not be a myth. Like so many discoveries in science, the fact that PK could be experimentally exhibited was almost accidentally uncovered. In 1934 a young gambler approached Rhine with his claim that he could mentally influence the fall of dice. Since each die face has a one-in-six probability of landing on a particular number when the die is thrown, the gambler's claim could be easily tested along the same lines as had been done in ESP testing. For example, in a run of twenty-four throws, chance could account for four hits, but no more, over a long period of time. Rhine and the gambler began to experiment informally with dice throwing, and Rhine was amazed by what he witnessed. This meeting initiated forty years of new explorations into PK, a subject which had fallen from favor in parapsychology as the general decline of PK mediums set in.

For his first formal experiment Rhine used two die and threw them by hand for high combinations (the total target being anything above eight, thus giving a possibility of fifteen out of thirty-six target combinations). Twenty-five subjects were used, each throwing their own dice. Usually they threw the dice against a wall to allow them to bounce randomly. As with ESP, some of the results for certain subjects were above chance, and out of a total of 562 runs (24 falls each), there was a deviation of 300 above chance, a probability of over a billion to one.[1]

In order to place better controls on the experiments, Rhine introduced into the tests a ten-inch-wide board covered with corrugated cardboard. The board was set on an incline and the dice were pushed off the top, rolling down and bumping randomly before coming to rest on a specified face or faces. Again, after 108 runs had been completed using this technique, above-chance scores were achieved. The introduction of the board was necessary to offset an obvious criticism of the first experiments. Throwing dice by hand could bias the results, since one can rig the dice by certain throwing techniques. The adoption of a more impersonal manner of rolling the dice by merely shoving them down a board considerably reduced this possibility.

A further innovation by Rhine in 1936 was the adoption of an even more rigid testing apparatus. This machine was an electrically driven, long, rectangular, meshed-in cage mounted on an axis. By activating the machine the axis would reverse the dice from one end of the cage to the other, hitting several baffles as they moved. By using this machine the subjects would not have to touch the dice at all, and this novel procedure permitted Rhine, J. L. Woodruff, and A. J. Linzmayer to act as subjects. (Remember that Woodruff and Linzmayer were talented ESP subjects also.) The dice used were specially made with the dots painted on. Conventional dice with indentations were often biased, since the indentations could affect the weight distribution. But even with these tight controls, Rhine and his co-workers achieved a rate of success of $p = .0008$, far beyond what coincidence could account for.[2]

So far the evidence for PK follows the same pattern as ESP. After Rhine began experimenting, results were so convincing that others attempted to confirm the PK effect, and like the story of ESP, they too were successful. A husband and wife team, Mr. and Mrs. E. P. Gibson in Michigan began to use a similar PK machine and achieved highly successful results. However, it was not merely the above-chance scores alone that forced recognition of the PK ability, but it was the discovery of an odd pattern which firmly placed PK on the parapsychological map. It had already been known that ESP followed a decline pattern during an experiment. At first the subjects score well, but the results gradually fall off as the testing proceeds. When World War II broke out and the United States was drawn into it, Rhine lost most of his graduate student help. Limitations in the amount of experimentation that could be carried out was serendipitous, since it allowed the researchers remaining time to give a fuller statistical evaluation to the data already accumulated. Since the PK test results were uniformly kept, recorded, and filed, there remained a large body of material to be evaluated. It was at this time that Betty Humphrey showed that the existing experimental results for PK had the same habitual decline as did ESP. Miss Humphrey demonstrated this by taking a typical PK score sheet and dividing it into equal quarters. Then, by counting the hits in each segment, one could see at a glance what the scorers' rate had been for each unit of the test. Analyzing several early experiments she found that, as the experiments went on, a countable decline of successes occurred. This decline was called the QD effect (quarter distribution). The importance of QD lies in the fact that chance, even if somehow contributing to above-chance scores, which is in itself highly unlikely, could not result in a habitual decline effect creeping in without being noticed by the original experimenters.[3] For example, in Rhine's first experiments, the tests were made in short cycles of three runs. Tallying all these brief tests, the decline, by comparing the first to second to third run of each minitest, showed an average of 6.09 to 5.15 to 5.05 successful hits. Further analysis of the QD was made by J. G. Pratt who at the time was on leave from the Navy. He reevaluated the Humphrey–Rhine data and came to a similar conclusion regarding the decline affect.

By this time several other experimenters had confirmed PK. Homer Hilton and George Baer tried an experiment to determine if different die sizes would affect PK. They did procure significant results, but the die sizes only gave inconsequential differential results. (See the *Journal of Parapsychology*, vol. 7, 1943.) Another young experimenter was Frank Smith who tested himself for PK and achieved good results. Harvey Frick experimented with a large number of dice thrown simultaneously, while Margaret Pegram threw for doubles. All this work was quite successful.

However, the most elaborate of the early explorations came from the Gibsons in Michigan. At first they worked under C. E. Stuart's coaching, and Mrs. Lottie Gibson became the prime PK subject. At first conventional PK tests were carried out wherein each run consisted of thirty-six throws of six dice, trying for a selected die face. Different targets were selected throughout the experiment. The first tests were carefully recorded and Lottie Gibson scored exceptionally well even for PK (p = .00058). Later, when the dice were thrown from a cup and the target faces were equally chosen to offset bias, she continued her scoring streak over a total of 200,000 die falls.[4] Subsequently, the Gibsons used Rhine's PK apparatus.

Since the Gibson material had been so diligently recorded, analysis of the results was an easy matter, and that project fell to J. G. Pratt who found that Mrs. Gibson's best success was on the first throw of the first run. Similar position effects were found so systematically that Pratt concluded that "These results, occurring as they did without the knowledge of either the subject or the experimenter, and being so far outside the immediate purpose of the tests that they remained undiscovered for ten years cannot be ascribed to biased dice, wishful thinking, recording error, or any other reasonable counter hypothesis. PK is left as the only adequate cause of these effects" (*Journal of Parapsychology*, vol. 10, p. 268).

Pratt later returned to the Gibson data for further analysis because of his own PK tests done in conjunction with J. L. Woodruff which seemed initially to be unsuccessful. Later examination of the scores did reveal a cancellation effect due to a decline pattern. Woodruff had begun by scoring well, but the decline to chance results had canceled out the mathematical significance of the success. Pratt also discovered a "preferential effect." When analyzing hits on high-numbered targets (four and above), they found that success had been achieved, but low-numbered targets had been psi-missed. A cancellation had occurred. Remember that this was before parapsychologists became fully cognizant that a preference for one task might be nullified by a dislike for another, both operating during one experiment.

The preferential differences were really only a trend in the

Pratt–Woodruff work and this led to the reanalyzation of the Gibson material. Indeed, when the analysis was complete, it became fairly obvious that, even though Lottie Gibson had achieved remarkable scores, she scored even better on certain die faces because of some undefined psychological preference.

These patterns lead Pratt to present his paper, "Rhythms of Success in PK Test Data" (*Journal of Parapsychology* 11 [1947]: 90–110) based on Margaret Pegram's experiments. As with ESP testing, the Pegram PK results showed initial success, decline, and a salience streak at the end of the run. This mapped out into a somewhat asymmetrical U curve. After analyzing the total results Pratt found that the best ones were achieved on the first column of a page, clustering at the top and bottom; the rest of the results were generally just chance. Pratt stated his view about the U curve effect: "This all adds up to the fact that the PK test . . . is a grossly inefficient instrument for measuring PK ability . . . It seems as if the test is choking off the very function which it was designed to measure." Pratt found a similar lawfulness in his reevaluation of the Gibson data.

The discovery of a demonstrable PK effect and its QD pattern led Dr. R. A. McConnell at the University of Pittsburgh to carry out an experiment designed specifically to bring these amazing implications to the attention of his scientific colleagues. Obviously, PK radically affects such physical sciences as physics and McConnell was eager to present his findings, if he could attain them, in a more conventional scientific publication than the *Journal of Parapsychology*. For his early 1950s experiments he used Rhine's PK apparatus with himself and two assistants as experimenters. Over a period of eighteen months, 393 subjects made 170,000 die throws. Each subject tried for a single target face and produced three pages of data—the last two using the machine, the first hand-thrown results. Although the total results were not significant, the QD showed an exceptionally strong decline effect. This, then, was evidence of PK. McConnell searched for a journal in which to publish his findings—one where the scientific community would be most likely to see it. Resistance to the idea of PK was strong, but eventually he placed his paper, "Wishing with Dice" in the *Journal of Experimental Psychology* 4 (1955): 245–269.

PK research was also carried out in Great Britain during this same period. Dennis Hyde tried to repeat the Duke tests but failed to achieve any significant results. Dennys Parsons also attempted to get evidence of PK but failed.

As with PK research, experiments during the entire period ranging from the 1930s to the 1960s tried to fathom the nature of PK—what physical, psychological, and physiological factors affected it. However, before turning attention to this material, a new chapter in the story of PK should be examined. So far PK had been attempted by making dice fall on certain faces or clusters of faces. However, W. E. Cox introduced a new technique in which the dice were "willed to fall" not on a certain face, but on a specified location on a landing platform. Placement PK, as it was dubbed, was shown to be doubly important when a Swedish experimenter-subject, Haakon Forwald, used a similar technique with astounding success.

Once PK research got under way there was a surge of interest in adopting it to new types of targets and experimental designs. R. H. Thouless, in England, tested PK on spinning coins, while Elizabeth McMahan at Duke tested children with disks painted different colors on each side. However, in the 1950s W. E. Cox began his long career at ingenious and successful PK testing. At first he used a typewriter case as an open experimental platform. He made the case into a checkerboard-like target area of 252 squares, each given a code number from one to six. Dice were thrown into it, willing them to land on certain squares. Cox used several subjects for his test and utilized twenty-four dice. He found that the original testing task did not pay off very successfully, but success was achieved eventually when he altered the task in this way: instead of the subject's trying for just pure placement, he also tried to make the die faces correspond to the numbered square on which it fell. Thus, if of the 252 squares several were marked as 6, the subject would throw not only to make a significant number of the dice land on the 6, but with the 6 face landing uppermost. This new technique was successful and showed that his subjects (or himself if we keep in mind the experimenter effect) could not only affect the die face to land with a specific number uppermost, but the ultimate position of the die as well.[5]

After carrying on further tests with cubes, coins, marbles, and other target materials, Cox had developed a new apparatus for testing PK. (Since then Cox has developed several other ingenious gadgets for PK testing.) This machine consisted of three tiers leading to a checkerboard platform made up of squares, each alternately designated as A or B. A cube or several cubes would fall and bounce randomly through the three tiers before coming to rest. Hopefully the subject could influence a majority of falling cubes to land on either A or B during the test. However, dice or other cubes could be "blocked" on the upper tiers with only a percentage of the original dice hitting the checkerboard. Since PK-missing had been observed during testing, Cox theorized that "negatively" influenced dice would be trapped in the upper tiers, while "positively" affected ones would make it to the bottom and to the correct target squares. The experiment was only marginally successful as a whole, but the total success rate on those dice reaching the bottom was quite high.[6] Cox later used a similar design for a five-tier experiment, and still later invented a machine to monitor the falling of drops of water. While none of his many experiments carried out over several years have been stunningly successful, many of them did offer small but solid evidence of PK. When analyzed together, Cox's runs of minisuccesses form into a huge mass of statistical evidence for PK. While Cox is prone to believe that PK, like ESP, is a natural ability that will become evident over long periods of testing, other parapsychologists have suggested that Cox himself is an exceptionally fine PK subject influencing his own experiments.

The fact that the experimenter might be his own best subject is aptly typified in the work of Haakon Forwald, a brilliant Swedish electrical engineer who has over five hundred patents to his credit. Forwald also has tested placement PK and has attained the same type of success as Cox. He began his experiments after successfully inducing telekinesis during table-tipping experiments. (In this type of experiment several people sit around a table with their hands placed on it, hoping that the table will begin to move. Often it will tip and gyrate. While usually it is only the unconscious muscular movement of those around the table causing it, similar to movements of a Ouija board, some of the motions become so complex at times that a PK force seems to be at the root.) This lead Forwald to contact Rhine in the late 1940s and begin more formalized PK testing. From 1949 to the present he has systematically experimented and published successful PK projects. At first he used a dice-throwing apparatus similar to the Duke device. However, the dice (ten) were allowed to fall onto a table divided into two target areas. Forwald alternately tried to make the dice fall on either side of the table. His second experiment was so successful that the probability was well over 1000 to 1, and his results were published in the *Journal of Parapsychology* as a paper by Rhine in 1951 (pp. 49–56).

As an engineer Forwald was just as interested in the nature of the PK force as in the evidence for PK itself, so he started experimenting with target material of different composition and mass such as wood, steel, aluminum, and so forth. Although no astounding successes were achieved, there were subtle indications of PK, especially when the target order for the sides of the table was AB instead of BA (letters represent the sides of the tables). Forwald was more successful when the target side was A and then B for some unfathomable psychological reason than when the order was reversed. His experiments also indicated a very shallow decline effect which was substantiated in his third experiment to an almost staggering degree. Forwald used cubes of different materials at the same time for the test, and consciously willed only those cubes of a certain composition to be affected. The experiment gave a CR of 4.0 or p= .0006. The "willed" dice fell consistently as directed mentally, while the others remained at chance. Oddly, though, Forwald did not find that objects of weightier mass were affected more by PK. For example, while steel seemed to be influenced less than wood, the ratio of success was not in accordance to their mass. Forwald also found some evidence for a decline effect which was confirmed when he tested two colleagues: the first half of the experiment gave + 41 hits, the second half − 86! [7]

Forwald also tried to determine the energy used during PK by measuring the probable deflections the targets were subjected to. The upshot of this was an attempt to experiment with the PK force along the conventional theories and principles of physics.

To do this Forwald designed an experiment using cubes with different surface roughness and different weights. An evenly distributed PK force, theoretically, would not affect dissimilar weights and surface textures in the same way. Forwald hoped to show that the PK force did not evenly affect targets of disproportionate structure as would not be expected of any conventional force affecting moving objects. The end results showed that rough cubes were more successfully moved, but this could have been due to psychological reasons as well as physical reasons. Ultimately, Forwald discovered that as soon as he tested a hypothesis, his results would immediately show a *reversal* from his intent. This suggests that PK was an unconscious process. For example, in a crucial test Bakelite cubes were pitted against heavier aluminum cubes. While the aluminum cubes were twice as heavy, five times more force had been applied to them. This ruled out the theory that there was a correlation between mass weight and exerted PK force.

After the exceptionally fine results obtained in Sweden, Forwald came to Durham in 1957 to work under new conditions with outside supervision, and he eventually succeeded in replicating his PK success under formal observation. In 1959 he ventured to the United States again to experiment in conjunction with R. A. McConnell in Pittsburgh, but was not successful at the PK tasks. However, when he returned to Sweden, successful results were again obtained. The difficulty in his Pittsburgh work may have been due to the time factor. Forwald did not have any warm-up time as he had in Durham to get used to the mechanism McConnell had developed for the experiments. Under such conditions it was not odd that his PK should abate temporarily, since it had been shown previously that ESP also disappeared when there was a sudden change of experimental conditions or when an observer was introduced. Forwald himself seems to have become a little disenchanted with a purely physical approach to PK and turned to target die-face experiments with some success. Ultimately he suggested that PK was involved with the gravitational field in the target area. He arrived at his conclusion by default, since he was unsuccessful at measuring any electrostatic, magnetic, or nuclear effects in the target area, and this only left gravitation as the most conspicuous alternative: PK, then, affected the gravitational field selectively to achieve a required result.*

The pioneering work of Rhine, Humphrey, Cox, Forwald, and others offered stunning evidence for the PK hypothesis, but it did little to reveal the actual nature of PK. Even Forwald's painstaking work actually told us more about what PK was *not* than what it was. Although research into the actual nature of PK has not been carried out as extensively as with ESP, there is some experimental evidence that sheds at least a weak light on the mind-over-matter mystery. Since PK was obviously a physical manifestation, researchers were interested in the question of how distance would affect the phenomenon. The pioneering work in this quest was initially carried out by Dr. Carroll Nash, a biologist who tested PK subjects at different distances from the target area. His first experiment showed no correlation between distance and success at PK between three feet and thirty feet from the experimental area. Nash's second experiment fared little better. Other distance tests failed to show that PK attenuated with distance as would be expected had a conventional physical force been operating.

So far, then, PK and ESP seemed to share common characteristics—they did not, at face value, conform to physical lawfulness, showed marked decline effects, and subjects successful at one could also achieve success at the other. In order to test if the basic PK process was in fact inherently related to the ESP process, several experiments were conducted in which PK and ESP were combined. The PK target (such as a die face) was concealed from the subject so that only by ESP could he determine the correct target for a given throw.

R. H. Thouless, testing for ESP-PK using himself as the subject, utilized die-face targets chosen by randomizing six numbered cards. Each throw was an attempt to match the specific concealed top card of the deck, and then repeating the test until he had accumulated 2592 trials. The results were encouraging but not fully significant. A further exploration was made by

* For a criticism of this view, see Joseph Rush's review of Forwald's monograph, *Mind, Matter and Gravitation* in the *Journal:* ASPR 65 (1971): 223–26. This monograph expounds the gravitational theory of PK.

Karlis Osis, then at the Duke Parapsychology Laboratory, who used three subjects, including himself, for the test which consisted of giving the subject a sealed envelope with a random number order of possible die-face targets numbered one to six. This order had to be matched by the subject's die throws during the PK task. The total results confirmed that ESP could be used to discover the target and PK to direct the die falls to match the hidden targets.[8]

A third search was made by Laura Dale, but it failed. G. W. Fisk, working in England, and Forwald made still further tests. Forwald correlated five of the die faces with the standard Zener card symbols which he then shuffled, creating a random target order. A die was thrown twenty-five times in an attempt to succeed at PK by using ESP to discern the targets. After 2500 trials he achieved a positive deviation of $+73$. This might not appear to be much, but statistically it calculates to $p = .0003$, a very significant probability.[9] Taken together then, the experiments confirmed the use of ESP-determined PK responses.

Experiments were also carried out to see if mental influences on PK could affect the gremlin-like ability. Laura Dale conducted a sheep-goat PK test, but did not find any clear-cut evidence that belief or disbelief had anything to do with PK as it had so strongly affected ESP. However, she did find that better experimental results were obtained with women than with men, which she attributed to her own feelings of ease when working with women. These experiments were carried out in the 1940s and published by the ASPR in 1946 and 1947.

Robert Van de Castle, at the time a graduate psychology student at the Duke Parapsychology Laboratory, tried to correlate PK to standard psychological test measurements. Like Humphrey's ESP work, he chose subjects who were rated as either expansive or compressive, and rated them on a five-point scale. Although his scores were not spectacular or even statistically significant, there was a consistent decline ratio from the more expansive personalities to the compressive subjects who psi-missed just as they had done in ESP testing. Next, Van de Castle carried out a sheep-goat test, the results of which were suggestive but not significant. Finally he turned to the Rorschach tests and found that subjects who were more spontaneous in their attitudes were better PK subjects.[10] It might be noted that PK tests were also carried out with hypnotized subjects, but with no meaningful results.

In essence, then, PK, although confirmed, was not as strong or easily directed as ESP. In fact, the most stunning evidence of PK, besides the slowly mounting and finally avalanching success of Forwald, has been inferential, notably the QD effect. PK effects seem so subtle and will-o'-the-wispish that even those psychological factors which fairly often affect ESP do not measurably affect PK. Nonetheless, behind all of this was the fact that PK did follow certain characteristics of ESP. It appeared that it was more a mental process than a physical one. It is difficult to do justice to the immense mass of experiments carried out on PK, but it is unfortunately true that these experiments, while telling us that PK does exist, offer very little more.*

Experimental PK offers a new order of telekinesis—a psychophysical influence on moving objects. Oddly, few star subjects have appeared out of the PK research, with the exception of Forwald, whose measurements of cube falls revealed considerable deviation from how they normally should have fallen. This type of PK seems to have replaced the older, more striking PK manifestations of the physical mediums. Nonetheless, the establishment of the PK force did alert parapsychologists to the feasability of using PK on static objects, a belief that had all but died out with the disappearance of the great mediums. Notably, PK research engendered a new interest in poltergeist phenomena.

Despite this situation PK on static targets has slowly been making a reappearance, and parapsychology today offers considerable modern evidence for PK on stationary objects.

In 1928 Professor Christian Winther of Copenhagen reported on strong telekinetic displays precipitated by his subject, Anna Rasmussen, which included movements of stationary objects, raps, and mental influences on a pendulum system. However, not long ago, in 1956, during the height of PK research, experi-

---

* A complete summary, review and interpretation of the PK problem outlining all these experiments was incorporated into a book *Mind over Matter* (1967) by Louisa E. Rhine. This volume should be consulted for further information regarding this subject.

ments with Rasmussen were recorded demonstrating the older form of PK on static targets. In some of these experiments Mrs. Rasmussen would stand several feet from a pendulum system and mentally attempt to move one or several of them to make them strike the sides of the glass casing in which they were often set. Several successful trials were made but unfortunately Mrs. Rasmussen's greatest achievement was with her own pendulums, not the experimenters', which does dull the significance of the evidence.[11]

A revival of an old form of PK jolted parapsychology in the 1960s when Jule Eisenbud, the Denver-based psychoanalyst, published a book, *The World of Ted Serios*, in which he outlined several successful experiments with a subject who was able mentally to influence photographic film. Serios could stare into a camera, then snap the shutter release and obtain unusual effects, including totally white or totally black prints. However, more notable were actual pictures, often blurry, that would be found inexplicably impressed on the snapshots. These pictures were often of buildings. Serios sometimes stared through a little device he called a "gizmo" which consisted only of a piece of rolled-up cardboard. Critics were quick to jump at his use of this device, claiming that it hid a fraudulent mechanism. However, no evidence of fraud was ever found with it or with Serios.

There are several incidents in the Serios experiments which are hard to account for by fraud. Occasionally a target picture would be shown to him which he would then try to impress onto the film. While Serios usually did not have much direct control over his ability, some of these tests were successful. (See *The World of Ted Serios*, p. 166.) Sometimes Serios' pictures showed inexplicable distortions from the original structure. One odd photograph showed a building at a Canadian airport which had the word Canada spelled CANAIDA! Other such anomalies have cropped up in the photographs which would not have occurred if Serios was faking the results. Most striking have been those experiments in which he tried to impress the snapshot with a concealed target, such as a target picture enclosed in an envelope. During such tests Serios would sometimes verbalize his impression of the target. When correct, this revealed not only his ESP ability, but a distinct relationship between his ESP and PK. On one rare occasion he stared into a motion-picture camera, and when the film was developed, a frame-by-frame analysis revealed the gradual formation of a mentally projected picture.

Eisenbud later carried out some novel tests with Serios including attempts to influence movie film and impress a camera through a lead-impregnated glass shield.[12]

The appearance of Ted Serios showed that PK was not restricted to the more conventional forms of PK. There were few attempts by outside investigators to test him, although Ian Stevenson and J. G. Pratt worked with him at the University of Virginia. They did get some results but would not commit themselves as to whether they accepted the genuineness of Serios' abilities. Like so many gifted subjects, Serios lost his abilities soon after.

Actually the phenomenon of thoughtography is not a new one, and the history of parapsychology offers several previous counterparts to Ted Serios. In France, Commandant Darget carried out several experiments at impressing photographic plates with mental pictures. Using himself as a subject in one experiment, Darget stared at a brandy bottle for half an hour, and when he placed a plate in the developing bath, he concentrated on an image of the bottle. When the plate was completely developed, a clear representation of a bottle was found. In Japan, Professor T. Fukurai carried out several similar experiments with amateur psychics which he eventually published as a book, *Clairvoyance and Thoughtography*. In these experiments the subjects were asked to imprint Japanese characters onto photographic plates. The subjects were often given a stack of plates and directed to imprint the character on one of the *inside* plates. Fukurai achieved stunning success, but his experiments, carried out from 1910 onward, were so criticized by the academic community that he lost his college position. And, around 1945 Hereward Carrington discovered a gifted subject, Joseph Ruk, who could impress pictures or odd light configurations on wrapped-up plates.[13] So, no matter how odd Serios' ability seems, his pictographic phenomena have considerable precedent.

The resurgence of interest in static PK has led to attempts to quantify experimentation in this area. One notable effort has been made by Gertrude Schmeidler with Ingo Swann. Swann, who has experimentally demonstrated several forms of psi ability, took part in an experiment in which his task was to change the surface temperature of a distant object. For the test Schmeidler set up a set of graphite and Bakelite pieces, hooked to thermistors which could be continually monitored. During these tests Swann could alter the surface temperature of the targets, making them either warmer or colder. Interestingly, when he concentrated on affecting one target, other targets in its immediate vicinity were found to alter similarly. However, more peripheral target objects also shifted in temperature, but in a negative direction. This suggests that somehow a field is being developed by PK which affects the area around the target. This is also reminiscent of the Stella C. experiments where it was proposed that the PK force generates energy from the atmosphere which subsequently cools. It is then redirected. Schmeidler suggested a similar phenomenon in the Swann experiments.[14]

Interest in this form of static PK has also resulted from the fact that once again parapsychology has found PK mediums whose abilities seem on par with the types of telekinetic demonstrations witnessed during earlier days. Notably, much of this material has emanated from the Soviet Union, although Western parapsychologists have been able to verify Soviet claims with at least one gifted PK medium, Nina Kulagina.

Originally Kulagina was studied not for PK but for "skin vision" (sensing colors, and so forth by touch) by the dean of Soviet parapsychology, Leonid Vasiliev. During the first PK experiments he asked Kulagina to attempt deflecting a compass needle by PK, and she was able to do it on one of her first tries. Formalized experiments were conducted by Zdenek Rejdak starting in 1968, and during these tightly controlled experiments Kulagina was able to deflect a compass needle while holding her hand a few inches away from it; move small objects, usually sliding them across a table by PK; and other similar tasks. Kulagina's physiology was carefully monitored, and it was found that she lost weight, her heart beat arrhythmically, her blood sugar level rose considerably, hormone secretions were affected, and she suffered considerable pain and general discomfort.

The chief Western parapsychologist permitted to observe Kulagina has been an English physicist, Benson Herbert, who traveled to the Soviet Union with his colleague, Manfred Cassirer. Herbert was one of the first to bring films of Kulagina's PK out of the Soviet Union.

On one visit Herbert brought with him a hydrometer (a sealed tube that measures the density of the liquid in which it floats) floating in a saline solution encased by a screen. Since electrostatic forces can often move objects that might mimic PK, the device was monitored by an electrostatic probe to guard against this.*

Despite all the controls Kulagina was able to affect the hydrometer:

> Kulagina, after moving her chair only a few inches nearer to the table, had apparently fallen into a state of concentration . . . and was gazing intently at the hydrometer . . . Kulagina slowly moved her arms, raising them so that the palms of her hands faced toward the instrument. Shortly after, the hydrometer began to move away from her in a straight line across the full diameter of the vessel, a distance of 2½″ and came to rest at the opposite side, the transit occupying some 90 seconds. She then lowered her arms and remained quite still. The hydrometer remained stationary for two minutes, then commenced to move again, at the same speed as before, retracing its path until stopped by the edge of the glass nearest her.

During Herbert's visit, both he and Cassirer also witnessed deflection of a compass needle and the precipitation of physical burns on Herbert's own arm by Kulagina's PK.[15]

Two other Western parapsychologists to visit the Soviet Union and witness Kulagina's PK were J. G. Pratt and H. H. J. Keil. As Pratt writes in his *ESP Research Today:*

> We had thought it would be valuable psychological preparation to show Kulagina some of the test objects we had brought in our luggage. We therefore placed a few objects on the table, where they were actually standing in the open pages of a large-sized guidebook of Prague we had brought. To our

---

* If a person is charged with static electricity by a Wimshurst machine and stands on a rubber insulated mat, the charge is enough so that the subject can move small objects by passing his hands over them.

surprise Kulagina began concentrating in her characteristic manner upon a small covered plastic cup, all the while saying that she had not tried her abilities in a year or more and was not sure she could do anything . . .

Suddenly Kulagina stopped holding her hands near the object and began breathing deeply for a few seconds. After that she resumed her efforts to cause the plastic cup to move, but with a distinctly different manner of going about it. She was obviously straining very hard and her hands were trembling from the effort. The empty cup between Kulagina's hands remained stationary, but a small wooden cube we had placed on the table and that was about four inches further back on the book moved two times. The block slid about one-half inch toward Kulagina but angled toward her left, then it moved again in the same way about five seconds later.

During an earlier trip Pratt had seen Kulagina slide a cylinder over aquarium gravel.

The fact that Kulagina's PK often misses its mark, so to speak, once again indicates that PK is not so much a mental force but some sort of field. Forwald had suggested this in his PK work, and the experiments with Stella C. and Ingo Swann also support this theory. Lastly, poltergeist effects seem to be shifted about by a moving field. In Kulagina's PK, photographic paper placed under the target objects have often been found clouded as though some force field had affected it. The field theory of PK was further substantiated by experiments with an American counterpart to Nina Kulagina, Felicia Parise.

Miss Parise was originally an ESP subject at the Maimonides Hospital's Dream Laboratory where research has been conducted for some years under the direction of Dr. Montague Ullman, Dr. Stanley Krippner, and Charles Honorton. Miss Parise, in addition to her ESP success, tried to imitate Kulagina's displays and discovered that she possessed a similar ability, including the power to deflect a compass needle guarded by a bell jar, and was ultimately able to slide small objects to and fro by PK. However, the most notable and revealing experiment with her was carried out by Graham Watkins and was reported by him at a symposium during the 1973 Convention of the Parapsychological Association. Miss Parise was able to deflect a compass needle by PK so that it pointed in the wrong direction. When the compass was moved to another location in the experimental room, the deflection ceased. Yet, upon returning the compass to the original target area, it deflected again. This suggested that some sort of PK field had been set up. Watkins also placed photographic film at varying distances from the subject and found that the film closest to Miss Parise was considerably fogged, while those at further distances were fogged to a much lesser degree. This would be in keeping with how normal energies act.

The experiments were discontinued when Miss Parise found that they were both physically and psychologically distressing. Nonetheless, these experiments continue to suggest that PK is not a quickly projected beamlike force, but an actual mentally constructed force field. Interestingly, the Parise experiments throw new light on one of Forwald's previous experiments in which he had procured significant success at PK tasks of getting doubles when two dice were used. Even though he suddenly changed the target, he continued to achieve above-chance results not for the new target, but for the doubles. This seems to indicate the operation of a similar type of psi-activated and radiated field hinted at by Watkins' discovery that the PK force became so localized that a compass placed back within its perimeters once again deflected. Could Forwald have set up a PK field similar to Miss Parise's which he could not affect? More evidence for this theory was procured by Watkins in later experiments with anesthetized mice.[16]

Graham and Anita Watkins began the experiments with the premise that a person might use PK to offset the effects of anesthetics. Two mice were anesthetized with chloroform, and a subject was then given the task of using psi to wake up the target mouse. For a typical test either the left or right mouse would be designated as the target for a series of trials with different pairs of mice. Not every subject was successful at the task, but certain subjects, usually those who had shown strong ESP in more conventional tests, could consistently wake up the target mouse and rouse it before the other drugged animal became animated. However, the Watkinses found a linger effect which is in keeping with the new concept of an actual PK field. If Watkins alternated the targets per trial between left and right mouse, subjects failed to achieve success. It was only when *one* side was consistently chosen as the target that they secured results. If the right side was chosen as the target area, and then after several trials the target was changed to the left side, the right-side mouse would still continue to wake first. The subjects seemed to have built up a PK field, not an on-and-off-per-trial force.

There were other fascinating sidelights to the Watkinses' research. As just stated, only gifted subjects were able to achieve any measurable success, and the total statistics of the experiments are astronomical. Watkins monitored his subjects to see if there were any physiological concomitants to their success, and he found that a state of hyperalertness and activity, such as speeded up heartbeat, seemed to be linked to success. He then took previously unsuccessful subjects, trained them through biofeedback to produce the same physiological states his successful subjects had employed, and then these subjects began to achieve results as well. As with his previous work with Miss Parise, photographic film left in the target area often fogged.

PK on living organisms is not a new idea in parapsychology. There have been experiments using PK to make microscopic animals such as paramecia travel in certain direction, or to affect the growth of fungus cultures. But the obvious implication of PK on living systems is the promise that it might contribute to the healing process. Psychic healing is an extremely problematic area of investigation in parapsychology. Since the human body is a mystery, it is difficult to isolate if PK is actually contributing to the healing of a diseased or wounded body or whether it is only some normal function of the magnificently complex biological organism. The anecdotal evidence for psychic healing is not very impressive, since proper medical reports are rarely brought forward to substantiate the claim of a healing. Dr. D. J. West did a critical analysis of eleven of the best authenticated healing cases which the Catholic Church has verified as occurring at the famous shrine at Lourdes, France. Despite the laudable attempt of the Church to verify these cases, West found that all of them could be harshly criticized on medical grounds and were close to being worthless as scientific evidence for healing. See West's *Eleven Lourdes Miracles* (New York: Garrett Publications, 1957). This is not to say that healings did not take place but only that, to be used as rigid scientific evidence for psychic healing, the cases were too faulty.

Despite these hazards there have been experimental studies of psychic healing that have shown that PK can contribute in the healing of biological organisms. The pioneer studies into this area have been chiefly the novel research of Dr. Bernard Grad of McGill University, using a gifted subject, Oskar Estebany, who claimed healing abilities. For his experiment mice were employed and placed into three groups after they were surgically wounded. In one group were the targets which Estebany would try to heal. One group was left to heal normally, and a control subject tried to heal the third group. The test consisted of Estebany's merely holding the mice's cage twice daily for fifteen minutes. By carefully watching the wounds it became clear that his group healed much faster than the other two.

For his next experiment Grad used plants as the target, and barley seeds were planted and watered either with containers of water which had been held by Estebany or with regular water. Again those seeds nourished from the treated water were affected by some form of PK. The treated water yielded more plants and larger ones. To rule out the possibility that Estebany treated his water chemically, the experiment was rerun using closed and sealed beakers. The success rate was the same.

After these initial successes, Grad ran a similar experiment but with different subjects. This test was to compare the effects of water held by a psychiatrically normal adult to water held by one of two mental patients. Better quality plants grew from the water held by the normal adult than by the water held by the two mental patients.[17]

In order to learn a little about Estebany's healing PK, a process-oriented experiment was designed by Sister Justa Smith, chairman of the chemistry department of Rosary Hill College, Buffalo, New York. Sister Justa's theory was that healing was caused by the subject psychically affecting enzyme activity in the body. Enzymes serve as chemical catalysts which speed up chemical activity in the body. To test this hypothesis she prepared bottles containing the enzyme trypsin and subjected them to ultraviolet light which reduces enzyme activity, or to a magnetic field which increases enzyme activity. Four bottles were used daily; the first remained as a control, the second was held by Estebany, the third was treated by ultraviolet light and then held by Estebany, and the fourth was exposed to strong magnetic fields. The enzyme activity in those solutions treated by Estebany equaled the effect of magnetic fields on the enzymes, and the bottle of ultraviolety treated enzymes that Estebany "healed," equaled the activity of the normal control bottle.[18]

Like ESP, PK seems to be a force that can be manipulated to carry out any number of different tasks. Although many theoreticians such as J. B. Rhine, Robert Thouless, and J. R. Smythies have tried to guess what relationship PK has to the way man functions in the world, we have practically no understanding of the physics of PK; why it is affected more by psychological than physical factors and determinates; why ESP and PK are so mysteriously linked; or how we might inadvertently use PK to control our own environment. One of the major problems is that PK is even more elusive in the laboratory than ESP. Despite these difficulties a few positive things might be said about the PK ability.

First, PK can assume various forms. Just as ESP, although a unitary system, can be either telepathic, clairvoyant, precognitive, or retrocognitive, PK can also assume different forms. It can move objects, heal tissue, become visible as suggested in the older mediumistic literature, set up fields, or project itself for one specific purpose, such as moving a target during a poltergeist outbreak. Secondly, PK does show a *few* similarities to physical laws, unlike ESP which completely transcends them. In this respect one can cite such factors as the vortex lawfulness that Roll found with poltergeist trajectories, or the Ingo Swann experiments which suggest that PK conforms to certain principles of thermodynamics. The third major finding about PK is that it is neither a completely physical nor a psychological manifestation, but a blend of the two—a psychophysical ability. This last finding is perhaps the most important, since it shows that mind and matter are not distinct entities but might actually be linked by some as yet unfathomable process.

9

New Horizons in ESP Research

The coming of the 1960s brought a mild cultural revolution that had an impact both upon science and society. The publicity and controversy over psychedelic or mind-expanding drugs evoked a new interest in the human consciousness and its various states. Interest in Eastern religion, and concomitantly Yoga, Zen, and other practices, psychedelics, the occult, and finally para- psychology spurred on a renaissance. Popular culture was im- mersed in a new fascination with the boundaries and mysteries of the human mind.

The fact that the mind is subject to varying states of aware- ness has given parapsychology another clue in its search for ESP. While we normally think of our conscious lives as existing in either sleeping or waking states, the human mind is capable of varying degrees and levels of consciousness. Besides our normal waking state, we are also subject to states of lethargy, rapture, hysteria, meditation, trance, reverie, stupor, and mystical awareness. Even though there are few solid facts about psi, the certainty that our waking alert hours are manifestly not con- ducive to ESP has been a major stumbling block in parapsycho- logical research. However, when it became obvious that the waking state is only one in a continuum of mental worlds, parapsychologists systematically began to explore other states of mind in the hope of finding psi-conducive levels of awareness. The relationship of ESP to altered states of consciousness has become one of parapsychology's many new horizons.

Thanks to such devices as the electroencephalograph, it is now easy to monitor the human brain and objectively determine when a subject has undergone a shift in his state of consciousness. The EEG records the electrical activity of the brain. Most mental states such as concentration, relaxation, and sleep have particular rhythms which are graphed by the EEG and are easily monitored. Relaxation, for instance, is typified by an alpha rhythm, which the EEG records as tight bursts of close-knit, jagged waves.

The mind in relaxation has begun to show that it can elicit psi better than its regular alert state. As mentioned in the chapter on ESP in the laboratory, R. J. Cadoret found that alpha activity in his subjects was related to ESP success. Later, Rex Stanford discovered that alpha abundance did not correlate with psi activity directly, but alpha decreases during certain portions of the ESP run corresponded with little ESP-induced variance and that alpha increases induce more active variance. Lastly, it was found that Lalsingh Harribance scored better during ESP tests when he was producing high amounts of alpha.

The search for a correlation between alpha and ESP has not been limited to these few studies. Rex Stanford carried out two further experiments which also showed a similar relationship. Working with students at the University of Virginia, the volunteers were asked to make fifty precognitive Zener card calls. The experiment was run while the students were lying quietly in a dark room and hooked up to the EEG. Before the formal experiment, the subjects were monitored to judge their base line of normal alpha activity. In both experiments Stanford found that his subjects scored better in ESP when alpha accelerated (measured by cycles per second increased over the subjects' base line.) [1]

The novel breakthrough, which is a natural outcome of alpha ESP research, is that one can now judge the level of alpha activity as it increases and wavers to see if these shifts correlate to similar fluctuations of the ESP ability. Three experimenters, Charles Honorton, Richard Davidson, and Paul Bindler, conducted an experiment using biofeedback techniques. (Biofeedback is a discipline in which the individual is taught by practice to scan his own internal automatic responses. For some reason becoming aware of these responses allows the subject actually to control them. With a little practice, the subject can control his own brain rhythms.) Using biofeedback, Honorton tested twenty-three subjects for clairvoyance with standard symbol cards while they relaxed in a darkened room. The subjects were then instructed either to generate alpha or suppress it. While no overall ESP results emerged from the experiment, nor any significance found between generation/suppression conditions, alpha shifts were marginally related to ESP success.[2] Before this experiment was designed, Charles Honorton ran a test with ten subjects and had found a significant correlation between ESP and alpha.

Despite these promising leads other alpha ESP tests have failed. While a few studies have shown no relation to psi, others have even shown psi-missing. But, it does seem that alpha might yet be some sort of key to psi for the following reason: in tests such as those conducted by Honorton and Stanford, it was not the overall ESP scores that were significant, nor a correspondence between a particular subject's amount of alpha and ESP scores as compared to other participants'. It was the correlation between the shift to increased alpha and a corresponding shift in ESP scoring. This would indicate that ESP is not, as had been widely believed, a one-shot transferred experience, but a natural ability that operates during certain mental states that we have as yet been unable to harness.

The failure of consistent alpha-ESP relationships during experimental testing (and despite this brief summary, the failures do outweigh the successes) had led Rex Stanford to state in his replication study paper: "The actual experimental work has so far failed to support, with any consistency, the so-called 'alpha ESP hypothesis.' " Despite Stanford's remarks, the "alpha ESP effect" has had sufficient, though scattered, verification to demand attention, even if the effect seems to be slight and capricious and even negatively correlated with ESP success.

However, it should not be thought that alpha is in any way a state of mind in itself. It is only an indicator of an overall psychophysiological state. In this respect some cogent remarks were included in the Honorton–Davidson–Bindler report which deserve quoting:

> It does appear that the simple presence of alpha is not, in itself, a necessary or sufficient condition for the activation of ESP. Honorton conceptualized the problem within the framework of an altered states of consciousness (ASC) paradigm and suggested that, "psi activity may be related to a relaxed, passive state of mind, relatively devoid of visual imagery, and in which there is a decrease in externally-directed attentive activity." Due to the wide individual differences in reported subjective states during alpha production, Honorton hypothesized that the "degree to which an S's [subject's] alpha output is related to his ESP performance may be a function of the degree to which he experiences an alteration of normal awareness or attentiveness during alpha." He therefore suggested that it might be advisable to include self-report scales and/or post-experimental interviews to ascertain the degree to which S's [subjects] report entering into a ASC during alpha production.

This is exactly what Honorton and his colleagues did with considerable success in their experiments. Subjects who gave high "state reports" (state reports can be loosely defined as the subjects' subjective evaluation of their own shift in consciousness) yielded good ESP scores.

The views expressed by Honorton are pregnant with ideas, for he suggested that ESP is correlated not to a specific brain state, as recorded by its electrical activity, but to a specific altered state of awareness. Such alterations have been known to occur through hypnotic suggestion, drugs, and, most significantly, rigorous meditative practices from Christian contemplation to Buddhist Zen and Indian Yoga, all of which have the achievement of altered states of consciousness (ASC) as their universal goal. And it is to these vistas that parapsychology has turned with increasing attention.*

---

* Because of space limitation it would be impossible to outline *all* experimental studies relating ESP to ASC. In the following sections only a few representative studies will be outlined typifying the type of parapsychological approach that can be made.

Meditation represents a truly unique control of consciousness. Oddly, even though all forms of meditation try to achieve a state of ASC, the techniques are often markedly different. For instance, many forms of Yoga are extremely passive, while some Zen schools are very active and even agitated as the student tries to solve a *koan* or unsolvable puzzle in order to achieve insight into the universe. During meditation the brain rhythm often goes beyond simple alpha into deeper rhythms which almost typify a waking trance. EEG recordings of Zen masters have showed extremely peculiar readings. In 1963, before the consciousness boom, R. H. Thouless wrote in his book, *Experimental Psychical Research:* "My own favorite hope for getting reliable ESP scoring is the practice of the meditational techniques used in Eastern religions. These include the adopting of certain postures, breath control, and voluntary inhibition of discussive thought. They are reported to produce paranormal capacities as a by-product."

One attempt to study ESP in subjects versed in meditational practices was made under the direction of Karlis Osis and Edwin Bokert at the American Society for Psychical Research. For their rather elaborate experiment, small groups of screened subjects met weekly for meditation sessions for a period of six months. The participants chose their own form of meditation. Following a half hour of meditation, an ESP experiment was run which was modeled after the Groningen experiments with Van Dam. A checkerboard-like apparatus was set up and the subject had to indicate which square had been chosen as the target by the experimenters. Like the Groningen tests, the subjects sat in front of a curtain, extended a hand through it, and blindly indicated which square they thought was the target. The experimenters remained in a different room and viewed the proceedings on a television monitor. A different type of ESP test was also used during this study in which an agent would concentrate on a photographic slide and send the theme to the percipient. The statistical evaluations made of the study were enormously complex. However, certain features did stand out. Primarily, Osis and Bokert, who had conducted in-depth interviews with the subjects, found that meditation led to certain stable psychological dimensions, including feelings of self-transcendence, and openness. These two dimensions, which seem to result from the meditation training, were linked to ESP success and manifested as both psi-hitting and psi-missing.[3] Those who showed these traits showed ESP.

The Osis–Bokert study was an attempt to elicit psi with experienced meditators, but a far different test was carried out by Gertrude Schmeidler who used subjects who were generally unacquainted with the subtleties of meditative practices. Each of six graduate students made an ESP run, and afterward a visiting swami gave a brief talk on meditation and instructed them in Yogic breathing techniques. Then the students carried out the brief exercize and made another test run. The first run showed only chance results, while the second gave ESP results at odds of 100 to 1. Unfortunately, the experiment was based on so few runs that it is hard to define clearly if the meditation had anything to do with the minimally significant ESP effects observed. Schmeidler herself offered seven possibilities for the success, some which she rated as probable, others as improbable: (1) a fluke of chance; (2) greater confidence in approaching the ESP task; (3) the result of greater interest; (4) a form of attentive appreciation of the lecture; (5) the effects of the breathing itself; (6) the psychic influence of the swami; (7) a combination of numbers 2 and 6.

Meditation is significantly linked to sensory deprivation (SD). As its name implies, sensory deprivation attempts to create altered states of consciousness by blocking off or depriving normal access to sensory stimuli. For example, the subject might be placed in a tank of water with eyes bandaged, and the water kept at body temperature. Or he might be placed in a pitch-black isolation booth. Subjects who have undergone severe SD experiments report bizarre changes in thought-processes, both pleasant and unpleasant. The subjects often report vivid hallucinations as well. Sensory deprivation offers certain parallels to meditation which sometimes requires extreme ascetic practices, such as isolation, hunger, and self-chastisement. These practices are undergone for just a single purpose—to block away the external world so that the student can delve into the mind's internal world without distraction. Simple meditation has a similar goal of turning off stimuli and intrusions from the outside world.

Sensory deprivation similarly coerces the subjects into such a state without, however, the requisite mental conditioning. Meditation and sensory deprivation have a similar product—the subject is occupied with nothing but his own thoughts.

There are scattered anecdotal accounts of ESP-type experiences occurring during sensory deprivation experiments.* More formal testing to find an SD–ESP correlation has been made by Charles Honorton and others. Thirty subjects were selected, and to facilitate the sensory-deprivation state, they were placed in an isolation cradle which consists simply of a floating platform supported by a metal frame. The subject is enclosed and strapped to the cradle to inhibit physical movement and is then blindfolded and his ears blocked. As the cradle gently gyrates, the subject loses space-time orientation, and shifts in states of consciousness often become a by-product.

During the test, the subjects rated their own shifts of consciousness, and at the end of thirty minutes an agent would start sending a randomly selected target picture. The subjects then reported their mental imagery. Outside judges compared the verbal reports to the target pictures and rated them on a one-to-eight scale. Ratings of one to four were judged hits, five to eight were considered misses. Similar to his work with alpha and ESP, Honorton found that the overall test was not successful; however those subjects who reported strong shifts in mental states did show ESP. Those who reported little shift in consciousness scored at chance level.[4]

Honorton has designed a similar test without the complication of the isolation cradle which has a significant bearing on ESP and sensory deprivation, and has so far been extremely successful at demonstrating ESP. In the ganzfeld experiments, as they are called, the percipient sits in a comfortable chair in front of a light in an isolated room; Ping-Pong ball halves are placed over the eyes, blocking vision and producing only an amorphous, diffused visual setting; a tape track of ocean waves is piped through earphones on the subject's head. The participant is thus partially

* For one such anecdotal account, John Lilly in his *The Center of the Cyclone* (New York: Julien Press, 1972) records his combined sensory-deprivation and LSD experimentation which prompted spontaneous ESP and out-of-the-body experiences.

sensorily deprived. At the onset of the experiment he begins to free-associate, talk and describe whatever thoughts or mental pictures come to mind. These are monitored and taped by an experimenter. At a randomly selected period during the test, an agent begins to send a target picture or a series of related pictures. After the test, the verbal associations can be compared to the target theme for the test period (both the subject and the monitor are not aware of the chosen target). The subject is also asked to pick out the likely target from a pool of targets.

Initial reports on these tests have been published in the *Journal: ASPR*, vol. 68, no. 2, and have shown exceptional promise. A television crew from Toronto even traveled to the Maimonides Hospital's Dream Laboratory where this research is being undertaken and filmed a session with one of its subjects, Ellen Messer. Miss Messer's verbal report at the critical time was of nightclubs and Las Vegas. The target chosen randomly by Honorton was a reel of pictures, *Tour of Las Vegas*. In such experiments both qualitative and quantitative evaluations can be made of the material.

The range and effects of the major psychedelic drugs (LDS, mescaline, and psilocybin) have been fiercely debated. When these drugs were first used in biological and psychological research, it was thought that they were a chemical replica of mental illness. Other researchers, however, discovered that their subjects experienced not the chaos of mental disturbance but rich introspective insights and even mystical-type experiences. It soon became clear that the psychedelics offered a chemical state so sensitive to psychological variables that the mind-expanding experience could produce an incredible gamut of different levels of awareness.

That the use of psychedelics might be a chemical road to ESP has long been suggested by anthropological research. Although purely anecdotal in scope, some of the reporters of drug-induced ESP experiences definitely felt that the drug caused the paranormal event. Since it is impossible to judge how often ESP occurs in day-to-day waking life, one cannot come to any definite conclusion as to whether the drugs really had much to do with the ESP experience. It could have occurred anyway. Since ESP occurs spontaneously during our conscious alert hours, it might be pure coincidence that some of these occurrences would take place while the individual is under the influence of a drug.

Nevertheless, many primitive cultures have specifically employed drugs for the purpose of inducing psi. Charles Danville-Fife, an Amazon explorer, recorded in his book, *Among Wild Tribes of the Amazons*, how he watched the natives brew a drug, known as yagé, from the vine *Banisteria caapi* which is an extremely powerful hallucinogen. Danville-Fife reported that a military officer, Colonel Morales of a nearby military attachment, took the drug himself and immediately gave details of the death of his father miles away. News verifying Morales' vision came several weeks later.

Similar anecdotal evidence of chemical ESP has cropped up spontaneously during formal drug research. The research team of Jean Houston and R. E. L. Masters pioneered drug research in the United States and noted ESP occurring during some of the experiments. However, these experiences were purely spontaneous and anecdotal. One woman, for instance, described a ship caught in an ice floe and reported its name, *France*. Two days later the team learned of a ship named *France* caught in ice off Greenland. The accident occurred at the same time the session was being held.

Although they are not parapsychologists, Masters and Houston did carry out some ESP experiments with their drug subjects which they reported in their book, *The Varieties of Psychedelic Experience*. Unfortunately, the experiments are not formally reported or described in detail. Standard Zener card tests were run, and although the results were insignificant, a few subjects did show increased scores during the LSD session. Next, Masters and Houston had an agent hold a slip of paper while the subject tried to discern the message on it. Sometimes this procedure was more successful. When the target was a "snake with arched head swimming in [a] tossed sea," the drug-influenced subject reported imagining a Viking ship thrown about in a stormy sea. This is only one of several successes that were reported.

Unfortunately, the scattered success of psychedelics to seemingly elicit ESP responses has never been confirmed experimentally. In fact, most psychedelic ESP experiments have been total failures. Two Italian researchers, Roberto Cavanna and Emilio Servadio, carried out a lengthy project of ESP testing with LSD and psilocybin in which several subjects had to describe pictures in sealed envelopes. Although there were one or two hits during the long run of tests, the entire project showed no evidence that psychedelics had any effect on producing psi. In fact, the project had so few hits that the entire plan was a dismal failure.[5] In Holland a group of experimenters headed by S. Van Asperen de Boer used psilocybin-influenced subjects for standard ESP card tests and psychometry. Again, no success was reported.[6] The long line of failures also included Zener card tests with LSD intoxicated subjects by J. Whittlesey. Karlis Osis tested gifted subjects while they were under LSD but found that they became so engrossed in the experience that they had difficulty carrying out the planned experiment. Walter Pahnke at the Maryland Psychiatric Research Center did ESP-LSD experiments where the subject had to designate a target square on a game board. Five subjects were used in the pilot experiment but no evidence for psi was found. Pahnke's accidental death soon after put a finish to the project.

Oddly, parapsychologists of the past did report some success with experimental ESP and drugs. Years ago mescaline had been used at the Pasteur Institute in Paris, where agents sent pictures telepathically to drug-intoxicated percipients with astounding success. Similarly, in the Soviet Union, Leonid Vasiliev conducted experiments with a single subject who took mescaline and then tried to get impressions of objects in sealed boxes. This series showed several good qualitative hits such as "something that is yellow, oval, hard, orange, and tinkles" when the hidden object was a small pendant compass. But the results have to be canceled out because the subject was not first tested in a normal state to see if she had any psi ability to begin with. So, we cannot tell if the drug really enhanced the psi ability.[7]

Although the experimental evidence for hallucinogenic ESP is poor, the prospect that these drugs might yet be a formidable tool for parapsychologists cannot be completely dismissed. The failure of many research projects might stem from the very type of ESP tests that have been undertaken. For example, both Osis and Masters-Houston found that their subjects were so preoccupied with the psychedelic experience itself that they lost all motivation in the ESP tests. Mainline psychologists have also reported on the difficulties of carrying out psychological tests with hallucinogenically intoxicated subjects. They too have found that the subjects lost all interest in carrying out tasks if they were distracted from the drug experience itself. It appears that parapsychologists have to develop new types of ESP tests particularly suited to the psychedelic experience.

Psychedelic ESP tests also have been based on the hypothesis that the drug state would produce ESP. As the work of Honorton and Stanford has shown with alpha, sensory deprivation, and the like, ESP may not be produced by the drug state itself, but only activated as the subject enters into a changed state of consciousness. This shift might produce the ESP, not the state itself. Previous researchers might have been looking for ESP in the wrong place. Also, Honorton's use of relating ESP to the introspective shift reports of the subject might also prove more fruitful. Psychedelic ESP experimentation run along lines similar to ganzfeld tests might conceivably be an easier media for psi to appear than the types of task-oriented experimentation that have so far been carried out. Unfortunately, the tight legal bind on drug research makes the prospect of future large-scale experimentation a pessimistic matter.

It should be mentioned at this time that, although the evidence for drug-induced psi is extremely shallow, the belief that one has experienced ESP is a common characteristic of the drug experience. Charles Tart, the University of California psychologist, polled several marijuana and psychedelic drug users for his book, *On Being Stoned*, and found this claim very frequent. However, as Stanley Krippner has stated, ". . . psychedelic drug usage typically gives an individual subjective impression that he is extremely psychic; whether this impression is valid remains to be empirically demonstrated."

The relationship between parapsychology and hypnosis has been a long and fruitful one. As has been pointed out the early history of mesmerism was imbued with reports of all sorts of paranormal events. However, when researchers such as Charles Richet, William Barrett, and later J. B. Rhine discovered that persons in the normal waking state also showed ESP ability, the cumbersome use of hypnosis as a catalyzing agent was soon discarded. All through the history of psychical research, and despite this development which showed ESP existed in normal states, there have been many attempts to show that hypnosis enhances ESP ability.

Intensive research into this area was undertaken by Emile Boirac, rector of the Dijon Academy in France, at the turn of the century. Like other researchers of the period, most notably the famous psychiatrist, Pierre Janet, he experimented with inducing hypnosis telepathically with gifted subjects. The following is his description of an informal experiment with one of his subjects:

> I seated myself on the terrace, and, while sipping my coffee, looked down on the scene beneath me. Dockmann was sitting in the garden with a friend who was reading a newspaper; his back was almost turned to me and he began to roll a cigarette. I do not know how, but the idea came to me to try the experiment here described, and with all the force of my will, I immediately put it into execution. Concentrating my mind entirely on this one thought, I looked steadfastly in Dockmann's direction, and commanded him to stop all movements and go to sleep. Dockmann did not appear to perceive that I was looking at him, but his actions quickly slackened, and his eyes became fixed. The unfinished cigarette remained in his hands, he suddenly dropped his eyelids, and remained motionless as a statue. His friend raised his head, perceived his condition, questioned him, but obtained no response. A singer seated at a neighboring table became frightened and screamed aloud. I hastened and went down, and in a few moments, by breathing quickly on his eyes awoke my improvised subject, who did not even seem to know what had happened to him.[8]

Not all of Boirac's experiments were so informal, and he successfully demonstrated this same peculiar telepathic feat before the Hypnological Society in France. He also experimented with the tranference of perceptions between subject and hypnotist. If the hypnotist placed something in his own mouth, the subject would describe it; if he pricked himself with a pin, the subject would likewise respond. Boirac's most notable experiments were in the externalization of sensibility wherein the subject would be told to project his sensibility into a glass of water. If the water was pricked, the subject would react by a physical jerk or an exclamation of pain. In some of these tests the water would be so far removed from the general area of the subject that ESP seems the most likely explanation of the success.

Despite this type of claim by relatively sophisticated parapsychologists, research into hypnosis and ESP has not taken any hints from these earlier reports. One notable exception has been Jarl Fahler, a Finnish parapsychologist, who reported a replication of Boirac's externalization of sensibility which showed great success.

Several tests have been made using hypnosis as an aid to ESP utilizing more standardized and conventional types of experimentation. By 1969 close to twenty ESP-hypnosis experimental studies had been reported.

J. J. Grela experimented with hypnotized subjects to see if suggestions to increase or decrease GESP scoring would be successful. The results did show a tendency for scores to fluctuate in accordance with the verbal suggestion. In 1957 Jarl Fahler tested subjects when awake and while hypnotized, under both clairvoyant and precognitive conditions. The overall results were significant; hypnosis had raised the psi scoring average from 4.96 hits per standard run to 5.57. This gave odds of 100 to 1 against chance. In 1958 Fahler and Cadoret published a replication study, again comparing subjects while awake and hypnotized. All three experiments were highly successful, the first of which gave a probability of p = .0000001.

Lawrence Casler studied ESP with hypnotized subjects and with other subjects who were given waking-suggestion treatment. GESP and clairvoyance were tried, and, although no difference in the scoring level for the two tasks was evident, the hypnotized subjects did produce better overall ESP scores. Casler later reported an experiment in which both agent and percipient were hypnotized and tested for GESP. The overall results were 100 to 1 against chance. A third major study on the effects of the subject's self-suggestion was a failure.

Several experiments into hypnotically induced ESP have been conducted by Charles Honorton. In his first test several subjects carried out eight clairvoyant runs in the waking state after having been given hypnotic suggestions to the effect that they would score above chance. Two groups of subjects were designated. The choice of the two groups was based on a psychological test which judged personality factors which Honorton believed would either engender or inhibit psi performance. The ESP test was extremely successful. The "good" subjects did even better after the suggestion, the "poor" subjects much worse. Honorton later replicated his findings in a follow-up study.

Other ESP tests have been run using more novel approaches than standard card guessing. One such attempt was made by Fahler and Osis with two selected subjects. The test was for precognition, and the hypnotized subject had to guess a series of target digits from one to ten. However, the main test was to determine the ability of the subjects correctly to identify upon which of their many responses they felt particularly confident of success. The correlation of those hits accompanied by confidence calls gave a staggering $p = .0000002$!

Charles Honorton and Stanley Krippner reevaluated all of these tests in 1969, graphing out the success rate and the experimental conditions of the thirteen main studies which consisted of nineteen experiments conducted between 1945 and 1969. Only seven reported experiments did not show that ESP was specifically aided by hypnosis. Of course, the main problem in evaluating these results is that a successful experiment is more likely to find its way into print than an unsuccessful one. Nevertheless, the high rate of experimental success during the tests does give credence to the old mesmeric claim that hypnosis is a psi-conducive state of consciousness.[9]

Most of these experiments were carried out before the consciousness boom, and since the mid-1960s interest in altered states of consciousness has become an even livelier topic in parapsychology. This was also coupled with a shift away from the standard card-calling type of tests. The merger between renewed interest in hypnosis and the search for novel ESP test situations led to some highly ingenious hypnotic ESP projects.

Dr. Stanley Krippner tested both hypnotically conditioned and suggestionized waking subjects for ESP, using pictures as the target. During the percipient's hypnotic state an agent would send an art print telepathically. Three different suggestions were given—to perceive the target print while hypnotized; in a dream during a nap after the session; or during dreaming accompanying regular sleep throughout the week. Using this technique both the verbal descriptions and the statistics were often remarkably accurate. One hypnotic subject whose target was Dali's *The Crucifixion*, reported during his nap, "crosses," and during a dream, "a book of Dali's paintings." [10] The overall results showed that while the nonhypnotically suggestionized subjects scored well, their ESP success seemed linked only to their dream records written down during the week. The hypnotically tested subjects scored highly during the posthypnotic nap. This led Krippner to believe that hypnosis speeds up the ESP process.

Charles Honorton and John Stump tried to make hypnotized subjects dream clairvoyantly of art prints set before them in sealed envelopes. After they were hypnotized, Honorton gave the following suggestion: "When I count to three you are going to have a very interesting dream. It will be a very vivid and realistic dream. You will dream about the target in the envelope. It will be as though you are walking right into the picture. You will participate in whatever action is depicted, and you will observe the picture from that standpoint. You will see everything very clearly because you will be part of it." (*Journal:* ASPR 63 [1969]: 175–84.)

Again, although the overall statistics calculated by judges trying to match dream protocols to the actual target art prints were not outstanding, several highly evidential hits were made. Often, although the actual target was only vaguely described, representative or striking colors were reported in the dream. In one case the target was Picasso's *Vase of Flowers and Sea Urchins*. The leaves of the flowers are blue; the sea urchins, orange and brown; the background is silvery with streaks of blue and yellow. Of this print one subject's ESP dream reads:

First I had this impression of color and jewels—purples and blues and deep reds in the bottom part of the picture. Everything was very blurred, but it was as if there were shining drops of jewel-like lights—Then it seemed like there was tinsel and it was Christmas. There was this tall shining silver streak down the right side of my vision. I saw the first impression once again and thought it was perhaps a multi-colored moth or butterfly—at the very end I was getting red and orange geometric shapes—mostly orange.

Although the target picture never completely jolted into dream awareness, this report reveals how the ESP impression nudged into the dream fragments. For instance the orange and brown sea urchins became "red and orange geometric shapes."

Since ESP appears to be particularly at home during the hypnotic state, an obvious question is: Can hypnosis be used to train gifted subjects? Throughout the history of parapsychology many systems have been proposed to help a person improve his ESP. During the early Spiritualist days, psychics often held "development circles" in psi-training. Hereward Carrington once wrote a novel book on the relationship of Yoga to psi training. However, in the 1960s a Czechoslovakian biochemist, Milan Rýzl, announced his ability to develop gifted subjects by hypnotic training. In 1966 he presented a complete description of his technique in a presentation, "A Method of Training in ESP," which appeared in the now defunct *International Journal of Parapsychology* 8 (1966): 501–32.

Rýzl outlined a six-stage method of psi development which he claimed to have employed successfully. In the first stage, the subject is given prehypnotic preparation which consists of an orientation period during which the subject is given motivation to increase his psi ability and is made familiar with the nature, scope, and uses of hypnosis. The second stage consists of normal hypnotic induction. In order to increase suggestibility the experimenter gives the subject verbal commands to hallucinate, carry out physical acts, and so on. According to Rýzl, particular emphasis should be placed on the induction of visual hallucinations, since ultimately they will be the vehicle for the ESP material. The subject is taught at this point to create and maintain mental images. The third phase begins the actual psi training wherein the subject is requested to create mental images of objects laid before his closed eyes. Hopefully the subject will be able to employ ESP in his visualizations prompted by the same type of verbal suggestion which the hypnotist has used to increase non-ESP hallucinations and images. Rýzl reported that at this point in the development of one subject, Miss J. K., when a pair of scissors was placed near her, she responded after some initial impressions: "I said two crossed pencils, but I now have the impressions of two things crossing each other . . . they are decidedly not pencils . . . The ends away from me are pointed . . . but those near me won't appear . . . It strikes me as though two circles are projected out of a thick fog . . . It is a pair of scissors."

Now that the subject can employ psi, in the fourth step he must be trained to identify and remove sources of error which might be mistaken for psi impressions: indistinct visions, errors due to suggestion, normal intrusions from the subject's own mind, and so forth. During this process subjects are trained by acquainting them with these sources of error and this helps them to distinguish true ESP from other intrusions. The fifth step is merely to enhance the subject's abilities by finding its scope, form, and limitations, and finally the last stage is training the subject to enter the psi-conducive state by autoinduction and place it under his own conscious control.

Rýzl's claims sparked a controversy in parapsychology even though the use of hypnosis to train ESP subjects was not novel. Gustav Pagenstecher had used hypnosis years before to develop Mrs. Zierold. However, Rýzl did demonstrate that certain of his subjects had allegedly developed remarkable psi by using his technique, including Miss J. K., a gifted clairvoyant, and Pavel Stepanek. (An American television network was able to film a successful session with one of Rýzl's trainees, but the film was hardly perceptible when developed. Czech government officials refused the team access to further sessions.) The case of Stepanek remains cloudy, since it cannot be firmly established that his ESP was developed by Rýzl. Rýzl did not test Stepanek's ESP before the training, and his ESP talents were only discovered after a few rather abortive hypnotic sessions. Nonetheless, Rýzl's claims, coupled with his gifted subjects, did create a stir in the parapsychological community.

It would be considered a pioneering breakthrough if it could be reported that other parapsychologists have successfully employed the Rýzl ESP-training program. However, despite the promise held by both Rýzl's technique and his gifted subjects, outside attempts to verify the efficacy of hypnotic ESP training following Rýzl's procedures have failed. Several parapsychologists replicated his work and then tested subjects with standard ESP card calls. These attempts failed to support any positive shift in the subject's ESP. It could be argued that Rýzl's techniques would develop free-response ESP material, and not necessarily affect card-calling ESP. John Beloff tried a pure replication of Rýzl's methods but did not find that any type of ESP task was aided by the method.

So when all the evidence is sifted we are left with several alternatives: Rýzl's subjects might have been psychic in the first place; his training procedure merely enhanced dormant ESP in the subjects; or the technique may work for him and no one else. This last option may well be the correct one. Just as there are gifted ESP experimenters, there are gifted hypnotists. It is quite feasible that Rýzl's multiple prowess as an experimenter and hypnotist, as well as his psychological makeup, is such that his method of hypnotic training is extremely useful as he works with his subjects. Other parapsychologists, not having these signal abilities, would not be able to use the same technique successfully.

Despite his reported successes, the Rýzl technique is one of many in parapsychology where a promising lead stops at a scientific dead end. This is not to say that future discoveries might not require a reevaluation of Rýzl's technique.

The value that the study of altered states of consciousness holds to further explorations into ESP is inestimable. While drugs per se do not seem to catalyze the ability, there is no doubt that as a whole ESP has occurred as a by-product of altered states of consciousness to a degree that appears inexplicable by coincidence. There are many possible reasons for this, chief among which are: the conscious and unconscious minds become in closer contact in this condition, which would facilitate the emergence of ESP from the subconscious; the mind searches for new sensory stimuli which might include the scanning for psi; the shift in thought processes might suppress the mind's censor which cancels out ESP impressions from the conscious; altered states often are represented by an onrush of subconscious and repressed material breaking into and preoccupying the mind which, like the first point, may contain much that is extrasensory; changes in awareness might produce transient personality patterns (such as more extroversion and expansiveness) which facilitate psi.

On an even more speculative level, one psychologist, Lawrence LeShan, has suggested that our lives are governed by a sense of individual (or consensus) reality where ESP is out of place in the "natural" world. However, as man alters his consciousness toward mystical states as described by religious ascetics and individuals who have undergone mystical cosmic, or "peak" experiences, he might partake of a new reality which consists of a direct link to the universe, nature, and man. In this new reality, ESP would be common and even expected, since contact with the universe would no longer be dependent on the five senses but perceived directly by the consciousness. ESP would be a natural outcome of this new reality.[11]

Although these views and paradigms are merely speculation, the interrelationships between ESP and ASC do suggest that the key to understanding ESP may not be along the lines of traditional psychology or physics, but along certain principles governing our own consciousness of which we are, as yet, unaware. The fact that hypnosis, sensory deprivation, and so forth reveal a measurably higher degree of ESP singles out the study of altered states of consciousness as one of parapsychology's most fruitful new horizons.

One avenue to understanding psi is by scientifically testing for ESP along lines suggested by spontaneous cases. There is little solid information revealed about psi in spontaneous ESP. However, one fact first pointed out by the ancient philosophers, then by Lambertini, and finally by modern parapsychology is that spontaneous ESP occurs more often during sleep than in waking hours. Thanks to the development of the electroencephalograph, along with other psychophysiological devices, science can now explore the mystery of sleep. It also gave parapsychologists the impetus to delve into the possibilities of experimentally induced telepathic dreaming. This, too, has led to another of modern parapsychology's more productive horizons.

The beginning of the quest came in 1953 due to Montague Ullman's interest in dream telepathy. As both a psychoanalyst and parapsychologist, Ullman had been fascinated by cases of dream telepathy encountered in his own clinical practice. In conjunction with another experimenter, Laura Dale, Ullman began an informal project to test for the possibility of telepathic dreaming. At this time there was no way to monitor dreams, so Ullman and Dale used a "Memory Trainer," a device which automatically set off tape recordings which at a specified time would activate. With the trainers placed under their pillows at night, set so the volume level of the tape was not loud enough to wake them, it was hoped that the same message, listened to subconsciously by both of them twenty miles apart, might effect a similarity in their dreams which would indicate telepathy. Usually the taped message was a nonsense syllable (such as *Zivid*) followed by a suggestion to remember and record the dream in the morning. Sometimes similar dreams were recorded; sometimes a dream would refer to a waking experience of the other; and other times a dream would be precognitive. The following is only a brief extract from the Ullman–Dale records: Dale awoke and recorded, "Someone (me?) was screaming and screaming for help." The same night Ullman's dream record reads, "There was someone like Saul standing in the background. I was reading a musical score. I suddenly said in surprise, 'This score spells out terror!' I awoke with a disagreeable feeling."

Often both Ullman and Dale would record the same theme but laid in a totally different context. When Ullman recorded in his diary a real-life attempt to construct a birdhouse and his thoughts about drilling three holes in the front of his home to help mount it, Dale dreamed of a man planting evergreen trees in a wooden board drilled with holes. There were many other successes, most notably precognitive dreams of actual events.

The year 1953 represented a breakthrough, not only for parapsychology, but also in academic psychology's interest in the phenomenon of sleep. At that time researchers from the University of Chicago were reporting the isolation of certain physiological concomitants to dreaming, including the fact that during the dream state the eyes flick to and fro. Called "rapid eye movements," their production, accompanied by certain rhythms recorded by the EEG, could tell when a subject was dreaming. So, in 1960 Ullman, in conjunction with Karlis Osis and E. Douglas Dean, began to experiment with telepathic dreaming. In order to facilitate this research, the Parapsychology Foundation supplied funds, equipment, and research rooms. Since the president of the foundation was Mrs. Eileen Garrett, the gifted psychic, she became the first experimental subject.

Mrs. Garrett would go to sleep in one room at the foundation after being hooked up to electrodes attached to the EEG. When it was determined that the subject was dreaming, an agent in another room would try to "send" a target picture, the theme of which would hopefully be amalgamated into her dream sequence. When the target was a golden metallic Indian mask, Mrs. Garrett dreamed of abstract paintings, and one "that looks as though it were a sunburst. There is a lot of yellow in it . . . their faces were slightly distorted as though they had just fallen down tired and were kind of sleeping . . . there was something gold."

During these early trials, several indisputable hits occurred when selected subjects were used. However, in 1964 the dream-telepathy research was altered to a more purely experimental procedure. Using new techniques, a qualitative evaluation could be made of dream records and their association to the target, while also giving statistical results which could be used to determine if the hits were beyond simple coincidence.

In order to achieve this, the primary scoring technique would be based on attempts by the subjects to identify the target picture (usually art prints) from a pool of targets and the ability of judges to match correctly a specific dream protocol to the chosen target. Although the dreams were often vague, subjects were able to isolate correctly and identify the likely target when confronted with a whole series of art prints. Even the judges were able to match dreams to targets. Using, at times, complex mathematical methods of evaluation, it was still clear that the results were not due to chance alone but to ESP. However, even if the statistics did not reveal any significance, there was a rich supply of obvious hits gleaned from the verbal reports. When the target was Orozco's painting, *Zepatistas*, which depicts a group of Mexican revolutionaries set against a background of mountains and clouds, one subject dreamed:

A storm. Rainstorm. It reminds me of traveling . . . approaching a rainstorm, thundercloud, rainy . . . For some reason I get a feeling of memory now, of New Mexico, when I lived there . . . There are a lot of mountains around New Mexico, Indians, Pueblos. Now my thoughts go to almost as though I were thinking of another civilization.

Even with obvious successes, the dream-telepathy research got even more provocative with the discovery of their first gifted dream-ESP subject, a psychologist, Dr. William Erwin. Erwin spent considerable time in a long series of ESP tests and scored consistently high when matching his dream records to the targets or when judges carried out a similar task. When the target for one night was Degas' *The Dancing School*, Erwin reported about "a class," "a school," and "one little girl that was trying to dance with me." Two lengthy series of tests were done with Erwin whose total success rate was staggering.

When the Parapsychology Foundation decided to close down its research division, the dream-ESP project fortunately found a new home at the Simon Maimonides Medical Center. Adopting the converted basement of the hospital, Ullman carried on the research with his collaborator, Dr. Stanley Krippner, and was later joined by Charles Honorton. During this new era of research, tests were carried out in clairvoyance, precognition, and long-distance ESP, using similar techniques to what had been done in earlier tests. For clairvoyance tests, the target picture merely was enclosed in a sealed envelope; for precognition the target was chosen after the subject had slept and dreamed.

It is not necessary to detail all these studies or give representative hits and successes. Using the same scoring techniques as outlined above, correlated with obvious qualitative success, subjects dreamed of scenes and pictures that closely resembled concealed clairvoyant targets or targets chosen the next day.* How-

* For example, a gifted British psychic, Malcolm Bessent, dreamed of birds and animals, and of a target of "emotional interest to Bob Morris," a parapsychologist who had done his Ph.D. dissertation on mating habits of ring-necked doves. The target chosen the day after was "birds." This might seem to be merely coincidental, but these "coincidences" went on night after night. At the end of the series Bessent had correctly dreamed precognitively of the target at odds of 1000 to 1 against chance.

ever, one notable experiment during this time was a novel attempt at long-distance ESP, coupled with "sensory bombardment." For this 1969 experiment an agent was placed at the Masters and Houston laboratory, fourteen miles from the Maimonides Hospital. The agent, when trying to send a target, would be immersed in a collage of sounds, projected images, lights, and so forth. One target was entitled *Artistic Productions of a Schizophrenic*, and during the "sending," the agent witnessed projected slides of abstract paintings drawn by a mental patient in Czechoslovakia. The percipients were Alan Vaughan and his wife Iris. Iris recorded of her dream:

> The bombardment . . . was . . . this silly imagery and a lot of it doesn't make sense . . . It was almost mental, more or less conveying a feeling than concrete terms as such . . . They weren't really images. They were like thoughts and moods that were sent out to a person. It was sort of a projection of a whole mood . . . It was weird. It was almost like some sort of psychiatric thing.

A similar experiment was carried out during a rock 'n' roll concert where the audience was shown a target picture, *The Seven Spinal Chakras* by Scralian, while undergoing a barrage of rock music. The Chakras represent a Yogic doctrine that the body has several energy centers, or Chakras, which are activated by a force, the Kundalini, rising up the spinal column igniting them. It travels from the base of the spine to the head. At this time the subject, Malcolm Bessent, dreamed:

> I was very interested in . . . using natural energy . . . I was talking to this guy who said he'd invented a way of using solar energy and he showed me this box . . . to catch the light from the sun which was all we needed to generate and store the energy . . . I was discussing with this other guy a number of other areas of communication and we were exchanging ideas as the whole thing . . . He was suspended in mid-air or something . . . I was thinking about rocket ships . . . I'm remembering a dream I had . . . about an energy box and . . . a spinal column.

The continuing success of the Maimonides research has given parapsychology one of its finest harvests of data about ESP. Not only have gifted subjects shown the ability to dream psychically, but even nonpsychic subjects have been found to show that ESP can affect their dreams. This is a breakthrough, since it has pointed to the possibility that sleep and dreaming can be systematically employed as a means to study or gain access to ESP. As of now this possibility is still only a hope, not a fact. But dream-ESP has opened an entirely new chapter in the search for the paranormal.

As with altered states of consciousness and psi, there are different theories which can account for dreaming-evoked ESP. The most natural is, of course, that ESP often reaches the subconscious and dreams are a normal method for this information to get to consciousness. This theory has been mentioned several times in the course of this book, but dream-ESP research indicates that this view, while not incorrect, may be too simple. Tests have been carried out which show that dreams are not only the carriers of ESP, but might actually be *infected* telepathically by the thoughts or emotions of another person. To explain this, Ullman has propounded what he calls the theory of "psi-vigilance." During sleep the mind is constantly scanning the environment in order to keep in check any threatening stimulus. Thus, we wake up when the phone rings and rarely fall out of bed. He believes that ESP impressions are potentially a very threatening invasion into the consciousness, so the mind's vigilance latches onto incoming telepathic or psi impressions which are then conveyed into the consciousness by any dream in process.[12]

Whatever the explanation for the unprecedented success of the dream-telepathy project, the research has supported Sigmund Freud who even before the birth of experimental parapsychology simply stated, ". . . sleep creates favorable conditions for telepathy."

Paradoxically, just as studying the transcending abilities of the human mind has led to a productive avenue to ESP, another of parapsychology's broad new horizons has been research in the opposite direction—ESP responses in animals (or an-psi research). The fact that animals might be good subjects is based upon many cases of spontaneous animal ESP. There have been many instances of animals acting peculiarly during hauntings, behaving strangely at the time of their master's death, and several well-documented cases of "psi-trailing," a phenomenon wherein an animal, deserted by its master, will travel many miles to rejoin him after traversing areas that it had never seen before. This type of homing suggests ESP in the same manner as if a human agent were clairvoyantly to discover an object hidden in a strange room.

One of the most amazing of these psi-trailing cases, and also one that gave strong corroborative evidence was the case of a collie named Bobbie. Bobbie's psi-trailing consisted of a cross-country trek from Indiana to Oregon. When the story hit the press, Colonel E. Hofer, president of the Oregon Humane Society, launched an investigation into the report and was able to talk with and cross-examine several persons who had seen or taken care of the collie as it made its journey. From these interviews, Hofer was able to verify the case and reconstruct it.

Bobbie's owner was Frank Brazier, a restaurant owner in Silverton, Oregon. On August 6, 1923, the Braziers began a cross-country trip. Arriving in Wolcott, Indiana, their car had to be taken to a garage to have the carburetor adjusted. Bobbie got into a tussle with a pack of dogs and was chased away from his owner. Heartbroken when they could not find their pet, the Braziers sorrowfully began the return trip to Oregon. From what Hofer uncovered, Bobbie began his amazing adventure by traveling upstate to Wolcottville where he was taken in by a hardware clerk. Leaving his newly found home he started his quest in the wrong direction, swimming across two rivers, but then reorientating himself in a westward direction, he crossed Indiana into Iowa where he was picked up by F. E. Patton. Staying with Patton only a day, Bobbie went on to Des Moines, through Nebraska, swam the Missouri River, and was next reported in Denver. What actually happened to Bobbie next is clouded in mystery, but the collie was miraculously able to transverse the Rockies in freezing winter weather. His next move took him through Wyoming and Idaho, and finally to Oregon. By this time it was February and the nearly dead dog found refuge with a kindly Portland woman, Mary Elizabeth Smith, who nursed him back to health. Despite her loving care, Bobbie departed once more and traveled the final seventy miles to Silverton, ending up not at his master's home but at the family's old farmhouse which they no longer occupied. Resting there and regaining his lost strength, Bobbie seemed to realize that something was wrong and set off for his master's restaurant where he was discovered by the Braziers. Bobbie's adventure had taken him a distance of three thousand miles along routes that the Braziers had never journeyed.[13]

In this case the psi-trailing was a return home through unfamiliar terrain. In other cases, ESP is even more suggestive, since the animal *followed* its master to a new and unfamiliar area.

J. B. Rhine and Sara Feather made an assessment of psi-trailing cases which had been sent to the Duke Parapsychology Laboratory. Their twenty-two-page report, "The Study of Cases of 'Psi-trailing' in Animals" (*Journal of Parapsychology* 26 [1962]: 1–22) reported on fifty-four cases which were chosen on the basis of the following criteria: (1) the original source was reliable; (2) a sufficiently specific trait was present by which the animal was recognized, such as a name tag or some unusual physical characteristic; (3) consistency within the report; and (4) corroborative testimony. Of the fifty-four cases, twenty-eight concerned dogs, twenty-two were of cats, and four of birds. Several were trailings over thirty miles. These cases cannot conclusively be held as evidence of animal ESP (or an-psi), since the range of animal sensory abilities, homing instincts, and so forth are still a mystery. Nonetheless, dismissing the idea that coincidence might explain some cases, ESP is a working hypothesis for psi-trailing.

During parapsychology's experimental history, animals have often been used as experimental subjects. Karlis Osis and E. B. Foster carried out research in the 1950s on the ability of cats to run a simple two-choice maze and correctly chose the one route which would lead to food. Fans were blown above the apparatus to eliminate olfactory cues. The test was a 1 in 2 odds, and it was found that some cats tended to select the correct maze route more times than chance would allow.[14]

Osis found that certain cats were better subjects than others. And, as with human subjects, parapsychology's history is impregnated with stories of gifted animal subjects. In 1959, R. J. Cadoret and G. H. Wood reported on their ESP tests with Wood's dog, Chris. In these tests, Chris was taught to paw a certain number of times, from one to five, representing the Zener card symbols. Using clairvoyant testing with a sealed order of cards, Chris made five hundred trials and scored extraordinarily above chance. This test was run by Wood, but when Cadoret came in to see the demonstration for himself, Chris's scores declined well below chance. Unfortunately, the inability to demonstrate consistently what looked like ESP ended Chris's novel career.[15] *

Early attempts at an-psi included testing mice to run a two-choice maze for food guided by ESP. For negative motivation, the mice that failed were killed. Other attempts were made to influence rats to travel a particular route in a T-maze by the experimenter concentrating on a desired path. This same test was later done with kittens. All the reports gave statistical evidence for ESP.

A different type of test was outlined and carried out by Dr. Robert Morris, the animal behaviorist, who has worked at the Foundation for Research on the Nature of Man and later as research coordinator at the Psychical Research Foundation. In his experiments Morris monitored the amount of movement made by the animals for a given period. Nineteen rats were used and their activity monitored. After the experiment several of the rats were killed, the decision to kill or spare being based on a random selection method. The theory was that the rats that were to be killed should precognize the event by much less activity. The results were not conclusive. Morris then designed a similar experiment using goldfish, but instead of killing them they were mercifully only held aloft, out of the water in a net, to provide a precognizable stress period. After the experiment was executed, those goldfish that had been removed from the tank were the ones who had been more active in the base-line period. This might be due to an ability of the animals to show anxiety because of an awareness of what would be happening to them.[16]

Despite the fact that all of these an-psi studies were often *suggestive* of ESP, the results were neither consistent nor over-

---

* J. G. Pratt also tested Chris and suggested that Wood himself was the ESP subject who, unconsciously aware of the targets through his own ESP, gave unconscious visual cues to his pet who responded to them.

whelmingly significant, and many of the experimental results could have had other normal explanations. (It might also be noted that experiments which employ killing or harming animals has caused a great controversy in parapsychology over the ethics of such experimentation.)

Since these studies have generally not been highly successful, why should an-psi research be considered a new horizon in ESP research? Like so many discoveries in parapsychology, the answer is really a story in itself.

In 1967 two French scientists, writing under the pseudonyms of Pierre Duval and Evelyn Montredon, presented a paper, in absentia, to the winter review meeting of the Institute of Parapsychology of FRNM, "ESP Experiments with Mice." Duval and Montredon reported on their experiment with mice which were placed in a small cage with a copper grid serving as its bottom. The grid was connected to a photoelectric cell and partitioned into two sections. By hooking the cage and cell to a random target selector, either side of the cage could be given a mild electric shock. The target selector worked entirely by chance so that after several trials both sides of the cage would receive an equal number of shocks. Mice placed in the cage were tested to determine if they could precognize which side of the enclosure would be the next to be shocked. This they would do by choosing the opposite side of the partition when the shock was administered over several trials. An automatic device recorded which part of the cage was activated and the position of the mouse. After all the results were tabulated, the mice had skillfully precognized the shock by avoiding it at 1 million to 1 odds against chance. The experiment was so novel that Duval and Montredon were awarded the McDougall Award for the year's most notable contribution to parapsychology.

The Montredon-Duval effect was replicated in the United States, but this material became suspect on the basis of possible mechanical flaws in the apparatus and inconsistencies in the tabulated results of later small rodent psi research carried out by the same team. At present parapsychology must wait for confirmation from a new team of researchers.*

* Since writing the above an initial confirmation has been made of the small rodent research by Adrian Parker in Great Britain although his results have yet to show consistent positive results.

The reason for pursuing psi in animals is built on a firm rationale. Unlike human subjects, animals may not have a built-in censor to keep psi impressions from affecting their behavior. Secondly, animals are probably not prone to boredom or uneasiness when observers are present, which drastically affects human subjects.

When Rhine began his research in the 1930s, one of the first discoveries made was that ESP was widespread among the human population. Parapsychology circa 1970 has shown it to be even more universal than that.

Parapsychology is such a blossoming and changing field that it would be hard to isolate all of its new leads and directions. Five years from now the directions outlined in this chapter may have been stalemated, become old hat, or have led to even further discoveries leading to even more questions. Already many of the older concepts about ESP are being challenged. Charles Honorton has used feedback to help his subjects score successfully on ESP tests; Russell Targ has reported on an ESP self-testing machine that he has found improves ESP scores. Both of these fields of inquiry go much beyond the "inability" of subjects to control their ESP which has been such a stumbling block in the search for psi.

Since parapsychology is an interdisciplinary study, new approaches to the study of ESP are continually being outlined even by the more mainline sciences. As parapsychology develops with the help and contributions of its sister sciences, it will orient itself toward new concepts and ideas. The investigation of altered states of consciousness, dreams, and animal ESP are only three areas, at present, that are being fruitfully explored. Only the imagination of an H. G. Wells or Jules Verne would be able to predict what new vistas ESP research might explore.

10

Psi, Death, and Survival

Parapsychology has supplied the scientific world with several startling discoveries—that one mind can become aware of another's thoughts without the use of the five senses; that one can know of a future event; and that one's mind can somehow influence physical objects. However, one of parapsychology's central issues is the survival question—does man survive death? Pre-Duke research was essentially concerned with investigating psychics who claimed they could receive information from the dead. Even though parapsychology today is mostly involved with the experimental study of ESP, survival research is still being pursued by some researchers. The rationale behind the survival question is briefly: if man can have an extrasensory contact with another living mind, can he also have a similar bond with the minds of those who have died? (Such agents are called by various names such as "discarnates," "incorporeal personal agents," "Theta agents," or simply, "the dead.") Throughout the history of parapsychology there have been reports of apparitions, haunted houses, and of certain people through whom the dead are purported to speak (mediums). Parapsychology was the first and only science which sought to explore these phenomena on a scientific and systematic level and the first science to see that the study of these alleged occurrences had a direct bearing on the nature of the human personality and the possibility of its survival of bodily death. In fact, some years before Freud wrote on the topic, one of the founders of psychical research, F. W. H. Myers, had already mapped out a concept of a subliminal mind, although his schema differed in several aspects from that of Freud.

Today, parapsychology is a very different science. Since J. B. Rhine began his researches at Duke University in the late 1920s, it has shifted to the more experimentally oriented study of statistical ESP testing. The reason for this was that the study of mediums, hauntings, and apparitions were all considered at that time to be unprofitable avenues of study. ESP research with the living was easier, apparently more fruitful, and promised to have a greater impact on the scientific community in general, as well as a help in learning about the ESP process itself.

Nonetheless, a core of parapsychologists has long been interested in the controversy surrounding the survival problem: Can man survive death and can he communicate with the living via some extrasensory process? One parapsychology laboratory, The Psychical Research Foundation in Durham, North Carolina, is endowed specifically to carry out survival research.

By no means do parapsychologists share common attitudes about the survival issue. In fact, no topic has sparked such wide divergence of opinion. Some parapsychologists such as J. B. Rhine consider the survival issue to be a bad risk, a stalemated issue which can never be resolved and that survival research should be indefinitely shelved so that more fruitful research may be carried out. Others such as Gardner Murphy consider the issue completely deadlocked—that no evidence can prove that man survives death. Still others argue that ESP among the living has no limitation, so that all evidence of survival, such as mediumistic communications, may be caused by a network of ESP rapports from the living. Others, such as Ian Stevenson and the late Hornell Hart, believe the evidence already amassed does prove survival. By far, though, most parapsychologists share the Murphy agnostic position.

What has caused this wide divergence of opinion on the survival question? What evidence has parapsychology amassed which can be considered as proof of survival? And now that some parapsychologists are showing a new awareness of the survival issue, is interest in survival research once again coming to the forefront?

To comprehend just how parapsychology became associated with the anecdotal and experimental study of death, one must understand the early history of parapsychology and the researches that were carried out. As was stated in the chapter on the beginnings of modern parapsychology, during the Victorian Age, Western society was undergoing a critical but subtle revolution. Darwin's writings had shaken conventional religious beliefs and the scientific writings of John Stuart Mill were seen almost as a new religion in the eyes of those who had been affected by the Darwinian challenge to Christian tenets. The prevailing view was that Darwin had disproved Christian dogma and that science would ultimately explain all the mysteries of man, his mind, his world, and his universe. A few scholars, mostly philosophers or students of philosophy and religion, grouped about Cambridge University, were in the midst of this controversy. Among them were the famous philosopher, Professor Henry Sidgwick and his friends, F. W. H. Myers and Edmund Gurney. These men felt that religious doctrines such as "immortality" needed revitalization, but that only scientific evidence in keeping with the new general interest in scientific methodology could satisfy this need. At this time a current fad was the religion called Spiritualism, which had migrated to Great Britain in 1852 from the United States. This religion taught that man could communicate with the dead through mediums and other channels. Tales of apparitions and hauntings were given new credence by this movement. Sidgwick and Myers agreed that perhaps here, if any genuine phenomena could be sifted from the obvious morass of fraud and malobservation which plagued "psychic phenomena," was the salvation of religion and the doctrine of personal immortality as well. This led to the founding of the Society for Psychical Research. It is rather safe to say that parapsychology, which ultimately turned to the laboratory study of ESP, was born and nurtured in a survivalistic milieu.

Parapsychology's early researches were twofold: the study of spontaneous psychical events which indicated that man survived death, and the experimental study of certain gifted subjects who claimed that the dead spoke through them.

This work is the backbone of the survival controversy. The study of apparitions was one of the first considerations of the early parapsychologists. While most people associate apparitions with figures of the dead, they actually represent a variety of phenomena. There are four types of apparitions: apparitions of the living; crisis apparitions, or forms seen while the actual person is undergoing an accident or death; postmortem apparitions; and continual apparitions (or ghosts). Oddly, a good proportion of apparitions represent living persons, and there are good cases on record of individuals who tried to send, by concentration, images of themselves to a friend or relative who correspondingly reported seeing an appartion of the living.

Many cases of apparitions of the dead and dying suggested that man survives death, and Myers was especially interested in collecting cases of apparitions of the dead. By rigorously examining the evidence in such cases, it was hoped that, from a catalog of cases which seemed in the light of the evidence to be genuine, it could be determined if these incidents demonstrated survival of death. The following case is illustrative of the type of event Myers was after, although this example was originally investigated by another researcher. Only initials were given, since in many cases the anonymity of the persons involved had to be preserved, though the real names and reports were always kept on file for any investigator to check.

F. G.'s sister died of cholera when eighteen years old. Nine years later, F. G., was on a trip to St. Joseph, Missouri, and was filling out some business reports one afternoon in his hotel room, leisurely smoking a cigar. Something caught his eye and upon turning around he saw the figure of his sister which stood staring at him. He was surprised to see a large red scratch on her cheek. When F. G. returned home to St. Louis he told this astounding story to his parents, whereupon his mother almost collapsed in shock, admitting that after the girl's death she had accidentally scratched her face but had carefully concealed it with powder. No one knew of the scratch but herself.

This was no idle story, since the testimony of all the witnesses was collected before the report was published.[1]

An even more famous spontaneous case is that of the Chaffin Will, also used as an argument that apparitions serve as evidence for survival of death. This, too, is illustrative of the type of case used by parapsychologists to study survival.

Chaffin, a farmer in North Carolina, died, leaving his entire estate to his third son, Marshall, disinheriting his other sons and his wife. Four years later, in 1925, one of the sons, James, had vivid visions of his father's form which kept telling him, "You will find my will in my overcoat pocket." Finally, locating the overcoat James found a slip of paper in it stating, "Read the 27th chapter of Genesis in my daddie's old Bible." The Bible was duly searched and in front of several witnesses a handwritten will was discovered just as the apparition had foretold, redistributing the property evenly. This later will was declared valid and its provisions carried out.[2]

To many of the early parapsychologists these cases were strong evidence of survival of death. However, several implications of modern ESP research has deadened this impact. The range of ESP suggests that it has no limitations. For example, distance does not affect it as it should by the inverse square law. Since ESP has no known or definable limits, cases such as the Chaffin apparition could be mental projections exhibiting extrasensorily received and assembled information. Young Chaffin became clairvoyantly aware of the will, and his subconscious projected a vision of a phantom as a method of communicating this information from his unconscious mind to his consciousness. This theory of an all-knowing, limitless, and selective psi ability is called the super-ESP hypothesis, and it is considered that if any evidence is to be offered for survival it somehow must not be explainable by the super-ESP explanation. Although several parapsychologists have argued whether or not we are entitled to believe that ESP is so broad and selective, the question of super-ESP versus survival is considered completely deadlocked.

A similar survivalistic study is of so-called haunted houses. For centuries there had been tales of haunted homes and haunted places, and the SPR set out to examine these reports. Their research led to the authentication of several cases.

In 1882 the Despard family moved into a new home in Cheltenham, England. One month later Rose, one of the daughters, saw a shadowy figure pacing the hallway outside her bedroom. The figure was that of a tall woman holding a handkerchief over her face. Rose followed the figure but gave up the venture when her candle blew out. During the course of the following years, most members of the Despard family saw the figure several times. Rose, who was a young medical student at the time, kept a detailed diary of her experiences. In order to test the figure's reality, she fastened delicately glued strings across a stairway down which the phantom often descended. Keeping vigil, she watched as the apparition walked through the strings without disturbing them.

Gradually the appearances became less and less frequent, but even after the disappearance of the wraith, footsteps could still be heard patrolling the house. These, too, gradually died away. Although no definite identification was ever made of the ghost, the figure did strongly resemble a previous tenant of the house who died of alcoholism.[3]

The Despard haunting is a rather typical case. However, hauntings can represent a diversified range of effects—the appearance of phantoms, odd sounds, and odors being the most common.

Another haunted house of this same period was Ballechin House in Scotland. The SPR was able to lease the house, and several of its members lodged there to investigate any odd occurrences. By the end of the SPR tenancy, several investigators had heard phantom voices, seen apparitions, heard inexplicable rappings and detonation-like sounds, and other haunting displays.

Despite the fact that apparitions seen during hauntings are often recognized as deceased persons who had lived in the house, they do not necessarily represent survival of death, and many theories about hauntings do not employ this belief as the crux of their explanations. One of the first comprehensive theories for haunted houses was put forward by Mrs. Eleanor Sidgwick who proposed that experiencing a haunting is similar to psychometry. Just as an object can somehow retain information-packed psi traces of its handlers or owners, so could the same type of impressions be stamped onto an entire house, so that it might, by some unknown process, become impregnated with the thoughts, emotions, and actions of past occurrences. An individual who comes into contact with these situations then physically "sees" or "hears" the impressions as though they were actually occurring in the present. What he really is witnessing is nothing more than a playback of past events ignited by "activating" the psi traces in the house. According to this theory, hauntings would not at all incorporate activity of the dead.

An Oxford philosopher, H. H. Price, offered a similar theory about hauntings which postulated the existence of a psychic ether—a psychic bridge between mind and matter amalgamating all matter and space. Under certain rare conditions, such as powerful emotion, thoughts and scenes might become impressed on this ether and leave a lasting mark on the atmosphere of a house. People coming into contact with the ether also experience these impressions as though a motion-picture film with sound track was being activated for and by the witnesses. Again, this theory, very little different from Mrs. Sidgwick's, does not imply survival of death, although Price admits the possibility.

One researcher who most decidedly *did* believe that hauntings represent the activity of the dead was an Italian parapsychologist, Ernesto Bozzano, who made a collection of several hundred cases. He broke down the characteristics of hauntings and applied them to all the standard theories, finally concluding that the theory that hauntings represent conscious personalities of the dead was the best explanation. Bozzano also substantiated the old theory that haunted houses were once the scene of death or tragedy which paved the way for the emergence of the haunting. In this respect, 80 percent of his 304 cases were linked to death or tragedy in the house. He based his survivalistic views on the premise that nonsurvivalistic theories could not explain several features of haunted houses: (1) phantoms of the dead are found to haunt places where they did not die, nor in a few cases even lived. (2) Hauntings often consist of physical phenomena such as the movement of objects. (3) Hauntings are particularly linked to death. Most other tragedies do not usually engender hauntings. (4) Hauntings are intermittent. (5) Certain actions, such as prayer or exorcism, carried out in the phantom's behalf or request often terminate the haunting. Such characteristics would imply that the "ghost" is a conscious, surviving entity.[4]

As with so many issues in psychical research, hauntings are a mixture of fascination and enigma. Whether or not they can serve as evidence for survival of death is a moot point.

As stated previously, the other area of early survival research was the study of mediums. The Society for Psychical Research was still an infant organization when William James discovered a psychic named Leonore Piper who demonstrated that she could receive information that looked as though it came from the dead. Later other great mediums were discovered such as Mrs. Gladys Osborne Leonard and in the United States, Minnie Soule.

Mrs. Piper was the best-known and most extensively tested medium of her day. Living in Boston, her reputation as a trance medium spread quickly and soon reached the ears of the great American psychologist, William James. James visited her in 1885 and after witnessing her trance state remained convinced that much of what she told him about his deceased relatives could only have been available to her through her extrasensory abilities, although he was not sure whether she was actually bringing through messages from the dead or whether she was reading his own mind for the information.

In order to study Mrs. Piper properly, James brought her to the attention of the Society for Psychical Research and arranged for test experiments to be carried out in Great Britain. In 1889 Mrs. Piper traveled to England in order to be tested by persons she had never seen in a country completely foreign to her. Her every movement was followed and her mail was opened to keep her under constant surveillance. Under these conditions if she could still bring forth veridical information about deceased persons, the evidence would be even more striking than that which she had offered to James and her American sitters.

The main type of evidence given the SPR group was simply messages from the allegedly dead friends and relatives of the English sitters. In most cases Mrs. Piper would go into a trance state with an anonymous sitter. Soon her control (a claimed discarnate who acted as a "master of ceremonies" for the seance), Phinuit, would appear to bring through the communicators (allegedly dead personalities) who would either speak or write through the medium. Often the information given was highly evidential. On one occasion Oliver Lodge, the famous physicist, sat with Mrs. Piper and gave Phinuit a watch via the entranced Mrs. Piper. Immediately a personality calling himself "Uncle Jerry" manifested, claiming that the watch had been his. Lodge pressed the communicator for further information about his life and "Uncle Jerry," who actually had been an uncle of Lodge's, then gave the names of his companions while alive, some adventures in a place called Smith's Field, almost drowning, killing a cat, owning a snakeskin, and other very trivial memories. Later Lodge contacted still-living relatives and verified as true much of what "Uncle Jerry" had told him.[5] Mrs. Piper had no way of knowing this information and could only have gotten it through ESP from some source, living or dead.

This case, typical of a large body of mediumistic material, also serves as a good example of the difficulties inherent in survival research. On one hand it seems altogether feasible that Mrs. Piper did receive the information from Lodge's deceased uncle. But can we prove that this was the source? If Mrs. Piper's own ESP were limitless, could she not have gotten the necessary information by tapping Lodge's own mind or the minds of Lodge's living relatives? Again, this is possible. Mrs. Piper's subconscious then could have constructed the information into an artificial personality drawn from her own mind which would employ the ESP-gathered and -assembled information and pass itself off as a deceased personality. It was because of this possibility that survival research ultimately had to turn in new directions.

On the other side, however, certain of these communications were extremely detailed and accurate. ESP as we know it is rarely so accurate. Also different communicators often had different difficulties in communicating. Some are crystal clear, yet others falter as if they were indeed trying to catch hold of vague memories. This all would be much in keeping with the spiritistic theory.

Another point that these communications were really from surviving personalities was not only the level and accuracy of the communications, but even certain characteristics they revealed while speaking through the medium—mannerisms, use of words, voice inflections, even physical traits such as squints, spasms, coughs, and so forth would be taken on by the medium. With mediums such as Piper and Leonard, their characterizations were often identical to traits of the communicators while alive.

Nonetheless, the SPR leaders were divided on the source of the communications. A chief experimenter of this period was Richard Hodgson. It was his view that Phinuit was merely a split-off personality from Mrs. Piper's normal personality. After hundreds of sittings, Hodgson felt that little of the evidence warranted the belief that the survival hypothesis was more credible than the telepathic hypothesis. Hodgson's first report was published in 1892. However in 1898 he wrote another report in which in an about-face he wrote, "I cannot profess to have any doubt that the 'chief communicators' . . . are veritably the personalities that they claim to be; that they have survived the change we call death, and that they have directly communicated with us whom we call living through Mrs. Piper's entranced organism. . . ." Hodgson added in his famous report that he at long last found the telepathic theory incompetent to explain Mrs. Piper's abilities.

What caused this abrupt change of view by Mrs. Piper's most experienced investigator? The main factor was a change in Mrs. Piper's own mediumship. Her communicators began using automatic writing more and more, although speech was still used as well. (In fact this allowed two communicators to carry on separate conversations at the same time.) Mrs. Piper's whole mediumship altered. The physiology of her trance changed and her communicators were much clearer. Phinuit, who had long been Mrs. Piper's control and whose communications about himself were often dubious and self-contradictory, began to fade from the scene and a new personality took charge calling himself George Pelham who began communicating in March 1892. However Phinuit still continued to manifest along with Pelham for a few more years but more intermittently. It was Phinuit who introduced Pelham through Mrs. Piper. (Actually George Pelham was the pseudonym used in the reports for George Pellew. He is usually initialed as G. P. in the reports.) Pellew when alive had been a friend of Hodgson's, and it was the G. P. messages and evidence that converted Hodgson.

In his voluminous communications G. P. would offer many veridical statements about his life. When sitters were anonymously introduced into the seances whom G. P. had known in life, he would without hesitation unfalteringly recognize them, call them by name, and take up conversations on familiar topics between them.

The following is an extract from one such sitting recorded by Hodgson in his second report, "A Further Record of Observations of Certain Phenomena of Trance," *Proceedings:* SPR XIII (1898). The sitters were Mr. and Mrs. Howard and their daughter Katherine who, while strangers to Mrs. Piper, had known G. P. Parenthetical notes are by Hodgson, those by the sitters commenting on what G. P. (Piper) was saying are initialed:

Phinuit: He (G.P.) has been to see his father, and he has seen, he has taken a book and carried it to have it printed. (His father had collected his poems and had them printed in a small volume, which appeared just before the first sitting of this series.)

During the early part of the sitting Katherine entered and sat down in a far corner. Almost immediately Phinuit said, "he wants to know who is Katherine?" Katherine comes over, and G.P. takes control of the voice, and personal greetings follow. . . . Recognition of dress, also of shawl, which was asked for, and which was placed over Mrs. Piper's shoulders.

"What is it takes me to Paris?" (The shawl has been worn in Paris frequently during a year, but there is no reason to suppose that G.P. living, was aware of this.)

G.P. inquired what had been done with a special picture which he had owned.

Mrs. H.: That got torn up after you passed out, but here is a picture that I don't know whether you will recognize, but you used to know the place. (G.P. puts picture on top of the head.) *

G.P.: What is this? This is your summer house.

Mrs. H.: Yes, you have it right.

G.P.: But I have forgotten the name of the town.

Mrs. H.: Don't you remember D———?

---

* During the sittings the entranced Mrs. Piper through her controls would often place objects given her during the seance on top of her head to gain impressions from them.

G.P.: Oh, the little brick house and the little vine, grape-vine some call them. Yes, I remember it all; it comes back as distinctly as the daylight . . . Where is the little out-house?

(All correct. The brick hen-house that, like the house itself, was solidly built of brick just did not come into the picture, but came to the very edge of it, so it was natural for George to ask where it was. The grape-vine that covered the whole house up to the roof was a striking feature of it—K.)

Mrs. H.: There is the painting (handing another picture).

G.P.: No, I have no recollection of that.

Mrs. H.: No, I painted it when you were not there. You never saw that.

G.P.: It is not fresh to me at all, but this (fingering the photo of the house) is very clear. Katherine.

Mrs. H.: She remembers it too.

G.P.: She was a little thing. Then you bought a place at some *ville*. (Katherine's age when we left D——— was six, nearly seven. We first bought the place at X———ville in 1886.) (Further references to personal incidents at D———.) Katherine, how is the violin? (She plays the violin.). . . . to hear you playing it is horrible, horrible.

Mrs. H.: But don't you see she likes her music because it is the best she has.

G.P.: No, but that is what I used to say, that it is horrible. (George was always more or less annoyed by hearing Katherine practise when she was beginning the violin as a little child.—K.)

G.P. (a basket is put into G.P.'s hands which he had given as a Christmas present): That is mine. Where is my lamp arrangement? I was very fond of that, you know. (He had also expressly got a small light-shade that could be moved round the shade of an ordinary lamp to cut off the light from the eye, and he had used this much when living. He had made other references to this in previous sittings.) . . .

Mrs. H.: I want you to see that (handing a paper).

G.P.: You wrote that to me this morning. (It was a poem on death written that morning with G.P. in mind, but no reference to G.P. in it). . . . (Another paper handed.) That is a letter. That is mine. That is my own, but that was written a long time ago. (Correct. A letter of his written many years before.) . . .

Give my regards to James Pierce. Tell him I could not speak to him, but I will again, and when you dine with him, think of me. (George occasionally dined at the house of James Pierce in company with Mr. Howard.)

Mr. H.: George, do you know whom this is from? (Handing an unopened newspaper enclosed in a wrapper as if just received in the mail.)

G.P.: Where is John Hart? I am too weak to tell you. Is that Orenberg?

Mr. H.: Yes.

G.P.: Yes, that is he. You take that away and I will tell you better (referring to the wrapper, which Mr. H. takes off).

That is Orenberg, dear old fellow. I would like to see him. His own hand folded it. (It was a foreign newspaper that Mr. H. had received from Orenberg that morning, and had at once hidden away without telling anyone of it.) . . . (To Mr. H.) Get the long pipe and smoke. (Mr. Howard was in the habit of smoking a long pipe in the evening, as was well known to G.P.) . . . (G.P. leaves, and at 9.16 Mrs. Piper comes out of trance, but as usual is somewhat dazed at first.)

Later on in her mediumship new controls took over Mrs. Piper and new communicators were brought through. Gradually after several years her mediumship began to collapse, but only after hundreds upon hundreds of cases like the G. P. communications had been placed on record. Ultimately she lost her trance state in 1911, regained it briefly in 1915, and gave her last official sittings in 1926–1927. After her retirement the SPR focused its attention on Mrs. Leonard who had achieved fame as a trance medium during World War I and had convinced Oliver Lodge of her gifts by detailed communications from his son, Raymond, who had been killed in the war (apparently predicted by Mrs. Piper). Ultimately Mrs. Leonard became known as the "English Mrs. Piper."

However the case for survival of death was not an easy subject to tackle even with this wealth of data. Researchers such as F. W. H. Myers, Lodge, and Hodgson did come to accept the spiritistic theory. Others such as Frank Podmore still favored telepathy (although he too began to modify his view shortly before his death). William James could not fully accept either theory and postulated that the medium was catching hold of free-floating personality and memory fragments of the deceased, not his actual personality, or was contacting a "cosmic reservoir" (as he termed it) of clairvoyantly available knowledge. In order to off-set the problem of telepathy from the sitter, new forms of mediumistic tests were developed.

In some cases an individual would sit with a medium, not to contact his own relatives, but to proxy for others miles away in order to offset the theory that the medium was getting the data from the sitter's mind. One famous case was the medium, Minnie Soule. The investigator was James H. Hyslop, who reported the incident in his book *Contact with the Other World*. Unknown to Mrs. Soule (named Chenoweth in most of the published material on her), Hyslop booked a sitting as a proxy for a woman, Mrs. Tausch, living in Germany, who wished to contact her dead husband. Hyslop and the woman's sister sat. It should be noted that the sister did not enter the room until after the medium had entered trance. Soon a communicator appeared describing himself in detail and finally wrote his name, "Tauch." He offered many incidents about his earthly life which Hyslop verified by contacting Mrs. Tausch. Hyslop spoke to the communicator in German, a language Soule did not know but which Tausch did, and received correct answers in the same tongue. This is known as "polyglot" mediumship or "Xenoglossy" and constitutes a whole area of survival evidence. Again, it would appear that a priori there is evidence that the ESP channel was between the medium and the alleged personality of the deceased agent. With Mrs. Leonard, proxy sittings were systematically carried out by her chief investigator, C. Drayton Thomas, with excellent results.

Cross correspondences were also used and as they are extremely complex, I will only give a brief summary of the principle behind them. A message would be given through one medium which in itself was meaningless. Then another medium would also be given a message which was related to the one given previously. Often the combined message then made sense. On some occasions the message was still cryptic until a third, fourth, or even fifth psychic was given the clue from the alleged communicator sending the message. The cross correspondences began in the communications of Mrs. Piper and other mediums being studied by the Society for Psychical Research shortly after the death of F. W. H. Myers who claimed to be constructing the messages from his world of the dead. The messages usually displayed a high command of obscure classical scholarship that Myers had specialized in when alive. Usually a riddle would be given piecemeal through various SPR star psychics—each kept in ignorance of what communications were coming through to the others.

These cross correspondences were strong evidence of survival for several reasons: (1) They occurred after Myers' death and seemed to be constructed by him. (2) They contained classical knowledge over and above what the psychics could have known. (3) So many mediums received the messages that one would have to believe that several psychics were in ESP rapport at all times to offset the survival theory. (4) The communications lasted for several years and outlived some of the mediums.

Mediumistic evidence was the cornerstone of survival evidence for many years, and most of the early investigators felt that this evidence alone proved survival. These included Myers, Hyslop, Lodge, and others. However, this evidence was soon challenged by advocates of the super-ESP hypothesis who argued that ESP among the living, which of course includes clairvoyance, could explain *all* mediumistic evidence. Since most of the early researchers had not spent much time experimenting with telepathy, their mediumistic evidence was not collected to argue against the ESP theory. Even though proxy sittings and cross correspondences were instituted to offset the theory that the medium received the information from the sitter or experimenter, it was felt that perhaps the medium could pick up knowledge from any living mind or even from some hypothetical "cosmic reservoir." After all, since most evidence was verified when the sitter contacted living relatives of the purported communicators, it is theoretically feasible that the medium could also have gotten the information via ESP from the same sources.

Even though there was scattered evidence that the medium's own mind was sensitive to ESP influences from the living, few researchers seriously considered that it would explain the huge bulk of survival evidence. However, the tide was soon to change with the Gordon Davis case which gave to super-ESPers their first real evidence.

In this case, S. G. Soal visited the medium Blanche Cooper, and during the sittings a personality called Gordon Davis was contacted. Davis was an old friend of his whom Soal had thought long dead. Davis told of his death, and, in typical communicator fashion, described details of his life, and so forth. The evidence was striking. Later, however, Soal discovered that Davis was very much alive, living in another part of London. Obviously, somehow ESP via the living was responsible. Cooper had apparently also used precognition, since Davis also described the furnishings of his home—a house that had been *seen* by the real Davis at the time of the sittings, but which he did not buy or furnish until later.[6]

The Gordon Davis case did not "disprove" the survival hypothesis, nor did it prove the super-ESP theory, and some parapsychologists such as Hornell Hart and others have written on how such cases could be compatible with survival evidence. However, again the case showed that mediumistic evidence, no matter how strong, could not surmount the super-ESP theory, and thus could not be considered definite proof of survival.

In light of these difficulties, modern studies of survival have been carried out trying to bypass the objections leveled at earlier work. However, before discussing this research some explanation should be made as to why survival research is making a comeback in parapsychology. First of all, the shift to purely experimental studies of ESP was very novel in 1930. But this novelty has slowly been wearing off, and some parapsychologists are beginning to feel that statistical studies of ESP are not paying off in the long run. Also, the evidence for the existence of ESP is now so strong that no one can legitimately dispute it, and so the time has come for parapsychology once again to enter the daring domain of survival research and the study of spontaneous cases. This view is not shared by all parapsychologists, and some research institutes, such as the Institute for Parapsychology of the Foundation for Research on the Nature of Man still carry out basic laboratory ESP research with a heavy reliance on statistical measurements.

The second reason for the upsurge in survival research was due to a rather complex court case concerning the will of James

Kidd. Kidd was an eccentric with a storehouse of secret wealth. When he was declared legally dead after his mysterious disappearance, his will stated that his money should be given to any person or organization that could prove that the soul leaves the body at death. Parapsychologists were quick to capitalize on this stipulation, and after a long and hard struggle the American Society for Psychical Research won the money for survival research. Now that parapsychology has a large amount of funds at its disposal, survival-oriented projects are being developed and new energy is being exerted to find ingenious methods of researching the survival question.

One area of survival research that was directly related to the older anecdotal approach was the study of deathbed visions. The leading modern parapsychologist researching this subject is Karlis Osis, formerly head of the Parapsychology Foundation's division of research and now research director of the American Society for Psychical Research.

For years doctors had reported that deathbed patients had strange visions—often of apparitions of the dead who came to lead them through the death experience. What was of importance was that these "hallucinations" were not explainable as being due to the degenerative nature of the fatal illness, nor to any medication given to the patients. Two early researchers, Sir William Barrett and James Hyslop, collected accounts of these experiences and pointed out that in several cases the dying persons could have had no knowledge that the "apparitions" they saw were persons who had only died a day or so before, the fact of which had been deliberately kept from them. Thus, these cases demonstrated at best that the apparitions were surviving entities or, at least, that ESP was somehow involved. A typical case of this phenomenon, a very important one in survival research, is recorded by Barrett's own wife who was a physician and who witnessed part of the occurrence. However, another witness, Miriam Castle, was present during the critical time and her testimony was collected by the Barretts:

I was present shortly before the death of Mrs. B., together with her husband and her mother. Her husband was leaning over her and speaking to her, when pushing him aside she said, "Oh, don't hide it; it's so beautiful." Then turning away from him towards me, I being on the other side of the bed, Mrs. B. said, "Oh, why there's Vida," referring to a sister whose death three weeks previously she had not been told. Afterwards the mother, who was present at this time told me, as I have said, that Vida was the name of a dead sister of Mrs. B's of whose illness and death she was quite ignorant, as they had carefully kept this news from Mrs. B. owing to her serious illness.[7]

The case was highly evidential, since the witnesses were compounded by the attending physician, Dr. Phillips, and the dying woman's mother who wrote out a corroborative account.

Osis was interested in judging the widespread occurrence of this phenomenon and also in seeing if a modern study of such events would give credence to the survival hypothesis. He thus sent out questionnaires to several thousand physicians and nurses and did a computer analysis of the results which were subsequently published as a monograph, *Deathbed Observations by Physicians and Nurses*. The results of the study were as follows: *

1. The dying often exhibit a period of exaltation shortly before death. This state is not due to the nature of the disease, education level, or sex, and only mildly by the patient's belief concerning survival of death.

2. The dying do have visual experiences near death enormously above the rate of visions or hallucinations observed by a normal population.

3. These visions, often of apparitions, occurred for the most part while the patient was in clear consciousness, not sedated, and were seen most commonly between one hour to one day before death.

4. These visions are most often of the dead, though other figures are seen.

5. Half of the percipients stated that the apparitions were going to take them into death.

Osis himself writes of his study, "Phenomena relevant to the survival hypothesis occur mostly when the physiological and psychological equilibrium of the patient is not markedly dis-

* These are my own summaries of Osis' results drawn from the study. They do not appear so ordered by Osis, but represent his major findings.

turbed." He also considered that his report did complement and confirm Hyslop's and Barrett's earlier anecdotal studies.

Another type of evidence for survival which has gone from the morass of anecdote to the domain of experiment is the study of the out-of-the-body experience (OOBE). Out-of-the-body experiences are enigmatic situations where the percipient feels that his consciousness has left the physical body, is existing without it, sometimes enveloped in an apparitional body, and which often times can travel, "see" and report occurrences that the person could not have known normally. If such a phenomenon could be shown to be more than hallucination, then a priori, such a phenomenon demonstrates that the consciousness can become independent of the body and feasibly survive the body's death. To give an example of an OOBE in which the ESP factor was somehow involved, I quote from a recent study of this phenomenon made by Celia Green reported in her *Out-of-the-Body Experiences:*

> I was in hospital having an operation for peritonitis; I developed pneumonia and was very ill. The ward was L shaped; so that anyone in bed at one part of the ward could not see round the corner.
>
> One morning I felt myself floating upwards, and found myself looking down on the rest of the patients. I could see myself, propped up against pillows very white and ill. I saw the sister and nurse rush to my bed with oxygen. Then everything went blank. The next I remember was opening my eyes to see the sister bending over me.
>
> I told her what had happened; but at first she thought I was rambling. Then I said, "There is a big woman sitting up in bed with her head wrapped in bandages; and she is knitting something with blue wool. She has a very red face." This certainly shook her; as apparently the lady concerned had a mastoid operation and was just as I described.
>
> She was not allowed out of bed; and of course I hadn't been up at all. After several other details; such as the time by the clock on the wall I convinced her that at least something strange had happened to me.

It is, of course, up to parapsychologists to determine more sophisticated methods of studying such accounts of purported OOBEs. Two scientists who have spent considerable time

studying this phenomena are Dr. Robert Crookall, a British ge-
ologist, and Dr. Charles Tart, the experimental psychologist.
Both have made important contributions concerning the nature
of the OOBE which bear on the survival hypothesis.

Crookall has been the leading collector of cases of the OOBE,
and his catalog of cases now exceeds seven hundred, most of
which he has published in his over a dozen books on the subject.
Crookall has been engaged during the past several years in a detailed content analysis of his collected narratives, hoping that by
breaking down the characteristics of the experience one could
verify that the experience is not hallucinatory; determine
whether an apparitional body really does project during the experience, gain insight into the mechanics of the experience; and
relate all of this data to the survival hypothesis. So far Crookall's
content analysis has paid off, and he has offered four lines of evidence about the OOBE.

Crookall's first analysis was to break down the characteristics
of the phenomenon. By doing so he found general patterns
within OOBE reports, such as specific traits concerning the
onset and end of the experience which could not be due to
chance and are hard to explain away as hallucinatory. Characteristics such as sensations of leaving the body through the head;
seeing a silver cord attached to the physical body; feeling a jolt
or "click" upon reentering the body; and other bizarre sensations. His cases were then broken down into groupings of
OOBEs occurring near sleep or in illness (natural) and these
were compared to those cases catalyzed by drowning, hypnosis,
and so forth (enforced). In this comparison Crookall found that
while all OOBEs have similar characteristics these two bodies of
OOBEs had statistically significant patterns differentiating
them. This, too, was evidence that the phenomenon was a genuine release of consciousness and not merely hallucination. Another parapsychologist, Hornell Hart, reanalyzing Crookall's
data, verified the statistical as well as the experiential significance of the breakdowns.

The next step was to compare OOBEs reported by the general public to those reported by famous psychics. A significant
difference was found. And finally the OOBE narratives were
analyzed to determine if certain set stages of release and reentry
of consciousness exist during the experience.

From these studies Crookall argues that the OOBE does represent a release of consciousness from the body in an "apparitional" form which could survive death.[8]

Hornell Hart had earlier compared apparitions of the living to apparitions of the dead. Since many people in the OOB state had been seen as apparitions by others, he felt that apparitions of the living probably were some sort of OOBE. When comparing apparitions of the dead to those of the living, including reports of OOBEs, he found they shared common characteristics, thus indicating that they are of a similar nature. Hart felt that this was concrete evidence for the survival theory and that OOBEs represent the release of an apparitional body that would ultimately survive death. The complete synthesis of his work with Crookall's was barely finished when Hart died and this final work has not been published.[9]

Despite Crookall's painstaking analyses, most parapsychologists have felt that a more experimental approach was necessary. Because of this, Crookall's research has been sadly neglected by the parapsychological community. However, the researches of Charles Tart soon reinforced the idea that the OOBE could be studied empirically and could ultimately be of aid in survival research. Tart himself, though, carried out his pioneering research without much interest in the implications of it to the survival hypothesis.

The study was based on the fact that not only have hundreds of persons recorded spontaneous OOBEs, but also that some individuals had written autobiographical accounts of recurrent OOBEs which the reporters were able either to control almost at will or at least have the experience repeatedly. It was Tart's hope to be able to study the OOBE through such a gifted subject in the laboratory where the experience could be monitored by the EEG and other such devices.

To date Tart has reported on two such subjects. One of them was able to induce an OOBE in a dream laboratory and correctly report what was occurring in an adjoining hallway. The EEG rhythm showed some similarities to a dream state during the experience. The other subject, more interesting and evidential, was a young woman who, during several successive nights in Tart's laboratory, encouraged several OOBEs. Finally, the subject was able to "float" up over her body and read a six-digit random target number on a ledge above her. This the subject reported correctly. The EEG readings were so enigmatic that neither Tart nor Dr. William Dement, the well-known authority of sleep research, could classify them as either sleeping or waking. Later Tart discovered that the number could have been read by a complex means of fraud, but it is highly unlikely that such means were used.[10]

Since it appeared that the OOBE could be tested experimentally, it was again Karlis Osis who developed a plan to test the OOBE in order to study its implications in the survival hypothesis. Simply, Osis wanted to see if during the OOB state, the subject's consciousness really left the body, or whether the experience was some form of dramatic ESP vision. His plan was a variant of Tart's original work. Could a subject correctly report a group of objects in proper perspective and proportion during the OOB state? ESP impressions are rarely so clear, and Osis hoped that the verbal reports by the subject would indicate whether the subject was actually "seeing" the target or if he was merely getting ESP impressions of it. The subject for this research was Ingo Swann who seems to be able to induce the OOB state while awake. Most people, including Tart's subjects, have to be asleep before manifesting the phenomenon. During experiments with Osis and his assistant, Janet Mitchell, at the American Society for Psychical Research, Swann has been able to perceive objects during the OOB state hidden in another room and report on them in proper perspective to each other. This then supports the survival theory that during the OOBE something actually "leaves the body" and uses a mode of perception similar to the laws of optics. The complete work with Swann has not as yet been published.

A vast amount of research is now being undertaken with a young Duke University psychology student, Blue Harary, at the Psychical Research Foundation under the able direction of Dr. Robert Morris. During these experiments Harary is placed in a laboratory usually some miles from the target area. He enters a relaxed state, induces an OOB state, and then tries to travel over the considerable distance to the target room where a test animal is under observation. Harary attempts to make the animal react to his presence. In some of these experiments a kitten, Harary's pet, would suddenly cease to move about, stop meowing, and become extremely passive. These periods of passivity corresponded to an astounding degree to those times when Harary was reporting OOBEs and being with his pet. Similarly, he has also been "detected" successfully by human targets who have reported seeing shadows, flashes of light, and so forth while Harary was actually trying to appear to them in the OOB state. The subjects knew only that an attempt would be made within a certain time period, but they did not know the actual time he would appear to them. Harary has also reported successfully on targets such as letter posters or objects on a table set up for him to view during his OOB state. However, since ESP could explain any success at these specific tasks, the use of detectors was adopted. Detection responses by people and animals argue that Harary is somehow actually present at the target site. Again, much of this material is unpublished but was reported to the 1973 Convention of the Parapsychological Association in Charlottesville, Virginia.

Although the shift has been away from mediumistic studies, a few parapsychologists still feel that evidence for survival might be forthcoming in experimentation with gifted mediums, but that this new type of evidence must be of a different nature and content from what has hitherto been recorded. Unfortunately, there has been a severe decline in the number of gifted subjects that parapsychologists have to work with, so that mediumistic studies have not been pursued. However, some plans have been put forward to test the survival hypothesis through mediumship.

Taking a cue from the old system of proxy sittings, Karlis Osis has attempted linkage experiments. In these experiments a whole number of agents separated various mediums from the widow of a deceased biologist. The experiments were actually cross correspondences combined with proxy tests. Despite these linkages, veridical information was communicated by or about the deceased target person.[11] Unfortunately, these tests, no matter how much "noise" is created between the various participants, still cannot overcome the super-ESP explanation.

Another area of exploration has been the study of "drop-in" communicators. All through the history of mediumship there have been cases of communicators appearing at sittings who were completely unrecognized by anyone present. Only later, after checking obscure records, have some of these drop-in personalities been traced and verified. Drop-in communicators are hard to explain by ESP for several reasons: no one immediately present could be the ESP donor of the information; there is no motive for the medium to conjure up, haphazardly, the personalities; and it is difficult to see why a particular personality should be selected with such detailed characterization and evidence from the thousands upon thousands of other personalities that have lived and died. Two parapsychologists most actively engaged in the study of drop-in communicators are Ian Stevenson and the British psychologist-parapsychologist, Alan Gauld. Gauld recently investigated a private group allegedly receiving communications from several drop-in communicators. In several cases detailed facts were given which could not be verified by any of the group involved at the sittings, but Gauld, following up clues given by the communicators, was able to verify several of them by checking into private or obscure documents, church records, and so forth. In these cases ESP from the living, while not entirely ruled out, is a difficult position to maintain.[12]

A third approach to mediumistic evidence is through what are called cipher tests. Again, modern parapsychologists have taken their cues from older researches. During parapsychology's early history several researchers left posthumous messages in sealed envelopes that they planned on communicating when dead. It was believed that if these letters could not be read psychically by sensitives during their lives, mediumistic communications after death which *did* reveal the contents would be evidence of postmortem survival. These tests were problematic for several reasons. Firstly, once a letter was opened, the test was ruined if the mediumistic communication was in error. Secondly, the super-ESP theory could account for them. For example, one investigator, J. G. Piddington, wrote a posthumous letter, but even during his lifetime the contents were spilled out in a cross correspondence via several SPR mediums. Also, memory might be impaired by the death experience, and the contents of such letters might be too hard to communicate. Although several investigators have left such messages, there has been no com-

pletely successful disclosure, though there have been partial successes.

To overcome these problems cipher tests were developed. R.
H. Thouless was the first to propose the use of such a code.
Plans are made for a key phrase to unravel a coded message
which perhaps could be communicated after the death of the instigator. Ian Stevenson, following Thouless' suggestion, worked
out a combination lock test, where a message would successfully
unlock a combination lock via a cipher technique. These pro-
posals are new concepts in survival research, so they, in conjunction with the dearth of first-rate mediums to receive the
communications, have not as yet given parapsychology any new
evidence of survival.

The final approach to survival research has been the sole project of Ian Stevenson who heads a division of parapsychology at
the University of Virginia School of Medicine. Stevenson's
long-term project has been to investigate cases of alleged reincarnation where usually young children report that they had lived a
previous life. In several of these cases Stevenson has been able to
verify that these subjects did show detailed information about a
deceased individual, his life, family, and mundane affairs. At
best this is evidence of reincarnation; at worst, of some weird
form of ESP. (See his *Twenty Cases Suggestive of Reincarnation*. New York: ASPR, 1966.)

One case is that of Imad Elawar. Imad claimed to have lived
before in a neighboring town in Lebanon. He gave his former
name, several family relations were identified by name, and the
nature of his death. Altogether Imad made fifty-seven statements about his former life in an area about which he could have
had no normal knowledge. Stevenson investigating the case was
able to verify that fifty-one statements referred to a genuinely
deceased person, although the actual identification of the donor
was confused.

In several cases the agent is born with birthmarks corresponding to injuries sustained by the donor personality. These
are hard to explain by any theory other than reincarnation. Of
course, reincarnation cases really are a rather back-door study of
survival inasmuch as they do not directly indicate survival after
death, only the reappearance of memory complexes in the living

state. Neither do all parapsychologists accept the reincarnation theory as explaining these cases. Recently, Gardner Murphy has offered a theory of retrocognition (ESP impressions of past events) of memory complexes which would in a way rework the super-ESP theory to include the evidence for reincarnation.

This is the historical and contemporary research that parapsychology has carried out in its study of death. The basic problem of man's ability to survive death is actually only a foundation leading to several issues that confront parapsychologists. No one in parapsychology seriously believes that the survival question will be successfully resolved to the satisfaction of the entire parapsychological community, much less the scientific community. However, the real problem underlying the survival hypothesis is not merely if man survives death, but *what* survives. For example, after studying several mediumistic communications, Hyslop came to the conclusion that we survive death in a conscious, aware state. However, William James came to the conclusion that the surviving personality was hardly anything more than a few fragments of personality held together in a vaguely conscious state and that this network would probably be incapable of long-term survival.

Oddly, both Hyslop and James reached their almost opposite conclusions through their study of the same medium, Mrs. Piper. Today, W. G. Roll, a leading theoretician on the survival issue, has argued that in life many of us go through short periods of total loss of personal awareness. These experiences were termed "religious experiences" by William James, "cosmic consciousness" by R. M. Bucke, and more recently "peak experiences" by Abraham Maslow. Could not the surviving personality be absorbed into a type of "field consciousness" as Roll terms it, where consciousness is lost? Such a theory, close to the Buddhistic concept of Nirvana, could hardly be called personal survival. This is only one of the many dilemmas facing survival research.

Despite the problems and controversy confronting the survival issue, it can readily be seen that parapsychology offers a most promising, unique, and fruitful approach to the study of death. Parapsychologists have long been aware that much ESP concerns or centers on the death experience such as crisis apparitions seen at the time of a serious accident or death; spontaneous ESP coinciding with death; and death coincidences, such as mysterious clock-stoppings and other physical effects that have accompanied death. Even if one were not interested in the survival problem per se, the very study of psychical phenomena is intricately related to the study and psychology of dying, and somehow intertwined with the actual process of dying whether survival after death takes place or not.

Because of this, no one interested in the psychological aspects of the phenomena of death and dying can afford to be unfamiliar with the history, literature, and evidence that parapsychology has to offer on the subject.

11

The Enigma of Psi

What does it all mean? This is a question posed not only by parapsychologists as they try to make sense of their data, but also by science and psychology as well, as they try to understand the implications of psi to their own disciplines. The fact that one's thoughts and dreams can be invaded by the thoughts or emotions of another has serious implications for psychology. That the mind can exert a physical force capable of deflecting an object opens a new chapter in physics. The ability of a gifted subject to awaken an anesthetized mouse confronts biology with a formidable enigma. And physical mediumship represents an unappreciated mystery within the human physiology. Trying to understand the meaning of psi is like trying to put together a jigsaw puzzle, only we have no box cover picture on which to model the pieces and several of the pieces have, unbeknown to us, been lost. We might further elaborate on the jigsaw puzzle model by suggesting that some of the assorted pieces don't even belong to the puzzle but have accidentally been thrown into the box. Thus, many elements of psi, dowsing, for instance, might ultimately be found to have natural physical explanations.

The enigma of psi is a product of two paradoxes. First, the occurrence of ESP is so rarely recognized by us, and few of us have more than one conscious psychic experience during a lifetime. Nonetheless we have considerable evidence that ESP is occurring all the time. To the early parapsychologists, ESP seemed to be a one-shot experience. Certain psychological conditions were met for some inexplicable reason and an ESP transfer took place. Stress seemed particularly linked to this transfer. Certainly, there were gifted subjects who could demonstrate ESP over and over again, but they simply had more ESP than anyone else. ESP was seen as an ability, and that under rare conditions even nonpsychics could suddenly exhibit the ability for a brief period during which an ESP transfer manifested.

This model and conception of ESP was built on a firm though incomplete rationale. Early parapsychology primarily consisted of collecting spontaneous cases where this one-shot theory of ESP was surely indicated. No one thought to test masses of individuals for any purpose other than to find gifted subjects.

Despite this, several of the pioneers of parapsychology did think that this model was incorrect and that ESP occurred continually but surfaced into consciousness only rarely. Among these were Henri Bergson, Hereward Carrington, Whately Carington, and G. N. M. Tyrrell. Time and date are often cruel, and the one-shot theory has had to be discarded. The new era of experimentation has confirmed that ESP does occur continually, although we are hardly ever aware of it. Although we are not conscious of it, ESP impressions may affect our everyday behavior and decisions. This X factor has a considerable bearing on psychology.

To illustrate this point one need only review a few of the experiments which have been designed to demonstrate the unrecognized influence of ESP. Rex Stanford had thirty subjects listen to a tape of a dream recollection. Unknown to the subjects, the dream was fabricated for the purpose of the experiment. After the subjects listened to the tape recording, they were given a four-possibility multiple choice quiz about certain aspects of the dream record. However, the questions were constructed in such a way that no correct answers were given for some in the dream record. The subjects would be expected to guess randomly at four possible answers. After the quiz was over Stanford randomly chose "correct" answers which he hoped his subjects would have precognized. On other questions which had correct answers, alternate target answers were selected in the hope that the subject's psi would override the correct answers. After making his choices Stanford then evaluated his subjects' responses and found that they had indeed clustered their answers around those later chosen as the target answer. True precognition had been demonstrated.[1]

In this case the subjects did not even know that an ESP test was being carried out, nor that they were unconsciously using psi. Nonetheless, ESP was operating and did affect their decisions. This type of masked experiment has in fact been employed with considerable success. Experiments have been designed and disguised as academic tests in which some questions have no correct answer other than the one choice chosen as the ESP target. Subjects, not aware of the hidden test and confronted by the unsolvable questions, can only guess at the answer—and sometimes a whole group will choose the target answers at rates far beyond chance. Similarly, even personality tests have been run on the same principle.

A rather post-hoc type of analysis of the effect ESP has in day-to-day living was undertaken by E. Douglas Dean and John Mihalasky. These two parapsychologists began by wondering if ESP may not play an unconscious role in everyday decision making. In order to test this hypothesis they started testing businessmen. Since success in business transactions is based on the ability of an executive to make cogent decisions day after day, Dean felt that the more successful businessmen might be making those decisions by unknowingly employing ESP (whether clairvoyant or precognitive) in their choices. Results of the subsequent testing showed that the more successful businessmen evinced more ESP ability.[2]

The fact that ESP does affect us unwittingly has led Rex Stanford to design his concept of the psi-mediated instrumental response. Although his view is an old one, he is the first modern parapsychologist to build it into an elaborate design. According to the PMIR model, an individual is constantly scanning his environment and situation via ESP. This is a bit different from older models which postulated that one constantly receives ESP impressions. Psi scanning is very much like Ullman's concept of psi vigilance. The scanning is employed to gather crucial bits of information, and when such a scrap is focused upon and relayed to the individual by ESP, a person often acts upon the data unconsciously. That is, he makes decisions or carries out actions often without proper reason and unaware he is acting on an ESP impulse. The PMIR can be used to explain much that we call coincidence: being at just the right place at the right time or serendipitous mistakes such as going to the wrong store and discovering an exceptional buy.

So, this is psi's first great puzzle: the fact that it is so common and recurring that it may affect our very behavior, but so disguised and repressed that we are only rarely aware of it. It is no wonder that many people question whether ESP is possible or that it even exists.

The second great paradox psi exhibits is its physical yet nonphysical aspects. We know that psi has both sensory aspects (ESP) and motor aspects (PK). The two are completely interrelated. They function together, appear jointly in the same subjects, and follow similar principles. Yet (and perhaps a neon light should shine on that word), although psi has obvious physical characteristics which can deflect, move, or even hurl objects, it manifests completely apart from time and space.

Thus the second puzzle is: Is ESP physical or nonphysical? If one were to judge those two alternatives, there are formidable barriers to believing that ESP in any way conforms to physical laws by conceiving it as some sort of wave or broadcast. For one thing, electromagnetic waves attenuate with distance. As the force travels, its power dwindles and finally its energy dissipates. The law governing the principle is the inverse square law, that the intensity of radiation falls off inversely to the square of the distance. It has long been known that ESP is not confined by distance. By the inverse square law there should be a proportional and quantitative difference between ESP tests done when the participants are close by and when they are far away. Yet no such relationship has been so neatly found. Mrs. Stewart's ESP worked well between London and Antwerp, and the early Duke successes were often achieved over several miles. Transatlantic ESP has shown no marked declines. The only oddity in the general law that ESP is not affected by distance has been some research of Karlis Osis working with one selected subject. However, the subject's attitude, beliefs about psi, or many other factors could have contributed to his failure at long-distance ESP while being successful at close-range ESP. Osis did find an interesting fact when he examined all published ESP distance experiments: there was a slight decline with distance, even though not as rigid, predictable, or lawful as the inverse square law.[3] However, as other parapsychologists pointed out, since all these experiments were run under grossly dissimilar conditions, it might not be the distance factor that impeded success. Although Osis also showed a distinct success-decline effect when he compared experiments run at seven different distances, these results could have been due to psychological, not physical factors. Another formidable objection, of course, to the idea that ESP has some physicality is that GESP and precognition are the same phenomenon. How could any physical ESP force explain precognition?

Another argument against an electromagnetic theory of ESP is the failure of electromagnetic shielding to stop ESP from occurring. It was the hope of Soviet parapsychologist, Leonid Vasiliev, to show that ESP was caused by "brain radiations." (As a historical note, this would have confirmed earlier research by the Italian, Ferdinando Cazzamalli, who claimed to have shown that ESP was caused by a force broadcasted from the brain.) In Vasiliev's experiments, the agent and percipient were separated by the use of a Faraday cage, an apparatus that grounds any electromagnetic waves. Vasiliev's theory was that this shielding would immediately halt ESP, and would of course demonstrate the physical nature of ESP and show that it is a normal and measurable force. Much to his chagrin, the Faraday cage had no effect on ESP and successful results were achieved despite it. With much embarrassment he had to publish his results and admit that he had failed to find a physical basis for ESP.[4]

There are, of course, other objections to the physical theory of ESP. The brain has no known receptor or sender for such a force; obstructions such as walls and other barriers have no effect on it, and physical instruments have failed to detect it.

Despite these formidable objections one could still argue the other side of the coin. For instance, there is growing evidence that ESP may be spatial. Both René Warcollier and Sir Alister Hardy, the well-known British zoologist, as well as Alan Vaughan, have noted that during mass ESP tests certain subjects in close proximity to each other show closely knit similarities in their ESP responses. Sometimes the common themes are related to the actual target while at other times the coincidentals are within the group with no relation to the actual target. In any event, ESP must be invoked to explain these spatially clustered successes. The earliest explanation was of telepathic infection between the percipients. But even by this theory ESP would have to be considered spatial, since only those in close proximity were infected. Another theory could be of an ESP field which affects a spatial area. This is similar to what Graham Watkins found in his PK research with Felicia Parise and with the anesthetized mice. In fact, one could even construct a PK theory for ESP. For example it might be said that what we call telepathy is really a PK projection by the agent directly onto the brain cells of the percipient. Even precognition research has offered a few tantalizing morsels which support an ESP field. If one reviews Croiset's precognition chair tests, it is apparent that, although some of his impressions did not apply to the target person, they did directly concern persons in close physical proximity to that person.

Of course, this is not to say that ESP is a field, but only to suggest that some data could support a physical field theory. Several parapsychologists have toyed with physical theories of ESP based on concepts borrowed from quantum physics. The world of subatomic particles is a bizarre one. That is, particles go forward and backward in time; there seem to be holes in space; and particles change position instantaneously without movement. The action of these particles shows some similarity to the upside-down world of ESP. So, a few theorists have suggested that ESP information may be transferred by subatomic particles or by a similar type of undiscovered ESP particle, a physical force not yet restricted by physical laws.

One parapsychologist who held this view was the late Adrian Dobbs. Dobbs supported his argument with a refutation of the absoluteness of the inverse square law. He argued that the inverse square law can be bypassed by electrical superconductivity. Some metals when cooled to the temperature of liquid helium can act as conductors for a flow of electric current which then travels irrespective of the inverse square law. Dobbs also argued that ionospheric conditions can often play havoc with the inverse square principle. His views become extremely technical, but basing his theory upon concepts borrowed from physics, he postulated the existence of psi-trons which can dart throughout different dimensions of space and time. These psi-trons, bearers of ESP information, could affect the neurons in a person's brain influencing the transfer of information within it.[5] A proper appreciation of Dobbs's theory requires considerable understanding of quantum physics, but his theory could conceivably explain ESP along the lines of physics. Nonetheless the psi-tron theory has been challenged not on the basis of the physics employed, but on the basis that the mind could not possibly have the ability to identify and isolate which one psi-tron or mass of psi-trons it needed for a particular bit of information, or how it could decode it. All information reaching the human organism is coded, transferred, and then decoded. Now if one were doing a clairvoyant-condition Zener card run, how could the brain find the power and ability to differentiate which psi-trons from the resulting jumble would relate to each specific Zener card in the deck? This is merely one of several arguments that have been proposed to dispute Dobbs's concept.

Obviously, these debates are highly speculative and have as yet no experimental confirmations or refutations. They have been built only on pointers here and there in a vast array of self-contradictory data.

How can one explain ESP? There is a very concise answer to that: We can't. Although we have some inkling about what forms it takes and what psychological factors affect it, we know little else. Despite this, there are several theories about the whys and wherefores of ESP which have been put forward by several of parapsychology's ingenious researchers. Some of these theories, such as Roll's psi-field hypothesis, and Dobbs's psi-tron postulation have already been discussed.

Semiphysical theories of ESP have often been suggested. For example, Ninian Marshall offered a "resonance" theory for telepathy,[6] according to which two similar complex organs might act on each other by direct resonance which overcomes time and space. These two similar brains might be able to influence each other directly despite physical barriers such as distance. As is easily seen, Marshall's theory explains practically nothing about telepathy nor takes into account the interrelation of telepathy, clairvoyance, and precognition. On a little more sophisticated level G. D. Wassermann theorized the existence of psi fields of the same nature as the physical fields suggested in quantum physics. These fields might radiate energy over vast distances, irrespective of obstructions; interact with physical fields; and carry ESP impressions.[7] This type of theory led to Roll's formal presentation of a psi-field theory.

A more philosophical approach has been offered by H. H. Price who bases his theory on the hypothesis of a collective unconscious. His theory is metaphysical and is closely allied to Eastern philosophy: none of us is a distinct, independent consciousness. We all share a common consciousness on a level beyond our sensory lives and we are all connected by this common bond of consciousness. According to Price, on this level, we each know others' thoughts because thoughts are not private but registered on this collective unconsciousness of which all can partake. Price's collective unconsciousness is a constant field of interaction which connects all of us at all times. A supersensory experience occurs when one dips into this matrix.[8] An almost identical theory has been proposed by Lawrence LeShan who found that psychics, mystics, and theoretical physicists independently agreed that all physical realities are part of a total "one," and are inseparable. During mystical experiences one contacts a higher reality in which one feels he cannot be separated from another person, nature, or divinity. Common products of the mystical experience include feelings of unity with all life and the transcendence of time. In such a state ESP and precognition become understandable. The individual contacts a level where he transcends time and becomes one with others and nature, and can thus partake of information on a supersensory level.[9]

A psychological interpretation of telepathy based on the laws of association has been outlined by Whately Carington in his famous book, *Thought-Transference*. According to this theory, when two people are faced with similar situations, certain associations might be shared by them. (Looking at a stream might suggest the common association of fish or fishing.) This type of situation leads to telepathy. For some reason the agent and percipient, set in a similar situation, will share common associations. These associations are shared by ESP via "K-ideas" which act as bonds between the two minds. Again, Carington's theory does little to advance our understanding of the fundamental problem of telepathy: How does information *get* from one mind to another?

To answer this puzzle, J. B. Rhine suggests that the organism has some agency that can "leave the body" and gather information; that some actual part of the mind is not bound within the confines of the body. Further, this part of the mind might employ energy, but an energy radically different from normal physical energy. (Thus, one might add, we may not have the resources to discover or measure it at this point in our scientific technology.) While this whole concept is similar to the idea of psi scanning, where a part of the mind is constantly scanning to latch onto ESP impressions and relay them to the mind, in Rhine's concept something actually "goes out" of the mind to gather the data.[10]

One cannot complete any discussion of theories about ESP, no matter how brief, without mention of C. G. Jung's concept of "synchronicity." To Jung anything that smacked of ESP was really a synchronous event or a "meaningful coincidence." That is, the events are not causally connected, but are coincidences which arise from the natural order of the universe. To cite an example, Jung related an incident of a woman describing a dream of a scarab beetle, and at that moment a similar beetle appeared on his windowsill. Now, these two events are unrelated but had great meaning. Jung felt that the universe is so ordered that a certain amount of these coincidences occur revealing an acausal lawfulness of their own, and this could account for what we call psi.[11]

It could be easy to rebut this theory. First of all, most ESP occurs due to the conscious volition of one individual over another such as in dream telepathy. There is nothing synchronous here. To employ the idea that the sending of the target and the corresponding accurate dream of the percipient is not based on a causal relationship would make nonsense out of psi and everything we know about it.

Nonetheless, we are often the center of unaccountable runs of coincidences, and this could reveal Jung's higher order of the universe affecting our lives, but coincidences could just as well be mediated by psi as explained by Stanford's model of the psi-mediated instrumental response. So, the problem of acausality versus causality remains deadlocked.

These theories about ESP have been outlined only briefly for several reasons. Primarily, many of them are speculations with little empirical backing. Secondly, these theories are often enormously complex and couched in technical, opaque language so that to understand them is a formidable task in itself. Further, some of them postulate "unknowns" (such as psi-trons and psi fields) to explain other unknowns (ESP or PK). Unfortunately it is extremely hard for anyone to design a foolproof experiment to prove any one theory of psi.

What is obvious, though, is that psi just doesn't make any sense in the physical world. It just can't exist in the world as we know it. It is this absurdity which has led the scientific world to view the whole subject of psi with suspicion. Any anomaly which so upsets our everyday view of things is bound to be shunned by conventional science. That mind affects matter; that two people share common thoughts not expressed by the senses; that one can foresee a random future event; all this is ridiculous. But it occurs.

Perhaps a key to understanding psi might be found by borrowing a concept from Eastern thought that closely parallels the views of Price and LeShan. According to some schools of Buddhist thought, what we see is a world of illusion. We differentiate the observer and the observed only because of our ignorance and reliance on categorical reasoning. If one transcends this type of intellectual reasoning, one discovers that we live in a very different world—one in which we are all merely different manifestations of a unified whole, each a finger on an infinite hand, but usually blind to this fact. When an individual experiences this state of realization (sunyata), all personality is lost and the person becomes one with time, space, and matter.

The empirical evidence for this claim is, of course, mystical experiences. People undergoing this state describe it as ineffable, blissful, and holy, as one loses all sense of identity and merges with either people or nature about him or even with the universe itself. And most religions have the search for this state as their central goal.

But, does this explain psi? No. For no matter how one experiences these ineffable worlds, the experience brings conviction only to the experiencer. He cannot share his experience with others. The mystical experience does tell us this—and this is a consideration that many parapsychologists are beginning to face—we have the possibility that we see only a slim part of reality. Our senses allow us only a glimpse of the whole that the universe represents. Secondly, our view of the universe is distorted by our narrow line of sensory experience. Psi makes no sense to us simply because our view of the universe, even our very language, is so distorted and based on misconceptions that we could never understand the universe using these senses and languages. The world of quantum physics is very different from our securely physical world. After all, as the old cliché goes, does not a table primarily consist of empty space? It is possible that only when our view of the universe is cleared of our illusions will psi make sense.

G. N. M. Tyrrell made some apropos remarks on this problem in his book, *The Nature of Human Personality*, which bear quoting:

> Matter in molar masses lends itself to the illusion of discontinuity and self-completeness, which are a necessity for the simple mind of man; and the way in which his mind and senses were evolved force this illusion upon him with tremendous power. Even when the human intellect begins to form, these basic features of adaptation condition the growing mind. That is why there is a universal tendency to dismiss as rubbish evidence for anything at variance with what the senses reveal— When this situation is realized, we begin to see where the real boundary of our world lies. It is not in the abyss of space, nor can either theory of space-time reveal it, nor is it to be found in the ultra-microscopical world of protons and electrons. There is no boundary existent in the Universe. All is continuous *ad infinitum;* but the way we are ourselves constructed limits what we perceive and forces upon us the necessary illusion that we perceive the whole.

Unfortunately, despite the revelations offered by mystical experiences, we are, as Tyrrell suggests, enchained within a limited world. Nonetheless, it is rather obvious that this conception of the world has worked well for us. We have been able to uncover some physical laws of the universe, principles behind astronomy, biology, physics, and chemistry.

However, the existence of psi alters this conception of a purely physical cause-and-effect world. In the field of biology, for instance, Sir Alister Hardy has suggested that psi might be an unknown factor guiding evolution. In the field of anthropology it has been suggested that the existence of psi led to the development of magical beliefs and rituals in primitive cultures. In the area of psychiatry it has been seriously suggested that ESP might be an implicating and even causative factor in mental illness. Even J. B. Rhine has suggested that the mind, brain, and body all interact by employing PK within the human system—a novel concept for physiology to consider.

It would take a volume in itself to discuss the implications psi offers to science. Psi might be more a contributing factor to them than was ever conceived.

Instead of ending this book with a lengthy conclusion or an attempt at an elegant argument about the importance of parapsychology, only a few words need be said. Simply, that whatever psi is, it promises to help science in its two most sacred searches—the search to understand man and the search to understand his universe.

Notes and References

CHAPTER I | PARAPSYCHOLOGY AND THE ESP CONTROVERSY

1. Glossary of the *Journal of Parapsychology*.
2. Henry Holt, *On the Cosmic Relations* (Boston: Houghton-Mifflin Co., 1914).
3. D. Scott Rogo, "The Academic Status of Parapsychology," *Parapsychology Review* 4, no. 6 (1973): 21–23.
4. J. B. Rhine, "News and Comments," *Journal of Parapsychology* 36 (1972): 167–76.
5. Bob Brier, "Goals in Parapsychology and Other Sciences," *Parapsychology and the Sciences*, proceedings of an international conference (New York: Parapsychology Foundation, 1974).
6. Gardner Murphy, *The Challenge of Psychical Research* (New York: Harper, 1961).
7. Charles Honorton and Stanley Krippner, "Hypnosis and ESP: A Review of Experimental Literature," *Journal: ASPR* 63 (1969): 214–52.
8. Murphy, op. cit.
9. K. Ramakrishna Rao, Review of "Five Years Report of Seth Sohan Lal Memorial Institute of Parapsychology," *Journal of Parapsychology*, March 1964. (For various rejoinders and charges see letters to the editor in the December issue of the *Journal*.)
10. E. G. Boring, "The Spirits Against Bosh," *Contemporary Psychology* 6 (1961): 149–51.
11. Ian Stevenson, "Scientists with Half-Closed Minds," *Harper's Magazine*, November 1958.
12. Ciba Foundation, *Symposium on Extrasensory Perception* (Boston: Little, Brown, 1956).

13. Robert Thouless, *From Anecdote to Experiment in Psychical Research* (London: Routledge and Kegan Paul, 1971).

14. Ibid.

15. J. B. Rhine, "Guiding Concepts for Psi Research" in J. B. Rhine, ed., *Progress in Parapsychology* (Durham, N.C.: Parapsychology Press, 1973).

CHAPTER 2 | THE FOUNDATIONS OF PSYCHICAL RESEARCH

1. S. Freud, *New Introductory Lectures in Psychoanalysis* (London: Hogarth Press, 1934).

2. J. de Vooght, "Les miracles dans la vie de S. Augustin," *Recherches de Theol. ancienne et mediévale* XI (1939): 5 ff.

3. E. J. Dingwall, *Some Human Oddities* (London: Home and Van Thal, 1947).

4. H. Carrington and Nandor Fodor, *Haunted People* (New York: Dutton, 1951).

5. Renée Haynes, *Philosopher King—the Humanist Pope Benedict XIV* (London: Weidenfeld and Nicolson, 1970).

6. Charles Honorton, "A Post-Mortem on Mesmerism and the Paranormal: Comments on *Abnormal Hypnotic Phenomena*," *Journal: ASPR* 64 (1970): 104–10.

7. E. E. Lewis, *A Report of the Mysterious Noises heard in the House of Mr. John D. Fox in Hydesville, Arcadia, Wayne County* (Canandaigua, N.Y.: 1848).

8. Ibid.

9. William Crookes, *Researches in the Phenomena of Spiritualism* (London: John Burns, n.d.).

10. Ibid.

CHAPTER 3 | ESP—THE SEARCH AND THE EVIDENCE

1. Symposium: "The Future of Parapsychology," *International Journal of Parapsychology* IV (1962): no. 2.

2. E. Gurney, F. W. H. Myers, and F. Podmore, *Phantasms of the Living* (London: Trubner's, 1886).

3. Professor Sidgwick's Committee. "Report on the Census of Hallucinations," *Proceedings:* SPR X (1894): 25–422.

4. L. Dale, R. White, and G. Murphy, "A Selection of Cases from a Recent Survey of Spontaneous ESP Phenomena," *Journal:* ASPR LVI (1962): 3–47.

5. Henry Sidgwick, Eleanor Sidgwick, and G. A. Smith, "Experiments in Thought-Transference," *Proceedings:* SPR VI (1889): 128–70.

6. H. J. F. W. Brugmans, in "Compte-Rendu du Premier Congress International des Recherches Psychiques à Copenhague," 1921.

7. L. T. Troland, *A Technique for the Experimental Study of Telepathy and other Alleged Clairvoyant Processes* (Monograph, Albany, N.Y.: n.d.).

8. G. H. Estabrooks, *Bulletin:* Boston Society for Psychic Research V (1927).

9. A. W. Verrall, "Report on a Series of Experiments in 'Guessing,' " *Proceedings:* SPR XXIX (1916): 64 ff.

10. Mrs. E. Sidgwick, "Report on Further Experiments in Thought-Transference Carried out by Professor Gilbert Murray," *Proceedings:* SPR XXIV (1924): 212 ff. and XXIV (1924): 336 ff.; *Journal:* SPR XXXII (1941): 29 ff.; *Proceedings:* SPR XLIX (1952): 155 ff. (Murray's SPR presidential address); E. R. Dodds, "Gilbert Murray's Last Experiments," *Proceedings:* SPR 55 (1972), pt. 206.

11. C. Miles and H. Ramsden, "Experiments in Thought-Transference," *Proceedings:* SPR XXI (1907), pt. 54.

12. Whately Carington, "Experiments on the Paranormal Cognition of Drawings," *Proceedings:* SPR XLVI (1940): 23–151, 277–334; XLVII (1944): 155–228. See also *Proceedings:* ASPR XXIV (1944): 3–107.

CHAPTER 4 | ESP IN THE LABORATORY
—THE SEARCH CONTINUED

1. J. B. Rhine, *Extrasensory Perception*. Reprint (Boston: Bruce Humphries, 1964).

2. Margaret Pegram Reeves and J. B. Rhine, "Exceptional scores in ESP tests and the Conditions. I. The case of Lillian," *Journal of Parapsychology* 6 (1942): 164–73.

3. G. N. M. Tyrrell, *Science and Psychical Phenomena* (New York: Harper Bros., 1938).

4. S. G. Soal and F. Bateman, *Modern Experiments in Telepathy* (New Haven, Conn.: Yale University Press, 1954).

5. R. G. Medhurst, "The Origin of the Prepared Random Numbers used in the Shackleton Experiments," *Journal:* SPR 46 (1971): 39–54.

6. J. B. Rhine, "Experiments Bearing on the Precognition Hypothesis, I," *Journal of Parapsychology* 2 (1938): 38–54; J. B. Rhine, B. Smith, and J. L. Woodruff, "Experiments Bearing on the Precognition Hypothesis, II, the Role of ESP in the Shuffling of Cards," *Journal of Parapsychology* 2 (1938): 119–31; J. B. Rhine, "Experiments Bearing on the Precognition Hypothesis, III, Mechanically Selected Cards," *Jour-*

nal of Parapsychology 5 (1941): 1–58; J. B. Rhine, "Evidence of Precognition in the Covariation of Salience Ratios," *Journal of Parapsychology* 6 (1942): 111–43.

7. John Palmer, "Scoring in ESP Tests as a Function of Belief in ESP. Part I. The Sheep-Goat Effect," *Journal:* ASPR 65 (1971): 373–408.

8. M. Anderson and Rhea White, "ESP score level in relation to students' attitude toward teacher-agents acting simultaneously," *Journal of Parapsychology* 22 (1958): 20–28.

9. Helmut Schmidt, "Precognition of a Quantum Process," *Journal of Parapsychology* 33 (1969): 99–109; "Clairvoyance Test with a Machine," *Journal of Parapsychology* 33 (1969): 300–307.

10. Malcolm Guthrie, "Further Report on the Experiments in Thought-Transference in Liverpool," *Proceedings:* SPR 3 (1885).

11. Robert Thouless, "Parapsychology During the Last Quarter of a Century" in J. B. Rhine, ed., *Progress in Parapsychology* (Durham, N.C.: Parapsychology Press, 1973).

12. P. Sailaja, "A Confirmatory study of the role of key cards in language ESP tests," Paper delivered at the Eighth Annual Convention of the Parapsychological Association, New York, 1965.

13. J. G. Pratt, "A Decade of Research With a Selected ESP Subject: An Overview and Reappraisal of the Work With Pavel Stepanek," *Proceedings:* ASPR 30 (1973): 1–78.

14. D. J. West and G. W. Fisk, "A dual experiment with clock cards," *Journal:* SPR 37 (1953–1954): 185–89.

15. S. Figar, "The application of plethysmography to the objective study of so-called extrasensory perception," *Journal:* SPR 40 (1959): 162–72.

16. E. Douglas Dean, "The Plethysmograph as an indicator of ESP," *Journal:* SPR 41 (1962): 351–53; E. Douglas Dean and C. B. Nash, "Plethysmograph results under strict conditions," as above: Sixth Annual Convention, New York, 1963.

17. C. T. Tart, "Possible physiological correlates of Psi Cognition," *International Journal of Parapsychology* 5 (1963): 375–86.

18. B. K. Kanthamani and K. Ramakrishna Rao, "Personality Characteristics of ESP Subjects. IV. Neuroticism and ESP," *Journal of Parapsychology* 39 (1973): 37–50.

19. Betty M. Humphrey, "Introversion-extroversion ratings in relation to scores in ESP tests," *Journal of Parapsychology* 15 (1951): 252–62.

20. Betty M. Humphrey, "Success in ESP as related to forms of response drawings. I. Clairvoyance experiments," *Journal of Parapsychology* 10 (1946): 78–106; "II. GESP experiments" 10 (1946): 181–96; Burke M. Smith and Betty M. Humphrey, "Some personality charac-

teristics related to ESP performance," *Journal of Parapsychology* 10 (1946): 269–309.

21. G. R. Schmeidler and L. LeShan, "An Aspect of Body Image Related to ESP Scores," *Journal: ASPR* 64 (1970): 211–18.

CHAPTER 5 | SPONTANEOUS ESP

1. Gertrude Schmeidler, "ESP Breakthroughs: Paranormal Effects in Real Life," *Journal: ASPR* 61 (1967): 506–25.

2. Robert Thouless, *From Anecdote to Experiment in Psychical Research* (London: Routledge and Kegan Paul, 1972).

3. Ian Stevenson, "Telepathic Impressions: A Review and Report of Thirty-five New Cases," *Proceedings: ASPR* 29 (1970): 1–198.

4. M. Ullman, S. Krippner, and A. Vaughan, *Dream Telepathy* (New York: Macmillan, 1973).

5. G. Pederson-Krag, "Telepathy and Repression" in G. Devereux, ed., *Psychoanalysis and the Occult* (New York: International Universities Press, 1953).

6. R. Heywood and I. Stevenson, "The Connections Between Previous Experiences and an Apparently Precognitive Dream," *Journal: ASPR* 60 (1966): 32–45.

7. Theodore Besterman, "Report of an Inquiry into Precognitive Dreams," *Proceedings: SPR* XLI (1933).

8. I. Stevenson, "A Review and Analysis of Paranormal Experiences Connected with the Sinking of the *Titanic*," *Journal: ASPR* 54 (1960): 153–71; "Seven More Paranormal Experiences Associated with the Sinking of the *Titanic*," *Journal: ASPR* 59 (1965): 211–25.

9. E. W. Cox, "Precognition: An Analysis, I," *Journal: ASPR* 50 (1956): 47–58; "Precognition: An Analysis, II," *Journal: ASPR* 50 (1956): 97–107.

10. Alan Vaughan, "Spontaneous Precognitive Dreaming," *Parapsychology Review*, September–October 1973, pp. 21–26.

11. C. Drayton Thomas, *Some New Evidence for Human Survival* (New York: Dutton, n.d.).

12. Rhea White, "The Mystery of Déjà-Vu," *Psychic* IV (1973): 44–49.

13. Ibid.

14. Gracia-Fay Ellwood, *Psychic Visits to the Past* (New York: Signet Books, 1971).

15. R. P. Greiner, Abstract: "An Investigation into the Personality Traits of People with So-Called Spontaneous Paranormal Phenomena," *Journal of Parapsychology* 28 (1964): 284.

CHAPTER 6 | ESP RESEARCH WITH GIFTED SUBJECTS

1. Gustave Geley, *Clairvoyance and Materialization* (New York: George H. Doran Co., 1927).

2. Gustav Pagenstecher, "Past Events Seership," *Proceedings: ASPR* 16 (1923): pt. 1.

3. W. F. Prince, "Psychometric Experiments with Senora Maria de Z.," *Proceedings: ASPR* 15 (1921).

4. W. G. Roll, "Pagenstecher's Contribution to Parapsychology," *Journal: ASPR* 61 (1967): 219–40.

5. W. G. Roll, "The Psi Field," *Proceedings:* Parapsychological Association, no. 1, 1957–1964.

6. Milan Rýzl, *Parapsychology—A Scientific Approach* (New York: Hawthorn, 1970).

7. A. H. Esser and L. LeShan, "A Transatlantic 'Chair Test,' " *Journal: SPR* 45 (1969): 167–70.

8. H. F. Saltmarsh, "Report on an Investigation of Some Sittings with Mrs. Warren Elliott," *Proceedings: SPR* XXXIV (1930–1931).

9. Gertrude Schmeidler, "Analysis and Evaluation of Proxy Sessions with Mrs. Caroline Chapman," *Journal of Parapsychology* 22 (1958): 137–55.

10. Ian Stevenson, "The Analysis of a Mediumistic Session by a New Method," *Journal: ASPR* 62 (1968): 334–55.

11. Judith Klein, "Lalsingh Harribance, Medium in Residence," *Theta #31*, spring, 1971.

12. Rhea White, "A Comparison of Old and New Methods of Response to Targets in ESP Experiments," *Journal: ASPR* 58 (1964): 21–56.

13. O. L. Trick, Abstract: "Psychological Studies of Two 'Mediums,' " *Journal of Parapsychology* 30 (1966): 301–2.

14. Gustave Geley, op. cit.

CHAPTER 7 | MIND, SPACE, AND MATTER—TELEKINESIS

1. Camille Flammarion, *Death and Its Mystery*, vol. II (New York: The Century Co., 1922).

2. Ibid.

3. H. Carrington and N. Fodor, *Haunted People* (New York: Dutton, 1951).

4. John Layard, "Psi Phenomena and Poltergeists," *Proceedings: SPR* 67 (1944).

5. H. Carrington and N. Fodor, op. cit.

6. Harry Price, "A Report on the Telekinetic and Other Phenomena Witnessed Through Eleanore Zugun," *Proceedings:* National Laboratory of Psychical Research (1927): pt. 1.

7. W. G. Roll, *The Poltergeist* (Garden City, N.Y.: Doubleday, 1972).

8. Hans Bender, Presidential Address to the Parapsychological Association, September 1969; J. Mischo, "Personality Structure of Psychokinetic Mediums," *Proceedings:* Parapsychology Association (1968): 388–92.

9. W. G. Roll, op. cit.

10. Raymond Bayless, *The Enigma of the Poltergeist* (West Nyack, N.Y.: Parker, 1967).

11. Ian Stevenson, "Are Poltergeists Living or Are They Dead?" *Journal:* ASPR 66 (1972): 233–52.

12. Hereward Carrington, *Eusapia Palladino and Her Phenomena* (New York: B. W. Dodge, 1909).

13. W. J. Crawford, *The Reality of Psychic Phenomena* (New York: Dutton, 1918); *Experiments in Psychical Science* (New York: Dutton, 1919); *The Psychic Structures at the Goligher Circle* (New York: Dutton, 1921).

14. J. Ochorowicz, "A New Mediumistic Phenomenon," *Annals of Psychical Science* 7 (1909).

15. Harry Price, *Stella C.* (London: Hurst & Blackett, 1925).

16. Harry Price, *Rudi Schneider* (London: Methuen, 1930); Anita Gregory Kohson, *The Ghost in the Machine* (unpublished manuscript on file at the SPR).

17. A. Schrenck-Notzing, *The Phenomena of Materialization* (London: Kegan Paul, Trench, Trubner & Co., 1920).

18. Gustave Geley, *Clairvoyance and Materialization* (New York: George H. Doran Co., 1927).

CHAPTER 8 | MIND, SPACE, AND MATTER
—PK IN THE LABORATORY

1. J. B. Rhine and L. E. Rhine, "The Psychokinetic Effect. I. The First Experiment," *Journal of Parapsychology* 7 (1943): 20–43.

2. J. B. Rhine, "Dice Thrown By Cup and Machine in PK Tests," *Journal of Parapsychology* 7 (1943): 207–17.

3. J. B. Rhine and Betty Humphrey, "The PK Effect: Special Evidence from Hit Patterns. I. Quarter Distribution of the Page," *Journal of Parapsychology* 8 (1944): 18–60.

4. E. P. Gibson, Lottie H. Gibson, and J. B. Rhine, "A Large Series of PK Tests," *Journal of Parapsychology* 7 (1943): 228–37.

5. W. E. Cox, "The Effect of PK on the Placement of Falling Objects," *Journal of Parapsychology* 15 (1951): 40–48.

6. W. E. Cox, "Three-Tier Placement PK," *Journal of Parapsychology* 23 (1959): 19–29.

7. H. Forwald, "Chronological Decline Effects on a PK Placement Experiment," *Journal of Parapsychology* 18 (1954): 32–36.

8. R. H. Thouless, "A Report on an Experiment on Psychokinesis with Dice and a Discussion of Psychological Factors Favoring Success," *Proceedings:* SPR 49 (1949–1952): 116–17.

9. H. Forwald, "An Experiment in Guessing ESP Cards by Throwing a Die," *Journal of Parapsychology* 27 (1963): 16–22.

10. R. L. Van de Castle, "An Exploratory Study of some Personality Correlates Associated with PK Performance," *Journal:* ASPR 52 (1958): 134–50.

11. Arne Olander, "Telekinetic Experiments with Anna Rasmussen Melloni," *Journal:* SPR 41 (1961): 184–93.

12. Jule Eisenbud, *The World of Ted Serios* (New York: William Morrow & Co., 1967).

13. D. Scott Rogo, "Photographs by the Mind," *Psychic* 1, no. 5 (1970): 40–46.

14. Gertrude Schmeidler, "PK Effects Upon Continuously Recorded Temperatures," *Journal:* ASPR 67 (1973): 325–40.

15. Benson Herbert, "Report on Nina Kulagina," *Parapsychology Review* 3, no. 6 (1972): 8–10.

16. Graham Watkins and Anita Watkins, Paper delivered at the 1972 Convention of the Parapsychological Association, Edinburgh, Scotland.

17. Bernard Grad, R. J. Cadoret, and G. I. Paul, "The Influence of an Unorthodox Method of Treatment on Mice," *International Journal of Parapsychology* 3 (1961): 5–24; Bernard Grad, "A Telekinetic Effect on Plant Growth, I," *International Journal of Parapsychology* V (1963): 117–33; Part II, *International Journal of Parapsychology* VI (1964): 473–98; Bernard Grad, "The Laying on of Hands; Implications for Psychotherapy, Gentling, and the Placebo Effect," *Journal:* ASPR 61 (1967): 286–305.

18. Note in *Parapsychology Review* 2, no. 4 (1971): 12.

CHAPTER 9 | NEW HORIZONS IN ESP RESEARCH

1. Rex Stanford and C. Lovin, "EEG Alpha Activity and ESP Performance," *Journal:* ASPR 64 (1970): 375–84.

2. C. Honorton et al., "Feedback—Augmented EEG Alpha, Shifts in Subjective State and ESP Card-Guessing Performance," *Journal:* ASPR 65 (1971): 308–23.

3. Karlis Osis and E. Bokert, "ESP and Changed States of Consciousness Induced by Meditation," *Journal:* ASPR 65 (1971): 17–65.

4. C. Honorton et al., "Shifts in Subjective State and ESP Under Conditions of Partial Sensory Deprivation: A Preliminary Study," *Journal:* ASPR 67 (1973): 191–96.

5. R. Cavanna and E. Servadio, *ESP Experiments with LSD 25 and Psilocybin* (New York: Parapsychology Foundation, 1964).

6. S. Van Asperen de Boer et al., "Is It Possible to Induce ESP with Psilocybin?" *International Journal of Neuropsychiatry* (1966): 447–73.

7. Leonid Vasiliev, *Mysterious Phenomena of the Human Psyche* (New Hyde Park, N.Y.: University Books, 1965).

8. Emile Boirac, *Our Hidden Forces* (also published as *Psychic Science*) (New York: 1917; London: Rider, 1918).

9. C. Honorton and S. Krippner, "Hypnosis and ESP: A Review of the Experimental Literature," *Journal:* ASPR 63 (1969): 214–52.

10. S. Krippner, "Experimentally-Induced Telepathic Effects in Hypnosis and Non-Hypnosis Groups," *Journal:* ASPR 62 (1968): 387–98.

11. Lawrence LeShan, *Towards a General Theory of the Paranormal* (New York: Parapsychology Foundation, 1969).

12. M. Ullman, S. Krippner, with A. Vaughan, *Dream Telepathy* (New York: Macmillan, 1973).

13. Charles Alexander, *Bobbie: A Great Collie of Oregon* (New York: Dodd, Mead & Co., 1926).

14. K. Osis and E. B. Foster, "A Test of ESP in Cats," *Journal of Parapsychology* 17 (1953): 168–86.

15. G. H. Wood and R. J. Cadoret, "Tests of Clairvoyance in a Man-Dog Relationship," *Journal of Parapsychology* 22 (1958): 29–39.

16. Robert Morris, "Psi and Animal Behavior: A Survey," *Journal:* ASPR 64 (1970): 242–60.

CHAPTER 10 | PSI, DEATH, AND SURVIVAL

1. F. W. H. Myers, *Human Personality and Its Survival of Bodily Death* (London: Longmans, 1903).

2. F. W. H. Myers, *Journal:* SPR, November 1927.

3. Rose Morton, "A Record of a Haunted House," *Proceedings:* SPR VII (1892).

4. E. Bozzano, *Les Phénomènes de Hantise* (Paris: Alcan, 1920).

5. Oliver Lodge, *The Survival of Man* (New York: George H. Doran Co., 1909).

6. S. G. Soal, "A Report of Some Communications Received through Mrs. Blanche Cooper," *Proceedings:* SPR 35 (1925).

7. William Barrett, *Deathbed Visions* (London: Methuen & Co., 1926).

8. Robert Crookall, *Out-of-the-Body Experiences—a fourth analysis* (New Hyde Park, N.Y.: University Books, 1970).

9. Hornell Hart, "Scientific Survival Research," *International Journal of Parapsychology* IX (1967): 43–52.

10. Charles T. Tart, "A Second Psychophysiological Study of Out-of-the-Body Experiences in a Gifted Subject," *International Journal of Parapsychology* 9 (1967): 251–58; "A Psychophysiological Study of Out-of-the-Body Experiences in a Selected Subject," *Journal: ASPR* 62 (1968): 3–27.

11. Karlis Osis, "Linkage Experiments with Mediums," *Journal: ASPR* 60 (1966): 91–124.

12. Alan Gauld, "A Series of 'Drop-in' Communicators," *Proceedings: SPR* 55 (1971): 273–340.

CHAPTER 11 | THE ENIGMA OF PSI

1. Rex Stanford, "Extrasensory Effects upon Memory," *Journal: ASPR* 64 (1970): 161–86.

2. D. Dean and J. Mihalasky, with L. Schroeder and S. Ostrander, *Executive ESP* (Englewood Cliffs, N.J.: Prentice-Hall, 1974).

3. Karlis Osis, "ESP over Distance: A Survey of experiments published in English," *Journal: ASPR* 59 (1965): 22–42.

4. Leonid Vasiliev, *Experiments in Mental Suggestion* (Church Crookham, England: Institute for the Study of Mental Images, 1963).

5. Adrian Dobbs, "Time and ESP," *Proceedings: SPR* 54 (1965): pt. 197.

6. Ninian Marshall, "ESP and Memory: A Physical Theory," *British Journal Phil. Science* 10 (1960): 265–86.

7. Ciba Foundation *Symposium on Extrasensory Perception* (Boston: Little, Brown, 1956).

8. H. H. Price, "Some philosophical questions about telepathy and clairvoyance," *Philosophy* 15 (1940): 363–74.

9. Lawrence LeShan, *Towards a General Theory of the Paranormal* (New York: Parapsychology Foundation, 1969).

10. J. B. Rhine, *Extrasensory Perception*. Reprint (Boston: Bruce Humphries, 1964).

11. C. G. Jung and W. Pauli, *Synchronicity* (New York: Pantheon, 1955).

Selected Bibliography

Capron, E. W. *Modern Spiritualism*. Boston, 1855.

Carrington, Hereward. *The Physical Phenomena of Spiritualism*. New York: Herbert Turner & Co., 1907.

———. *Eusapia Palladino and Her Phenomena*. New York: B. W. Dodge, 1909.

Coover, John. *Experiments in Psychical Research*. Stanford, 1917.

Dingwall, E. J., ed. *Abnormal Hypnotic Phenomena*. New York: Barnes & Noble, 1967.

Dunne, J. W. *An Experiment with Time*. London: Faber & Faber, 1927.

Dunraven, Earl of. *Experiences in Spiritualism with D. D. Home*. London: Society for Psychical Research, 1924.

Ehrenwald, Jan. *Telepathy and Medical Psychology*. London: George Allen & Unwin, 1947.

Eisenbud, Jule. *The World of Ted Serios*. New York: William Morrow, 1969.

Flammarion, Camille. *The Unknown*. New York: Harper & Bros., 1900.

———. *Death and Its Mystery*. 3 vols. New York: The Century Co., 1921–1923.

Flournoy, Theodore. *Spiritism and Psychology*. New York: Harper & Bros., 1911.

Forwald, Haakon. *Mind, Matter and Gravitation*. New York: Parapsychology Foundation, 1969.

Fukurai, T. *Clairvoyance and Thoughtography*. London: Rider & Co., 1931.

Gauld, Alan. *The Founders of Psychical Research*. New York: Schocken, 1968.

Green, Celia. *Out-of-the-Body Experiences*. Oxford: Institute of Psychophysical Research, 1968.

Hansel, C. E. M. *ESP: A Scientific Evaluation*. New York: Charles Scribner's Sons, 1966.

Hyslop, James H. *Contact with the Other World*. New York: The Century Co., 1919.

Jaffé, Aniela. *Apparitions and Precognition*. New York: University Books, 1963.

Leroy, Oliver. *Levitation: An Examination of the Evidence*. London, 1928.

Lilly, John. *The Center of the Cyclone*. New York: Julian Press, 1972.

Lodge, Oliver. *The Survival of Man*. New York: George H. Doran Co., 1909.

Lombroso, Cesare. *After Death—What?* Boston: Small Maynard & Co., 1908.

Masters, R. E. L., and Houston, J. *The Varieties of Psychedelic Experience*. New York: Holt, Rinehart & Winston, 1966.

Moberly, Ann, and Jourdain, E. P. *An Adventure*. New York: Macmillan & Co., 1911.

Mowbray, Major. *Transition*. Reprint. London: L.S.A. Publications Ltd., 1947.

Ochorowicz, Julien. *Mental Suggestion*. New York: Humboldt Publishing Co., 1891.

Osis, Karlis. *Deathbed Observations by Physicians and Nurses*. New York: Parapsychology Foundation, 1961.

Osty, Eugene. *Supernormal Faculties in Man*. London: Methuen, 1923.

Owen, A. R. G. *Hysteria, Hypnosis and Healing: the Work of J. M. Charcot*. New York: Garrett Publications, 1968.

Pratt, J. G. *ESP Research Today*. Metuchen, N.J.: Scarecrow Press, 1973.

Prince, W. F. *Human Experiences*. Boston: Boston Society for Psychic Research, 1931.

Rao, K. Ramakrishna. *Experimental Parapsychology*. Springfield, Ill.: Charles C Thomas, 1966.

Rhine, J. B. *Extrasensory Perception*. Reprint. Boston: Bruce Humphries, 1964.

———. *New Frontiers of the Mind*. New York: Farrar & Rinehart, 1937.

Rhine, J. B. et al. *Extrasensory Perception After Sixty Years*. Boston: Bruce Humphries, 1940.

Rhine, Louisa. *ESP in Life and Lab*. New York: Macmillan, 1969.

———. *Mind Over Matter*. New York: Macmillan, 1970.

Richmond, A. B. *A Reply to the Seybert Commissioners' Report*. Boston: Colby & Rich, 1888.

Sinclair, Upton. *Mental Radio*. Reprint. Springfield, Ill.: Charles C Thomas, 1962.

Sudre, René. *Treatise on Parapsychology*. New York: Citadel, 1960.

Tanagras, A. *Psychophysical Elements in Parapsychological Traditions*. New York: Parapsychology Foundation, 1967.

Tart, Charles. *On Being Stoned*. Palo Alto, Calif.: Science & Behavior Books, 1971.

Thouless, R. H. *Experimental Psychical Research*. Baltimore: Penguin, 1963.

Tietze, T. R. *Margery*. New York: Harper & Row, 1973.

Tyrrell, G. N. M. *Science and Psychical Phenomena*. New York: Harper Bros., 1938.

West, D. J. *Eleven Lourdes Miracles*. New York: Garrett Publications, 1957.

Zoellner, Johann. *Transcendental Physics*. London: W. H. Harrison, 1880.

————. *Report of the Seybert Commission*. Philadelphia: J. B. Lippincott, 1920.

————. *Confessions of a Medium*. London: Griffith, Farrar, Okeden & Welsh, n.d.

————. *Revelations of a Spirit Medium*. London, 1922.

Index

Aberfan disaster, 136–37
Adare, Lord, 51–52
Adler, Alfred, 130
Akers, C., 110*n*
Albe, Fournier d', 193
Albert, Gretl, 95–96
alpha ESP effect, 108, 166, 227 –30
altered states of consciousness (ASC), 226–44
American Society for Psychical Research (ASPR), 56–57
an-psi research, 110, 249–54
analysis, in psi, 81
Anderson, Margaret, 101
anesthetics, and PK, 222–23
Angela, Saint, 31
Angoff, Allan, 40
animals, psi in, 110, 249–54
apparitions, 15, 48, 65–67, 176, 184, 258–59; crisis, 60, 64, 65, 258; of the dead, 65, 67, 258–59, 271–72, 275; of the living, 258, 275. *See also* visions
apports, 195, 197
Aquinas, Saint Thomas, 31
Aristocritus, 29
Aristotle, 29–30
ASC, psi and, 226–44
Augustine, Saint, 31

Baer, George, 207
Baggally, W. W., 189–91
Bailey, June, 89, 110, 168
Ballechin House, 260
Barker, J. C., 137
Barrett, William, 43*n*, 55, 58, 176, 194, 236, 271
Baterbaugh, Coleen, 143–44
Bayless, Raymond, 184
Bell, John, 44
Beloff, John, 103, 109, 243
belomancy, 30
Bender, Hans, 170, 176, 182–84
Benedict XIV, Pope, 34–35
Bergson, Henri, 283
Bertrand, Alexandre, 38–39
Bessent, Malcolm, 247*n*, 248
Besterman, Theodore, 135
Bindler, Paul, 227, 229
biofeedback, 228. *See also* alpha ESP effect
Birge, W. R., 163, 165
biting poltergeists, 176, 178, 180
Bjelfvenstam, Erik, 40
Blume, Johann, 32–33
Bobbie (collie), 250–51
Boirac, Emile, 237–38
Bokert, Edwin, 230–31
Bond, Esther, 90–91

Bourg de Bozas, Count Guy de, 151
Bozzano, Ernesto, 261
Braid, James, 40
brain radiations, 286
Brazier, Frank, 250–51
Brier, Robert, 15
Brown, G. Spencer, 21
Brugmans, H. J. F. W., 70–71
Buchanon, J. Rodes, 153
Bucke, R. M., 280
Burt, F. P., 77
Bush, George, 51
Busschbach, Van, 101

Cabibbo, C., 106
Cadoret, R. J., 108, 166, 227, 238, 251–52
Callihan family, 181
cantilever theory of PK, 194
capnomancy, 30
Capron, E. W., 44
Carington, Whately, 77–78, 94, 283, 289–90
Carrington, Hereward, 32n, 34, 176, 189–93, 199, 241, 283
Casler, Lawrence, 238
Cassirer, Manfred, 220
Cavanna, Roberto, 235
Cazzamalli, Ferdinando, 286
Census of Hallucinations, The (SPR), 64–67
Chaffin Will case, 259
chair tests, 159–63
Chapman, Caroline, 164
Chari, C. T. K., 142
Chiaia, Professor, 185
children: ESP in, 90–91, 101; and poltergeists, 178–83, 185
Chris (dog), 251–52
cipher tests, 278–79
clairvoyance: defined, 14; hypnosis and, 238–40; medical, 31, 37–39, 41; and precognition, 15, 138–39; and telepathy, 72–73,

126; tests for, 85–88, 94, 102; traveling, 31
Clement XIV, Pope, 31
clock stoppings, 120, 173, 174
coincidence, 284–85, 290
collective unconscious, 289
community of sensations, 38–39, 41, 153–54, 237–38. See also healing, psychic; medical clairvoyance
compass deflection, 219, 222
control (spirit), 140, 262
Cook, Florence, 54
Cooper, Blanche, 270
Cooper, T. C., 89, 110
Coover, John, 72–73
cosmic reservoir, 267–68, 269
Cox, W. E., 137, 210–11
Crandon, Mina ("Margery"), 203n
Crawford, W. J., 193–95
Creery sisters, 70
crisis apparitions, 60, 64, 65, 258
crisis cases, 60–61
crisis telekinesis, 173
critical ratio (CR), 84n
Croiset, Gerard, 159–63, 167, 169, 197, 287
Crookall, Robert, 274–75
Crookes, William, 47–50, 52–54, 147
cross correspondences, 268–69, 277
Cumberland, Stuart, 19–20
Cumberlandism, 19–20

Dale, Laura, 215, 245
Dalton, G. F., 141
Damgaard, Jacqueline, 166
Danville-Fife, Charles, 234
Darget, Commandant, 218
Darwin, Charles, 43, 49–50, 257
Davey, A. J., 62
Davidson, Richard, 227, 229
Davis, A. J., 42–43
Davis, Gordon, 269–70

De Puységur, Marquis, 37–38
Dean, E. Douglas, 112, 246, 284
death, life after. *See* mediumship;
  survival issue
death coincidence, 65
deathbed visions, 271–73
decision-making, and psi, 284–85
decline effect, 74, 90, 99–100, 209;
  explanations for, 104–6; in PK
  tests, 207–9, 212; types of, 104
déjà vu, 141–42
Delmore, William, 110
Dement, William, 276
Democritus, 29
Despard family, 259–60
Dessoir, Max, 70
Deutsch, Helene, 30, 129
Di Ligouri, Alfonso, 31
dice throwing tests, 205–10
Dieppe Raid case, 144–45
differential scoring, 107
Dingwall, Eric, 32–33, 40–41,
  76–77, 152, 201
displacement effect, 78, 94, 96,
  106–8
dissociation, in psi, 80
distance tests: ESP, 79–80, 89–90,
  160–63, 248, 285–86; PK, 214
divination, 30
Dobbs, Adrian, 287–88
Dodds, E. R., 29, 30, 34
dreams, 30, 48; contemporaneous,
  127–28; precognitive, 131–36,
  138, 140–41; realistic, 119,
  127–28, 131, 133, 138; symbolic,
  119, 127–28, 131–33, 138; telepathic, 244–49; tests on, 240–41
Driesch, Hans, 203
drop-in communicators, 277–78
drugs, and ESP, 87–89, 233–36
Drummer of Tedworth, 35–36,
  176
Ducasse, C. J., 58
Duesler, William, 44
Dunne, J. W., 133–35, 139–41
Dunstan, Saint, 32

Dupré, G., 124
Duval, Pierre, 253

ectoplasm, 200. *See also* materializa-
  tions
Ehrenwald, Jan, 30, 130, 170
Eisenbud, Jule, 30, 58, 129, 130,
  141, 217–18
Elawar, Imad, 279
electromagnetism, 286
Elliot, G. Maurice, 32*n*
Elliot, Mrs. Warren, 159, 163–64
Elliotson, John, 39, 41, 153
Ellis, Albert, 130
Ellwood, Gracia-Fay, 146
emotion, and ESP, 102, 112–23
Erwin, William, 247
Esdaile, James, 39
ESP: contemporaneous, 119–30;
  controversy about, 15–27; culti-
  vation of, 241–43; defined, 11;
  disappearance of, 88, 96; forms
  of, 14; inhibition of, 65, 105–6,
  120–21, 127; mass effect of, 73,
  80, 97, 101, 136–38, 287;
  patient/therapist, 30–31,
  129–30; patterns of, 103–11; personality and, 101–2, 113–16,
  146–47, 169–71; physics of,
  285–89; PK and, 11–12, 98–99,
  104, 174–75, 197, 214–18; precognitive, 130–41; principles of,
  111–16; sporadic, 107–8, 283;
  super-ESP hypothesis, 259,
  269–70; theories about, 282–91;
  unconscious, 111–13, 120,
  137–38, 283–85. *See also* clairvoyance; mediumship; parapsychology; precognition; psi; retrocognition; telepathy
ESP cards, 83, 86, 90, 102
Esser, A., 160
Estabrooks, George, 74, 104
Estebany, Oskar, 224–25
Eva C., 199–201

evolution, 293
expansion/compression, 115–16, 215
experimenter effect, 89, 108–11, 130, 141, 203–4
extrasensory perception. *See* ESP
extroversion/introversion, 114–16, 170

Fahler, Jarl, 238, 239
Feather, Sara, 251
Feilding, Everard, 189–91, 195, 199
Ferenczi, Sandor, 129, 130
field consciousness, 280
Figar, S., 112
fire igniting, 176
fire immunity, 51
Fisk, G. W., 93*n*, 109, 215
Flammarion, Camille, 67, 188, 192
Flournoy, Theodore, 139
focusing, 107
Fodor, Nandor, 34, 178
Forwald, Haakon, 210–15, 222
Foster, E. B., 251
Fox sisters, 43–47, 171
fraud, 18–20, 46, 48–49, 70, 118
Freud, Sigmund, 30, 117, 128, 249, 256
Frick, Harvey, 207
Friedrich, Johann, 32–33
Fukurai, T., 218
Furness, H. H., 46

gamma telepathy, 172
ganzfeld experiments, 232–33, 236
Garrett, Eileen, 83, 170, 246
Gauld, Alan, 45, 67, 278
Geley, Gustave, 149–50, 152, 171, 199, 201–3
general extrasensory perception (GESP), 84–85, 88; and hypnosis, 238; precognition and, 131–33

ghosts, 258
Gibson, E. P., 206, 208
Gibson, Lottie, 206, 208–9
Glanvill, Joseph, 35, 36
Godric, Saint, 34
Goligher, Kathleen, 193–95
Grad, Bernard, 224
Green, Celia, 119, 131, 273
Greiner, R. P., 146–47, 169–70
Grela, J. J., 238
Groningen experiments, 70–72, 230
group testing, 100–1. *See also* mass ESP effect
Grunewald, Fritz, 178
Gurney, Edmund, 55, 59–64, 70, 257
Guthrie, Malcolm, 68–69, 74, 104–5, 110

hallucinations, 65–66, 120, 124–26, 131; auditory, 66, 176, 184. *See also* visions
hands, materializations of, 186, 191–92, 198, 199, 202
Hansel, C. E. M., 19, 87, 95
Harary, Blue, 276–77
Hardy, Alister, 80*n*, 287, 293
Hare, R. M. D., 48–49, 51
Harribance, Lalsingh, 104, 165–67, 197, 227
Hart, Hornell, 58, 256, 270, 274–75
hauntings, 15, 34–36, 175, 259–62. *See also* poltergeists
Hayden, Mrs., 47
healing, psychic, 14, 223–24. *See also* community of sensations; medical clairvoyance
Herbert, Benson, 220
heredity, and ESP, 170–71
Hermann family, 179
Heymans, G., 70–71
Heywood, Rosalie, 135
Hilton, Homer, 207

Hodgson, Richard, 57, 62, 188, 264–65, 267
Hofer, E., 250
Holt, Henry, 12
Home, D. D., 50–54, 185
homing, 250–51
Honorton, Charles, 18, 41, 106–8, 221, 227–29, 232–33, 236, 238–39, 240–41, 247
Houston, Jean, 234, 236
Howard family, 265–67
Hugh of Maus, Bishop, 34
Humphrey, Betty, 113, 114–15, 207
Hurth, Mrs., 122
Hyde, Dennis, 210
hyperesthesia, 42, 76, 93
hyperventilation, 198–99
hypnosis, 13, 236–38; and clairvoyance, 238–40; ESP and, 17–18, 153–54, 238–43; GESP and, 238; and PK, 216. *See also* mesmerism
Hyslop, James, 57, 268, 269, 271, 280

impressions, 119–24; patterns of, 122; precognitive, 131–32
intuitions. *See* impressions
involuntary utterances, 48

Jaffé, Aniela, 118, 131
James, William, 20, 73, 262, 267, 280
James of Illyricum, Saint, 32
Janet, Pierre, 237
Jephson, Ina, 74, 104
Johnson, Alice, 64, 69
Johnson, Gertrude, 92–93
Joire, Paul, 173
Jones boys, 18–19, 170
Joseph of Copertino, Saint, 32–33
Jourdain, E. P., 145
Jung, C. G., 58, 118, 290–91

K-ideas, 290
Kanthamani, B. K., 110 and *n*, 114, 115
kappa telepathy, 172
Kappers, Jan, 146–47, 169–70
Keil, H. H. J., 220
Kidd, James, 270–71
Klemme, Herbert, 144
Kline, Nathan, 161
Kluski, Franek, 53*n*, 202
Krippner, Stanley, 18, 221, 236, 239–40, 247
Kuhn, Thomas, 25–26
Kulagina, Nina, 219–21

Lambertini, Prospero, 34–35, 244
Lange, George, 150
latency, in psi, 80, 94, 96
Layard, John, 178, 181
Leonard, Gladys Osborne, 140, 262, 264, 267
Leppo, Luciano, 40
Leroy, Oliver, 33
LeShan, Lawrence, 116, 244, 289, 291
levitation, 32–34, 176, 184, 186, 190–91, 193
Levy, J., 110*n*
life after death. *See* mediumship; survival issue
light boxes, in psi tests, 73–74, 92–93
linkage experiments, 277
Linzmayer, A. J., 84–85, 89, 106, 168, 206
Lodge, Oliver, 68–69, 77, 104–5, 186–88, 263, 267, 269
Lombroso, Cesare, 24, 176–77, 185, 192
London Dialectical Society, 50
long-distance psi. *See* distance tests
Losey, Chauncey, 44
Loyola, Saint Ignatius of, 32
luminous phenomena, 186, 191, 197, 202; defined, 48

Lundholm, Helge, 83
Lynn, T., 195*n*

McConnell, R. A., 20, 209, 213
McDougall, William, 82
McFarland, J. D., 109
McMahan, Elizabeth, 210
malobservation, and psi validity, 61–63
Mapes, James, 49, 51
Margenau, Henry, 58, 59
Marshall, Ninian, 288–89
Maslow, Abraham, 280
mass ESP effect, 73, 80, 101, 287; precognitive, 97, 136–38
Masters, R. E. L., 234, 236
materializations, 48, 186, 191–92, 195, 199–202
Maxwell, Joseph, 193
Medhurst, R. G., 95
medical clairvoyance, 31, 37–39, 41. *See also* community of sensations; healing, psychic
meditation, and ESP, 230–31
mediums, 255, 262–70. *See also* sensitives
mediumship, 83, 262–68; defined, 14; physical, 14, 185–204; polyglot, 268; Spiritualism and, 42–47, 56; trance, 42, 48. *See also* survival issue
memory lapse, and psi validity, 61–63
"Memory Trainer," 245
mental contagion. *See* mass ESP effect
Mesmer, Franz Anton, 37, 40
mesmerism, 37–42. *See also* hypnosis
Messer, Ellen, 233
Mihalasky, John, 284
Miles, Miss C., 77
Mill, John Stuart, 257
mind over matter. *See* PK
miracles, 31–32

Mitchell, Janet, 276
Moberly, Ann, 145
molds, impressions in, 189*n*, 202
Mompesson, Mr., 35–36
Montredon, Evelyn, 253
Morales, Colonel, 234
More, Henry, 35
Morris, Robert, 110*n*, 163, 247*n*, 252, 276
Morselli, Professor, 189, 190–92
Moser, Liselotte, 40
movement, in psi, 81
Mowbray, Major, 195*n*
Murphy, Gardner, 16, 58, 79, 144, 256, 280
Murray, Agnes, 75
Murray, Gilbert, 75–77, 148
Myers, A. T., 64, 69
Myers, F. W. H., 55, 56, 59–60, 67, 142, 186–88, 256–58, 267, 268–69
mystical experiences, 291–92

Nash, Carroll, 112–13, 214
Nelson, G. K., 49
Neri, Saint Philip, 32
Nicol, J. Fraser, 24, 58
Nomine, Yvonne, 165
Norton, Agnes, 144–45
Norton, Dorothy, 144–45

observers, and ESP success, 87
occult, 13, 15, 29–30, 42
Ochorowicz, Julien, 42, 70, 187, 195
Orme, John, 137
Osis, Karlis, 215, 230–31, 235, 239, 245–46, 251, 271–73, 276, 285–86
Ossowiecki, Stephan, 149–53, 157, 168*n*, 197
Osty, Eugene, 139, 157–59, 198–99
out-of-the-body experiences (OOBE), 15, 273–77

Owen, A. R. G., 41
Ownbey, Sara, 85, 88–90, 110, 149, 168

Pagenstecher, Gustav, 153–55, 242
Pahnke, Walter, 235
Palladino, Eusapia, 185–93, 197, 199
Palmer, John, 114
parallelism, in psi, 80
parapsychology: boundaries of, 13–15; defined, 11; criticisms of, 17–24; as science, 15–27; Spiritualism and, 42–57. See also ESP; PK; psi
Parise, Felicia, 221–22, 287
Parke, H. W., 29
Parker, Adrian, 253n
Parsons, Dennys, 210
passivity, 71
patient/therapist ESP, 30–31, 129–30
Pearce, Hubert, 85–89, 100–1, 104, 149, 168
Pederson-Krag, Geraldine, 129
Pegram, Margaret, 91, 207, 209
Pelham, George, 264
Pellew, George. See Pelham, George.
perception, subliminal, 42, 76, 139
personality: and ESP, 101–2, 113–16, 146–47, 169–71; and PK, 215–16
Phantasms of the Living (SPR), 59–67, 118, 125
photographic film, PK and, 217–18, 222
physical mediumship, 185–203; defined, 14; experimenter effect and, 203–4; explanations of, 192–93
physics: of ESP, 285–89; of PK, 12, 183–85, 212–14, 221–23, 225
Piddington, J. G., 278
Piper, Leonore, 262–67, 280

PK: characteristics of, 174–75, 212–14, 216; defined, 11, 14; and ESP, 11–12, 98–99, 104, 174–75, 197, 214–18; experimental, 103, 202–25; explanations of, 173–75; forms of, 14, 225; personality and, 215–16; physics of, 12, 183–85, 212–14, 221–23, 225; placement, 210–12; and precognition, 98–99, 141; principles of, 194; spontaneous, 120, 173–75; static, 216–22. See also healing, psychic; parapsychology; physical mediumship; poltergeists; psi; telekinesis
placement PK, 210–12
Planck, Max, 25
plants, and PK, 224–25
plethysmograph tests, 112–13
PMIR, 284–85, 291
Podmore, Frank, 59–61, 64, 178, 267
poltergeists, 34–36, 43n, 175–81, 202–4; characteristics of, 178, 184; defined, 14; physics of, 183–85; as projected repression, 178, 181–83. See also hauntings
polyglot mediumship, 268
possession, 48
prägnanz, in psi, 81
Prasad, J., 119, 131, 133
Pratt, J. G., 19, 85–87, 109, 163, 165, 179–80, 207–9, 218, 220–21, 252n
precognition, 94, 96–97, 119, 130–31; clairvoyance and, 15, 138–39; defined, 14; and déjà vu, 141–42; in dreams, 131–36, 138, 140–41; explanations of, 138–41; GESP and, 131–33; hypnosis and, 238, 239; mass effect, 136–38; and PK, 98–99, 141; tests for, 97–99, 102–3, 159–63, 283–84; unconscious, 137–38
predestination, conditional, 135
preferential effect, 208–9

Prel, Baron du, 186
premonition, 134–35, 139. *See also*
    impressions; precognition
presentiments, 48
previsions, 48
Price, George, 19, 20, 22
Price, H. H., 261, 289, 291
Price, Harry, 176, 178–79, 195–99
Prince, W. F., 24, 63, 155–56
probability, 84*n*. *See also* statistics
proxy sittings, 268, 277
pseudoprecognition, 98
psi: in animals, 110, 249–54; and
    ASC, 226–44; characteristics of,
    64, 80–81, 99–100; cultivation
    of, 241–43; defined, 13;
    paradoxes of, 282–91; religion
    and, 31–35; in sensitives,
    151–53, 155, 163, 167–71. *See*
    also apparitions; ESP; hauntings;
    out-of-the-body experiences; PK
psi field theory, 158–59, 184, 288,
    289
psi-mediated instrumental re-
    sponse (PMIR), 284–85, 291
psi-missing, 74, 106–7
psi scanning, 284–85
psi-trailing, 250–51
psi-tron theory, 287–88
psi-vigilance theory, 249, 284
psychedelics, 233–36
psychic ether, 261
psychic shuffle, 98*n*
psychics. *See* mediums; sensitives
psychoanalysis, 128–30
psychokinesis. *See* PK
psychometry, 154, 156–59;
    defined, 153; and hauntings,
    260–61
Pulver, Lucretia, 44

QD effect (quarter distribution),
    207–9, 216

Race, Victor, 37
Ramsden, H., 77

Ramsey, M., 106
randomness, in ESP tests, 93 and
    n, 95, 102–3
Ransom, Champe, 17–24
Rao, K. Ramakrishna, 102, 107,
    114, 115
rapping, 43–47, 176, 184. *See also*
    poltergeists
Rasmussen, Anna, 216–17
Rayleigh, Lord, 20, 55
recurrent spontaneous psycho-
    kinesis (RSPK), 176. *See also*
    poltergeists
Reichenbach, Baron von, 40, 55
reincarnation, 279–80
religion, 31–35
research: automation in, 74 and *n*,
    92–93, 102, 106*n;* bias in, 23–24;
    early, 68–74; in groups, 100–1
    (*see also* mass ESP effect); masked
    experiments, 284; nonrepeatabil-
    ity of, 17–18; parapsychological,
    12–13; perfect scores, 85, 91;
    precautions in, 85–86; time fac-
    tor in ESP tests, 96. *See also*
    under specific phenomena and
    equipment
resonance theory of telepathy,
    288–89
retrocognition, 142–46, 280;
    defined, 14
rhabdomancy, 30
Rhine, J. B., 13–14, 26–27, 41,
    57–59, 68, 71, 82–92, 97–100,
    103–5, 109, 118, 205–6, 212,
    236, 251, 256, 290, 293
Rhine, Louisa, 82–83, 115, 118,
    119–21, 126, 131, 142, 173–74
Richet, Charles, 20, 70, 149–50,
    186–88, 199–200, 203
Richmond, A. B., 46*n*
rigid rays, 195
Rogers, Carl, 18
Roll, W. G., 141, 156–57, 158,
    170, 176, 179–82, 184, 225, 280
Romanus, 31
Rosenthal, Robert, 111

Rosma, Charles, 44
RSPK, 176. See also poltergeists
Ruk, Joseph, 218
Rush, Joseph, 59
Rýzl, Milan, 241–43

Sailaja, P., 107
salience, 99, 104, 209
Salter, W. H., 76
Saltmarsh, H. F., 163–64
Sannwald, G., 119, 170
Schiaparelli, Giovanni, 186
Schmeidler, Gertrude, 58, 101,
    114, 116–18, 164, 219, 231
Schmidt, Helmut, 102–3, 104,
    107, 110 and n
Schneider, Rudi, 53n, 170, 197–99
Schneider, Willie, 170, 197–98
Schrenck-Notzing, Baron Albert
    von, 152, 198–203
science, parapsychology as, 15–27
seances, 48
sensitives: patterns of, 167–71; re-
    search on, 148–67. See also
    mediums
sensory bombardment, 248–49
sensory cuing, 42, 92
sensory deprivation (SD), 231–33
Séré, E. Louis de, 38
serial time theory, 135
Serios, Ted, 217–18
Servadio, Emilio, 130, 235
Seybert, Henry, 46
Seybert Commission, 45–46, 50
Shackleton, Basil, 94–97, 110
sheep/goat effect (SGE), 101, 114,
    215
Sidgwick, Eleanor, 69, 76, 131,
    260
Sidgwick, Henry, 55, 60, 64, 69,
    257
Sinclair, Mrs. Upton, 78–79, 148
Sinclair, Upton, 78–79
Sittig, Georg, 33
skin vision, 219

Skinner, B. F., 68
Slade, Henry, 46 and n
sleep, and ESP, 244–49. See also
    dreams
Smith, Frank, 207
Smith, G. A., 69
Smith, Justa, 224–25
Smythies, J. R., 225
Soal, S. G., 18–19, 94–96, 103,
    170, 270
Society for Psychical Research
    (SPR), 50, 55, 257
Soule, Minnie, 262, 268
spirit music, 48
spirit slate writing, 62
spirit writing, 48
spiritual impersonation, 48
Spiritualism, 42–57, 257; defined,
    41
Stanford, Rex, 108, 227–28, 236,
    283–84, 291
Stanislawa P., 201
statistics, 20–22, 70, 84n; for free-
    response material, 163–66
Stekel, Wilhelm, 129
Stella C., 195–97, 199, 219, 221
Stepanek, Pavel, 107, 109, 116, 242
Stevenson, Ian, 23, 58, 87, 119,
    122, 126, 131, 135–38, 163–65,
    184, 218, 256, 278–79
Stewart, Gloria, 94, 96, 100–1, 285
stone-throwing, 176
Stuart, C. E., 85, 89, 110, 114–15,
    208
Stump, John, 181, 240
suggestion, 40. See also hypnosis;
    mesmerism
Sudre, René, 79, 152
super-ESP hypothesis, 259,
    269–70
survival issue, 255–70; research on,
    270–81. See also mediumship
Swann, Ingo, 219, 221, 225, 276
Swedenborg, Emanuel, 43
synchronicity, 290
syncretism, in psi, 81
synthesis, in psi, 81

table-tipping experiment, 211–12
Tanagras, A., 141
Targ, Russell, 106n, 254
target material, 102
Tart, Charles, 113, 165, 236, 274–75
telekinesis: defined, 14; explanations of, 173–74, 192–93; miracles as, 31–32; research on, 50–54; spontaneous, 173–76, 202–4. See also physical mediumship; poltergeists; RSPK
telepathic apparitional theory, 60
telepathy: and clairvoyance, 72–73, 126; collective, 79–80; defined, 14; dreams and, 244–49; explanations of, 172; laws of association and, 289–90; resonance theory of, 288–89; spontaneous, 60–61, 64; tests for, 60, 68–70, 72–74, 87–89, 94. See also thought transference
teleportation, 176, 179, 183, 184
temperature changes, 197, 219
Tenhaeff, W. H. C., 159, 163, 169, 170
Teresa, Saint, 32
Thaw, Blair, 70
Thomas, C. Drayton, 140, 268
thought transference, 55, 58, 68. See also telepathy
thoughtography, 217–18, 222
Thouless, Robert, 25–26, 86, 103n, 105–6, 118, 172, 175, 210, 214, 230, 279
Tillyard, R. J., 179
time: in ESP tests, 96; and mass precognition, 137
Titanic, precognition of sinking, 136–37
token object reading, 153n. See also psychometry
Tomczyk, Stanislawa, 195, 197
trance mediumship, 42, 48
traveling clairvoyance, 31
Trick, O. L., 170

Troland, L. T., 73–74, 102
Turner, May, 89–90
Tyrrell, G. N. M., 92–93, 102, 103–4, 158, 283, 292–93

U curve effect, 209
Ullman, Montague, 221, 244–47, 249
Urban, H. J., 114
Usher, F. L., 77

Van Asperen de Boer, S., 235
Van Dam, A., 70–71, 230
Van de Castle, Robert, 215–16
variance, 107–8
Vasiliev, Leonid, 219, 235, 286
Vaughan, Alan, 138–39, 141, 167, 248, 287
Vaughan, Iris, 248
Venzano, Professor, 189, 192
Verrall, Helen, 170
Versailles case, 145–46
Villecourt, Cardinal, 31
Virginio, Giovanni, 186
visions, 48, 51, 66; deathbed, 271–73. See also apparitions; hallucinations
voices, 66, 176, 184

Wallace, Alfred Russel, 50
Warcollier, René, 58, 79–81, 110, 287
Wassermann, G. D., 289
Watkins, Anita, 222–23
Watkins, Graham, 221–23, 287
weight changes, 193, 194, 219
Weinberg, A. A., 70
Wells, David, 51
West, D. J., 109, 223
West, Hilda, 61
White, Rhea, 67, 101, 142, 167
Whittlesey, J., 235
Wiesner, B. P., 172, 175
Winther, Christian, 216–17

Wood, G. H., 251–52
Woodruff, J. L., 90, 110, 206, 208

Xenoglossy, 268

Zener, Karl, 83
Zener cards, 83, 86, 90, 102

Zielinski, Ludmilla, 40
Zierold, Maria Reyes de, 153–56, 242
Zirkle, George, 88–89, 100–1
Zoellner, Johann, 46n
Zorab, George, 40, 51
Zugun, Eleanore, 178–79